R I V E R

Isle Cochon

Ottawa Village

PLAN
of
DETROIT
with its Environs

A. The Town

B. Out Posts

C. Pondiacs Encampments

D. Capt Dalyells defeat

By John Montresor

IN DARKNESS
DWELLS THE
PEOPLE WHICH
KNOWS ITS
ANNALS NOT

Imposing oak doors open from the Great Room to the Rare Book Room, home to the Library's greatest treasures. Hanging on the walls are portraits of William L. Clements and the three directors who administered his library from 1923 to 2007.

AN AMERICANA SAMPLER

*Essays on Selections from the
William L. Clements Library*

Edited by
Brian Leigh Dunnigan
and
J. Kevin Graffagnino

Ann Arbor
William L. Clements Library
The University of Michigan
2011

Decorative vaulting of the porch ceiling.

*Capital of one of the columns
supporting the porch.*

For more information about the Clements Library, visit our website: www.clements.umich.edu

ISBN 978-0-615-46683-5

Printed in the United States of America by Walsworth Publishing Company

Endpapers:
Front: John Montrésor, Plan of Detroit with its Environs, [1764]. Pen and ink with watercolor.
Back: [Étienne Verrier], Plan de la ville de Louisbourg à l'Isle Royale, [ca. 1740].
Pen and ink with watercolor.

Book Design: Kathy Horn, Blue Skies Studio

Typeface: headlines: Trajan; author's names: Bickham Script Pro; text: Minion Condensed

Number of copies: 1,000

TABLE OF CONTENTS

The William L. Clements Library, designed by Albert Kahn (1869–1942) and dedicated in 1923.

William L. Clements (1861–1934) as portrayed by Hermann Hanatschek in 1928.

A LIBRARY OF
AMERICAN HISTORY

— J. Kevin Graffagnino

"This day and hour mark the conclusion of a book-collector's career. A library of American history has been created, and a disposition made of it. There has been constructed a building, that the integrity of this library may be preserved, and that there may be special facilities for historical research work. My interest in the Library is transferred, with its work and development, to its new owner— the University of Michigan."

The day was June 15, 1923, and the hour was the dedication of the William L. Clements Library on the campus of the University of Michigan. In his presentation remarks, Clements paid homage to such great Americana collectors as John Carter Brown and James Lenox, and he expressed the conviction that with the opening of his library Ann Arbor would attract a large number of serious students of early American history. "Inspiration and written expression in full measure will come from those who see and use such books," he said, "along with a realization of the great things they stand for, and the pivotal events they first narrate." Clements loved the rarities he had accumulated, and he was confident that future generations would share his fascination with "the treasures in this library."

William Lawrence Clements was born in Ann Arbor on April 1, 1861, the sixth and last child of James and Agnes Clements. James Clements was a gas engineer with interests in several Michigan cities, and on graduating from the University of Michigan in 1882 with a degree in engineering William began work at the Bay City Industrial Works, in which his father was a principal investor. Young Clements became manager of the company in 1883, and in the succeeding decades he made it a national leader in the manufacture of steam shovels and other heavy railroad equipment. By the time he turned 50 he was moderately wealthy, chief investor in the First National Bank of Bay City, and a member of the University of Michigan board of regents.

Clements began his collecting career later in life than most bibliophiles. He filled his "fine residence" in Bay City with an assortment of everyday books in the 1880s and '90s, and then in 1903 he bought the Americana collection of Civil War veteran and Bay City merchant Aaron J. Cooke. Because Cooke and Clements were close friends, as the older man neared the end of his life he welcomed the opportunity to transfer his books to Clements. Cooke's library was "rich in Americana and other volumes from the sales of Brinley, Barlow, Menzies, and other great nineteenth-century book collectors," so acquiring his 1,000 volumes gave Clements a strong foundation on which to build. At the age of 42, he had the money, leisure and inclination to make the most of this good start, and in the remaining three decades of his life he did just that.

With the Cooke nuggets in hand, Clements began buying Americana from Francis P. Harper in New York, C. F. Libbie in Boston and the sales of the Anderson Auction Company. He met legendary dealer George D. Smith in 1905, but apparently Smith's emphasis on supplying rarities to Henry E. Huntington kept him from selling much to Clements. By the early 1910s, Clements had the Americana bug in a serious way. Mostly shut out by Huntington's much fatter wallet at the first two of the fabulous Robert Hoe auctions in 1911, the next year Clements purchased 140 choice early American titles that had belonged to New York City collector Newbold Edgar from Lathrop Harper for $17,500. These included Anne Bradstreet's *Tenth Muse* (1650); Adriaen Van der Donck's *Beschryvinge van Nieuw-Nederlant* (1656); William Smith's *History of the Province of New-York* (1757); and Bernard Romans, *East and West Florida* (1775). In 1913 Clements brought his first full-time librarian to Bay City to care for and catalog his 3,000 volumes. A year later, perhaps encouraged by his acquisition of Thomas Hariot's *A Briefe and True Report of the New Found Land of Virginia* (1588), which he described as "the star of all Americana," he had sufficient pride in his holdings to publish

Christopher Columbus' Epistola (Rome, 1493), his account of New World discoveries, is one of the many rare volumes in the Clements Library's Book Division.

Uncommon, Scarce and Rare Books Relating to American History . . . from the Library of William L. Clements.

Issuing his catalogue did nothing to slow Clements' pace of acquisition. He plunged with enthusiasm into the bibliographic tar pit of Theodor de Bry's *Voyages* (1590–1634), Levinus Hulsius' *Sammlung von sechs und zwanzig Schiffahrten in verschiedene fremde länder* (1598–1660) and the *Jesuit Relations* (1632–72), building superb collections of those seminal sources on early America. Expanding his horizons from books and pamphlets, in 1918 he bought 3,000 volumes of duplicate eighteenth- and early nineteenth-century American newspapers from the American Antiquarian Society. When high-priced rarities became available—James Rosier's *True Relation of . . . the Discovery of the Land of Virginia* (1605) in 1918 from Philadelphia dealer A. S. W. Rosenbach for $6,000; Richard Hakluyt's *Principal Navigations* (1599–1600); along with John Smith's *True Relation of . . . Virginia* (1608) and *Description of New England* (1616) for a total of $13,000 from George D. Smith in 1919—Clements invariably noted how much his hobby was costing him (in 1919 he spent $60,000 on acquisitions, making his total expenditures on books since 1903 more than $400,000) and then wrote the check. "I am adding Americana as fast as opportunity offers," he wrote to Clarence Brigham at AAS. "I do not know what I would do if I did not have this interest."

By the end of the 1910s, Clements had begun considering what to do with his collection. He had visited the great Americana libraries in New York and New England, and that experience shaped his thinking. In September 1919, at a meeting of the University of Michigan regents, he informally offered his library to his *alma mater*. The following month, as chair of the board's Library Committee, he led a delegation of University regents and librarians back to the East Coast so they could share his vision of how to proceed, and in February 1920 he placed a formal offer before the regents. They accepted immediately, and over the course of the next three years Clements and the University crafted an agreement. Clements pledged to donate his library and to provide $175,000, plus $15,000 for furnish-

Columbus signed his Epistola *with his new title, "Admiral of the Ocean Fleet."*

ings and equipment, to build a suitable home for it if the University would guarantee an annual appropriation of $25,000 for staff salaries, acquisitions and operating expenses. While both sides agreed quickly to these details, the relationship of the Clements Library to the University's central library system became a key point. At the outset Clements had stipulated that the head of his library would work "under the general instruction and supervision of the General Libraries of the University," but as negotiations proceeded he changed his mind. The autonomous Elizabethan Club Library at Yale and the John Carter Brown Library at Brown University were better models, he declared, so in October 1922 he demanded that Michigan set up a structure in which a separate five-person Committee of Management would oversee his library. University of Michigan officials and library administrators were surprised and dismayed by the change, but they went along rather than argue with Clements about it.

All the while Clements kept buying. Purchases, large and small, added quantity and quality alike to his collection. In February 1920 he acquired John Brereton's *A Briefe and True Relation of the Discoverie of the North Part of Virginia* (1602) at a New York auction for $4,050. On a trip to England in July 1921 he bought 220 volumes of the papers of Lord Shelburne, Britain's Prime Minister during the American Revolution, at auction for $7,000, a remarkable bargain that nonetheless contributed to his book-buying expenses of $70,000 that year. Realizing that he had neglected cartographic early Americana, in 1922 he paid Henry N. Stevens of London $5,500 for 149 maps of Revolutionary America. When the library of the late Henry Vignaud, eminent collector and student of early American history, became available in Paris in the fall of 1922, Clements brokered a deal in which he and the University of Michigan would split the $17,700 cost based on how much of the collection he added to his holdings. The amounts Clements was spending may not seem impressive to a 2011 eye, but when you adjust 70,000 1921 dollars for inflation and come up with more than $800,000, then couple that with the fact that Clements was never close to membership in the rarified financial echelon of fellow collectors J. P. Morgan and Henry E. Huntington, his spending merits more respect.

Clements may have expected that he would be done with his hobby when his library opened in June 1923, but in fact he was far from "the conclusion of a book-collector's career." Spurred on by first Clements Library Director Randolph G. Adams, instead he remained as avid a collector as he had ever been. In December 1925 he paid Miss Frances Clinton $88,500 for 16,500 manuscripts of her illustrious ancestor, Revolutionary War general Sir Henry Clinton, eclipsing his purchase that same year of 5,000 manuscripts of Clinton's American counterpart Nathanael Greene for only $30,000. Two years later Clements added a large collection of the papers of Lord George Germain, Secretary of State for the American Colonies 1775–82, for $20,000. He concluded his remarkable decade of Revolutionary War acquisitions by purchasing 20,000 manuscripts of British general Thomas Gage for $100,000. These collecting coups, in which Clements and his agents negotiated long and skillfully with the descendants of important leaders in the Revolution, elevated his library from a sterling collection of printed materials to an unequalled archive of unique sources on Revolutionary America. In each case, Clements outmaneuvered collectors, dealers and institutions with far deeper pockets than his, blend-

with a number of small Arms

Four Brass Cannon and two Mortars or Cohorns, in the Cellar or out Houses of Mr. Barretts a little on the other side the Bridge where is also lodged a Quantity of Powder & Lead.

Ten Iron Cannon before the Town=House and two within it which Town=House is in the Center of the Town, The Ammunition for said Guns within the House

Three Guns of 24 Pounders, lodged in the Prison yard with a Quantity of Cartridges and Provision

A Quantity of Provision and Ammunition in other Places, The near the meeting Principal Deposits are the Houses of Messrs. Hubbards, Butler the name of Jones the Sailor, near Hubbards two men of Bond; and particularly at Mr. near Whitneys who lives on the Right Hand at the Entrance of the at a Town, the House plaistered white a small yard in front and a railed Fence a large Quantity of small arms Powder and all is reported to be deposited in his stores adjoining the House

A Quantity of Ammunition and Provision together as number of cannon and small arms having been collected at Concord for the avowed Sir, You will march with the Corps of Grenadiers and purpose of opposing the Lawful government Light Infantry put under your Command with the utmost expedition and secrecy to Concord, where you will seize and destroy all the Artillery and Ammunition Provisions Tents & all other military Stores you can find, you will knock and destroy the Carriages off one Trunion at least of each of the Iron Guns, and beat in the the rest burnt Muzzles of the Brass ones so as to render them useless. The & flour Powder may be shaken out of the Barrells into the Water, and the Pockets Men may put the Balls & Lead into their knapsacks throwing them away by Degrees into the Fields Ditches Ponds, &c. to be have a Plan with on which is marked you shall I give you a Return of the Places where the Artillery & Ammunition &c. is reported to be lodged, and after destroying the same you will return; and if your Men appear much fatigued you may halt them at Lexington or Cambridge and let them rest in

---

The War for Independence began at Lexington Green on April 19, 1775. General Thomas Gage (1721–87) sparked the fighting when he dispatched British troops from Boston to seize military supplies stored at Concord, Massachusetts. His April 18 draft of that order is among the Gage Papers in the Manuscripts Division.

ing finesse, perseverance and outright luck to come out ahead. In the process he also demonstrated that it is far easier to start collecting antiquarian treasures than it is to stop.

Clements kept a close eye on "his" library after 1923 as well. He was in constant contact with Adams, sometimes to the latter's consternation as the founder tried to set Library policies and procedures for the new director. Although Adams fit perfectly Clements' desire for a trained historian with a passion for antiquarian books and manuscripts rather than "just a librarian" to run his creation, like

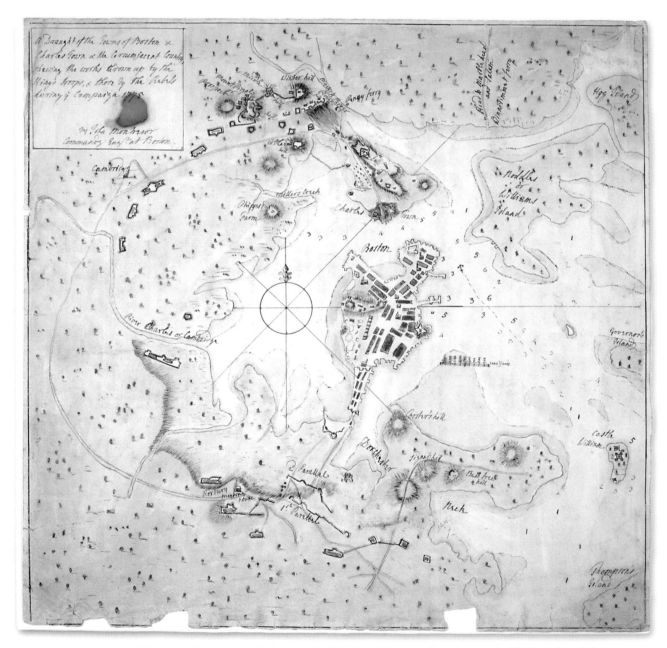

"A Draught of the Towns of Boston & Charles Town & the Circumjacent Country…." was drawn in the fall of 1775 by British engineer John Montrésor (1736–99) to identify the fortifications of the American army besieging the city. The Clements Library's collection of manuscript maps of the American Revolution is arguably the finest in the world.

many founding donors Clements found it difficult to pass the torch even to his hand-picked and very capable administrator. Dealing with requests that were really orders from Bay City and advice on what kinds of researchers were worthy to use the Library (in his dedication remarks Clements had excluded University of Michigan undergraduates or "the ordinary graduate student" from the list, declaring that if a handful of eminent historians used the collections annually he would be happy) required considerable tact and patience on Adams' part, and he proved equal to the task. On balance Clements and Adams got along quite well, and Clements' ongoing interest certainly worked to the Library's benefit, but occasionally Adams must have pondered the wisdom of the age-old axiom, "Never take a job heading an organization where the founder is still alive."

The last years of Clements' life brought a mix of happiness and distress. His wife divorced him in 1930, but he remarried the following year. In the summer of 1931 his Bay City bank closed, and Clements poured a great deal of his own money into getting it reopened in 1932. A Democratic landslide in Michigan's spring 1933 elections cost him his seat on the University board, ending his 24-year tenure as a regent. Working with Adams to advance the Library in Ann Arbor provided a much-needed diversion from the battering that the Depression wreaked on his corporate and personal finances. Much to his own dismay, early in 1934 Clements felt compelled to inform the University that he or his estate would have to sell rather than give to the Library the great Revolutionary War manuscript collections that he had kept in Bay City. He hoped for an economic upswing that would restore his capacity to donate as he had always intended, but it did not come before his death on November 6, 1934. After three years of negotiating and helped by a $100,000 donation from Detroit collector Tracy W. McGregor, the University paid Clements' heirs $300,000 spread over a decade for the Gage, Shelburne, Germain, Clinton, and Greene papers.

Seventy-five years after his death, William L. Clements stands as one of the great Americana collectors of his or any other generation. In assembling his collection, he acquired prized titles from the libraries of such noteworthy predecessors as Elihu D. Church, Henry Huth, William Menzies, and Brayton Ives. He worked successfully with many of the principal American and British dealers of his time—Francis and Lathrop Harper, Henry N. Stevens, Alfred Quaritch, A. S. W. Rosenbach, Bernard Maggs—to bring the best copies of the rarest volumes to his shelves. When it came time to plan the Clements Library, he consulted with and gathered advice from leading authorities like George Parker Winship, Wilberforce Eames, Clarence Brigham, and Worthington C. Ford. At auction, in relationships with dealers and in negotiations with private owners he more than held his own against Henry F. De Puy, Beverly Chew, Henry E. Huntington, Herschel V. Jones, and the other leading collectors of his day. Looking back on his collecting career, Clements wrote, "If a man is even moderately enthusiastic, and has actually collected a sufficient number of books to make a foundation of a library as a specific subject, he, by general understanding among his co-sufferers, has been inoculated with the disease and has a case of Bibliomania." Few individuals have caught the virus more permanently or accomplished more under its influence than Clements.

Today the William L. Clements Library is an impressive monument to its founder. The Library's first three directors—Randolph G. Adams, Howard H. Peckham and John C. Dann—averaged 28 years on the job, and each excelled at strengthening the collections in ways that broadened the Library's parameters while maintaining the depth important to scholars. As a result, for any collector of Americana prior to 1900 the Clements is a remarkably attractive destination. From the architectural beauty of Albert Kahn's 1923 building, modeled after a 1587 casino on the grounds of the Villa Farnese in Caprarola, Italy, to the rare books, pamphlets, maps, prints, photographs, and manuscripts that shed light on American history from Columbus through the nineteenth century, the Clements offers collectors and researchers alike a wealth of unique resources. On almost any aspect of the early American experience—military history, politics and government, religion, gender and ethnicity, culinary history, the creative arts, travel and exploration—the holdings at Clements are among the best in the world. Like such peer institutions as the American Antiquarian Society, the John Carter Brown Library at Brown University, the Newberry Library, the Huntington, the Massachusetts Historical Society, and the Beinecke Library at Yale, the Clements collects, preserves and makes accessible a breathtaking array of primary sources on our heritage. Henry E. Huntington once wrote, "The ownership of a fine library is the surest and swiftest way to immortality." If Huntington was right (and what self-respecting bibliophile could doubt him?), the name of William L. Clements will live forever.

The Clements Library has grown significantly since our founder's passing in 1934. We remain one of the best collections of primary sources on America from Columbus to 1800, the chronological parameters established at our opening, but our collecting scope has gradually moved forward in time. Under Randolph G. Adams, first Director here (1923–51), we began to collect the early nineteenth century. Second Director Howard H. Peckham (1953–77) moved us up to the American Civil War, and third Director John C. Dann (1977–2007) extended the flexible stop-date to 1900. We will halt there for the foreseeable future; absent the facilities, staff and budgets of the country's largest academic libraries, attempting to establish great collections strength on twentieth-century America would be foolhardy. Instead, we'll remain a serious research library of primary sources in their original format on early American history, with "early" defined as covering the Age of Discovery through the nineteenth century. There will be fingers of interesting source material here beyond 1900, but for the time being at least we will not push later than that with real depth and preeminent collections as our goals.

The essays in this book reflect the growth of the Library since 1923. Readers will see a number of entries on our traditional strengths of discovery and exploration, politics, and military history, as with Katie Heddle's essay on Peter Martyr's *The Decades of the Newe Worlde or West India* (London, 1555), which Mr. Clements acquired from fellow collector Grenville Kane. Emi Hasting's essay on

Benjamin West's monumental history painting, "The Death of General Wolfe" is the largest of thousands of images held by the Library's Graphics Division. This, the third of five known copies painted by West (1738–1820), was executed for the Duke of Waldeck in 1776 and purchased by William L. Clements for his library in 1928.

John Eliot's Indian Bible both places that landmark of early Native Americana in its seventeenth-century context and traces the path it took from the library of Queen's College, Oxford, to the Clements shelves. The "White Hills" and "Wine Hills" variations in William Hubbard's 1677 map of New England, which Clements Library Director Randolph G. Adams was the first scholar to discuss critically, form the basis of Mary Pedley's text. Brian Dunnigan continues the early cartography theme, a subject near and dear to Mr. Clements' heart, in his essay on our manuscript "Cantonment of the Forces in N. America 1766," from the papers of William Petty, second earl of Shelburne. The Library's unique copy of Anthony Bacon's *Considerations on the Present State of the North American Colonies* (London, 1769), with its sensible recommendations for changes in British colonial policy, serves as the lens for Christine Walker's examination of the growing gulf between Britain and her American subjects. David Hancock writes eloquently about the Library's voluminous primary sources on the war that followed by zeroing in on our manuscript accounts of the events of April 19, 1775, the prelude to the conflict that ended in American independence.

The middle essays in this book tie the pre-1800 Americana that Mr. Clements emphasized in his collecting to the nineteenth-century history the Library began to acquire after 1934. As Brian Dunnigan's second essay demonstrates, John Fitch's 1785 *A Map of the north west parts of the United States of America* is one of the cartographic treasures in our holdings, and our pursuit of it stretched across seven decades. Philadelphia artist Edward Clay's impact on nineteenth-century American attitudes on race and ethnicity comes to life in Martha Jones' review of his 1828 *Life in Philadelphia,* and Mary H. Parsons follows with a moving account of ex-slave Matthew Matthews' long years of efforts to secure the freedom of his wife and children, as his letters in our Masters-Taylor-Wilbur Papers detail. Barbara DeWolfe rounds out our trio of essays on antebellum African American history with a poignant look at Sarah Forten's April 15, 1837, letter to Angelina Grimké, in which the challenges and prejudice that people of color faced in her generation come vividly to life. Diana Sykes writes about the Library's very strong West Indies collections as epitomized in an 1838 lithographic

This colorful lithograph celebrates the Southern California Citrus Fair, held in Chicago in 1886 and made possible by the newly developed refrigerated railroad car. The Clements Library's remarkable collection of primary source material relating to American food and cookery forms the Janice Bluestein Longone Culinary Archive. Much broader than simply a cookbook collection, the archive includes thousands of pieces of ephemera and many other sources relating to American food ways.

portrait of Toussaint L'Ouverture, whose military success and abolition of slavery in Haiti made a lasting impression in the United States and Europe alike.

New areas of collecting for the Clements constitute the jumping-off points for the last third of this volume. Clayton Lewis discusses the remarkable Niagara Falls daguerreotypes of Thomas Martin Easterly, the highlights of a growing early American photography archive. Our primary sources on westward expansion shine in Terese Austin's essay on William Clayton's *The Latter-Day Saints' Emigrants' Guide* (St. Louis, 1848). The Civil War, in which the Library's holdings went from very little to deep and rich through the donations of James S. Schoff in the early 1970s, is the backdrop for Bethany Anderson's assessment of the wartime correspondence of volunteer nurse Cornelia Hancock. The breadth and depth of early American culinary history, in which the Janice Bluestein Longone Culinary Archive ranks among the finest collections in existence, become obvious in Jan Longone's essay on Malinda Russell's *A Domestic Cook Book* (Paw Paw, 1866), the first cookbook by an African American author, and JJ Jacobson's review of three Swedish American cookbooks dating from 1882 to 1936. Finally, Cheney Schopieray's discussion of Stephen Brown's 1917–18 manuscript diaries points to the Library's collection of selected twentieth-century military letters and papers for scholars to compare with our extensive sources on earlier conflicts in which Americans participated.

In 1998 the Clements published *One Hundred and One Treasures from the Collections of the William L. Clements Library* in observance of its 75th anniversary. Given that "the *101*" featured many of our greatest rarities, creating a new overview of the Library's holdings with fresh selections a mere dozen years later took some doing. We hope the result is a book that complements rather than replaces the *101*, and that readers will find both volumes interesting either singly or in tandem. Collectors should learn from the pair that the Clements' shelves and cabinets contain treasures beyond the envious imaginations of antiquarians not born in the mid-nineteenth century. Scholars should take note, as hundreds of their publishing predecessors have done to good effect, that the Library collections are rich in primary sources for research on all aspects of early American history. Readers in the middle will realize that for anyone interested in America's past the Clements is a destination of extraordinary appeal. All are welcome at the Library, where the spirit of dedication to advancing the study of our national heritage remains as strong as when William L. Clements opened our doors in 1923.

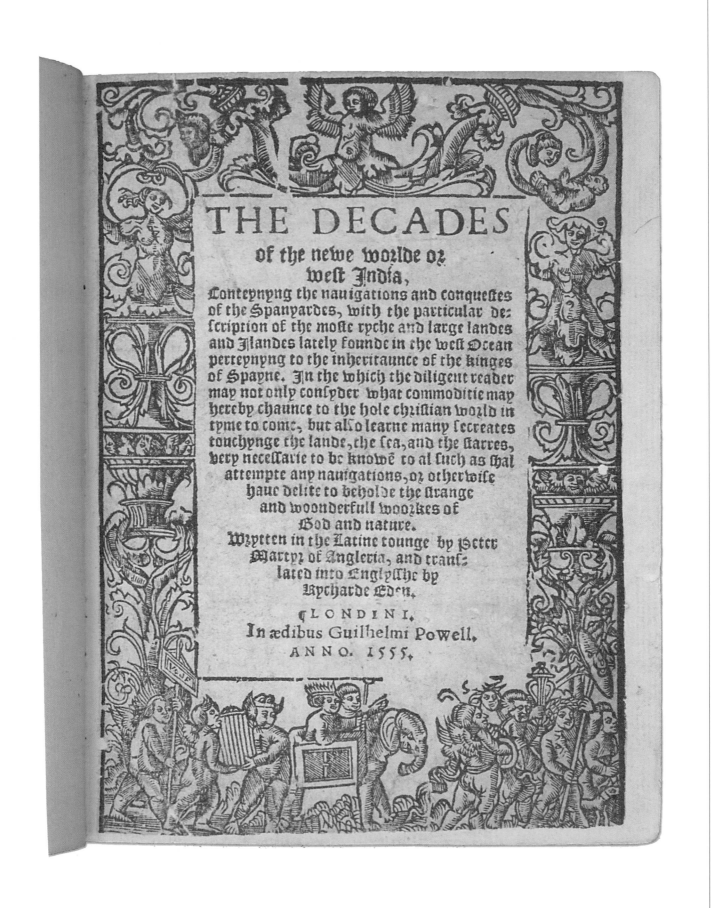

THE DECADES

of the newe worlde or
west India,
Conteynyng the nauigations and conquestes
of the Spanyardes, with the particular de=
scription of the moste ryche and large landes
and Jlandes lately founde in the west Ocean
perteynyng to the inheritaunce of the kinges
of Spayne. In the which the diligent reader
may not only consyder what commoditie may
hereby chaunce to the hole christian world in
tyme to come, but also learne many secreates
touchynge the lande, the sea, and the starres,
very necessarie to be knowē to al such as shal
attempte any nauigations, or otherwise
haue delite to beholde the strange
and woonderfull woorkes of
God and nature.
Wrytten in the Latine tounge by Peter
Martyr of Angleria, and trans=
lated into Englysshe by
Rycharde Eden.

¶LONDINI,
In ædibus Guilhelmi Powell,
ANNO. 1555.

DOCUMENTING A "NEWE WORLDE"

— Katie Heddle

*"It was a gentle custom of the ancients to number amongst
the Gods those heroes by whose genius and greatness of soul
unknown lands were discovered."*

Thus begins the first of the *decas,* or "decades," Pietro Martire (Peter Martyr) d'Anghiera's carefully compiled accounts of the earliest European explorations of the Americas, events that changed the human landscape of the world forever. Martyr (1457–1526), an Italian-born scholar and cleric, had risen by his talents and ability to hold religious and academic positions in the courts of Ferdinand and Isabella of Spain, including a seat on several occasions on the Council of the Indies. He was uniquely positioned and qualified to deal with the information flowing back to Europe as Columbus and succeeding explorers and voyagers began to unravel the mysteries and catalog and exploit the riches of what Martyr himself first dubbed *orbe novo* or the "New World." Peter Martyr became their chronicler, compiling and preserving much of what we know of the earliest period of exploration of the Caribbean and the Central American mainland.

Martyr's work was just the thing to attract the attention of William L. Clements, who possessed a strong collecting interest in the books that revealed the voyages and discoveries of the age of European exploration and the progress of the earliest colonies in the Americas. Martyr's published works would join classics such as Christopher Columbus' *Epistola* (Rome, 1493) and the writings of Hernán Cortés and many others on the shelves of the Clements Library's Rare Book Room. Among them is the first English-language text that incorporated some of Martyr's work, *The Decades of the Newe Worlde or West India* (London, 1555), translated by Richard Eden (1521?–76). It was this book, an anthology incorporating the first four of Martyr's eight decades, with additional narratives by other explorers, that first introduced Tudor England to the wonders of more than a half century of exploration and made the more adventurous look to the opportunities of the Americas.

Peter Martyr d'Anghiera was born in Arona in Italy in 1457 and studied locally before moving to Rome at the age of twenty. Having an amiable personality and obvious ability, he was welcomed into prestigious academic circles thanks to the likes of the Archbishop of Milan, Giovanni Arcimboldo, the antiquarian and scholar Pomponious Laetus and Ascanio Sforza, brother of Duke Ludovico Il Mordo. These names mean little to most of us today, but during Martyr's time the church wielded great authority and influence, thus making his connections and place amongst theo-political circles extremely important. Sforza, a future cardinal, would become his most important ally and patron.

In Rome, Martyr continued his education with the assistance of his influential patrons within the Catholic Church hierarchy. In 1487 he was persuaded by the Spanish ambassador to return with him to his country, one of a number of Italians who carried with them some of the spirit of the Renaissance and introduced it to the much more religiously conservative Spain. Martyr arrived just as the long conflict with the Moors over the Iberian peninsula was nearing its climax, and the end of the fighting left a unified, Christian Spain that would soon be looking to the West and the broad reaches of the Atlantic Ocean beyond which lay the Americas.

It did not take long for Peter Martyr to gain a reputation as a promising scholar with influential patrons. Soon after the return of Columbus from his first voyage, Martyr began compiling information on his explorations based on reports, letters and interviews with the participants themselves. His account of Columbus' 1492–93 voyage was first presented as a pair of letters addressed to C ardinal Sforza in 1493 and 1494. In 1501 Martyr was urged to supplement these with eight more on Columbus and his contemporaries. This established a format of "decades," each comprising ten books or chapters, which Martyr would use for all of his later accounts of New World exploration. In 1511 he was appointed chronicler of the Council of the Indies, and in the same year he published the first of his decades as *Opera Lagatio Babylonica Occeani Decas.* This, his first historical account of the earliest Spanish discoveries, incorporated much information on Columbus' voyages and a wealth of detail on the people and places he had encountered.

The printing of Martyr's first decade was followed in 1516 by the publication of two more, the first of which chronicled the activities of Alonso de Ojeda, who had sailed with Columbus on his second voyage, and conquistadors Diego de Nicuesa and Vasco Núñez de Balboa. The third decade recounted Balboa's sighting of the Pacific Ocean, the expeditions of Pedrarias Dávila, and Columbus' fourth and final voyage. It was the 1516 work that first used in its title the term *orbe novo* for the lands we still think of as the New World.

In all, Martyr produced eight decades before his death in 1526, the last five covering such topics as the conquest of the Aztec empire by Hernán Cortés, explorations on the Pacific coast of America, Magellan's attempt to circumnavigate the globe, and early accounts of the natives of Cuba, Haiti, Mexico, Central America, and even the North American mainland. All eight were published together in 1530 as *De Orbo Nouo,* providing the complete chronicle as recorded by Martyr. The title-page illustration depicts, appropriately enough, the labors of Hercules.

Martyr's narratives are wide-ranging in their subject matter and include everything from detailed accounts of the voyages, explorations, and both peaceful and violent encounters with the natives to descriptions of the plants, animals, and natural resources of the new lands. His narratives are written in a clear and lively style, with much detail about the exotic people and surroundings encountered by the Spanish during their explorations. They are filled with highly descriptive anecdotal accounts of events, from battles with the native peoples to the size and appetite of New World serpents. Accounts of cannibals, a warlike people known as the *Caraibes,* occur often in the first

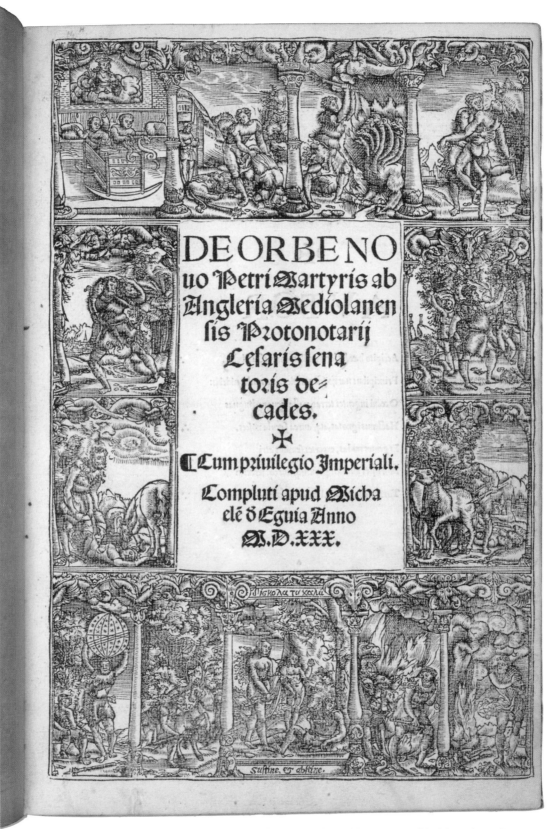

DE ORBE NO
uo Petri Martyris ab
Angleria Mediolanen
sis Protonotarij
Cęsaris sena
toris de=
cades.
✠
❡ Cum priuilegio Imperiali.
Compluti apud Micha
elé ð Eguia Anno
M.D.XXX.

The title page of Peter Martyr's De Orbe Nouo *(Alcala, 1530) is enlivened by depictions of the labors of Hercules.*

several decades, in part because of their impact on the more peaceful natives of the Caribbean islands and, of course, because of Spanish fascination and disgust with their practice of hunting other men for food. Gentler facts are included as well, such as the first printed mention of the potato, one of many New World foods that would influence the European diet, and the introduction of native words, many of which are used today, such as *hurakan* for the violent storms of the region.

Martyr's narrative even includes flashes of humor in its recounting of contacts between Spanish explorers and native peoples. In explaining how the Yucatan peninsula gained its name, for example, he claims that when the Spanish arrived there they were greeted by the natives, and, having no interpreters present, both parties attempted to communicate by using gestures. The explorers tried to ask the name of the land in this way, and the natives replied "yucatan, yucatan." The name stuck, but, according to Martyr and unbeknownst to the sailors, "yucatan" in the native language meant "I don't understand you."

The decades are not arranged in chronological order, but rather as the events were told to Martyr and as new information became available. The result is a lot of skipping around in the timeline. Whereas Martyr begins the first book of the first decade with stories of Columbus, by the third decade

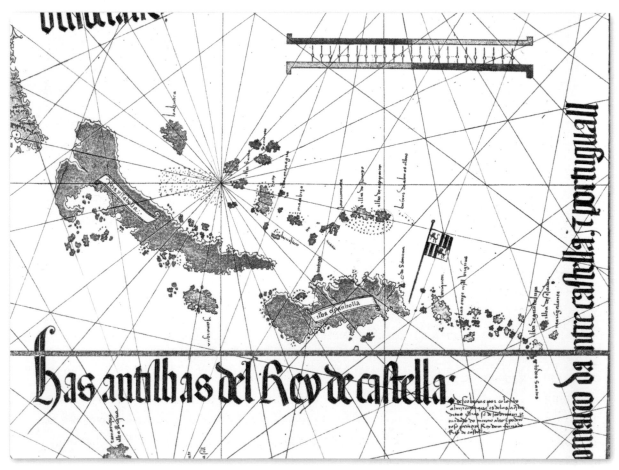

The Greater Antilles was the first region of the New World to be exploited by the Spanish. This is a detail from a nineteenth-century facsimile of Alberto Cantino's 1502 manuscript map of the recently discovered lands.

he backtracks from Vespucci to Columbus and from Columbus to Columbus' brother Bartholomew. Despite this seemingly haphazard chronicle, Martyr's writing transitions from each subject with ease and one is never lost in the reading of his decades.

Peter Martyr's several works were all written in Latin, but the middle of the sixteenth century saw their first translation into English, an event that would influence the attitude of Englishmen toward the new lands on the opposite side of the Atlantic. *The Decades of the Newe Worlde or West India . . . Wrytten in the Latine tounge by Peter Martyr of Angleris, and Translated into Englysshe by Rycharde Eden* was published in London nearly thirty years after Martyr's death and may be considered the first English collection of accounts of voyages to America. Although Eden took his title from Martyr's *De Orbe Nouo,* his book includes translations of only the first four decades, which make up about half of the volume. The remainder of the text is comprised of other accounts of exploration and discovery, including "The historie of the Weste indies," translated from the work of Gonzalo Fernández de Oviedo y Valdés and first published in 1526, and extracts from Antonio Pigafetta's 1525 account of the first circumnavigation of the globe undertaken by Ferdinand Magellan and under his command until he was killed in the East Indies. Another section relates "Other notable thynges as touchynge the Indies," based on the work of Francisco López de Gómara and other authors, and introduces the voyages of Sebastian Cabot, the first trans-Atlantic navigator sailing for England. The book includes, as well, accounts of travel to Moscow, Cathay and the northern regions and of the first two voyages from England to Guinea in Africa.

In spite of Eden's inclusion of more current material that he must have judged would be of interest to his English audience, it is Martyr's decades that begin and dominate the work and present the context for Spain's incursions into the Americas. Englishmen could now read of Columbus' first voyage, a story that is so familiar to us today but was wonderfully exotic in the sixteenth century:

> *Christophorus Colonus (other wise called Columbus) . . . perswaded Fernando and Elysabeth, catholike prynces, that he doubted not to fynde certayne Ilandes of India, nere vnto owre Occean sea. . . . At the length three shyppes were appointed hym at the kinges charges.*

To read these recollections told to Martyr by Columbus himself is as fascinating today as it must have been in sixteenth-century England. Leaving Spain with three ships and 220 men, Columbus set out to find land to the westward, stopping briefly in the Canary Islands to replenish food and water. He then sailed southwest for 33 days seeing nothing but water and sky. On the thirtieth day the increasingly impatient crew tried to overthrow Columbus' leadership; literally, they wanted to throw him overboard, claiming that he was leading them on a wild goose chase and had no idea where he was going. It is a testament to Columbus' powers of persuasion that he calmed the sailors and assured them that not only did he know where they were headed but that if they would just hold on a few more days they would reach land. Three days later, on the morning of October 12, 1492, "with cheerfull hartes they espied the lande longe looked for."

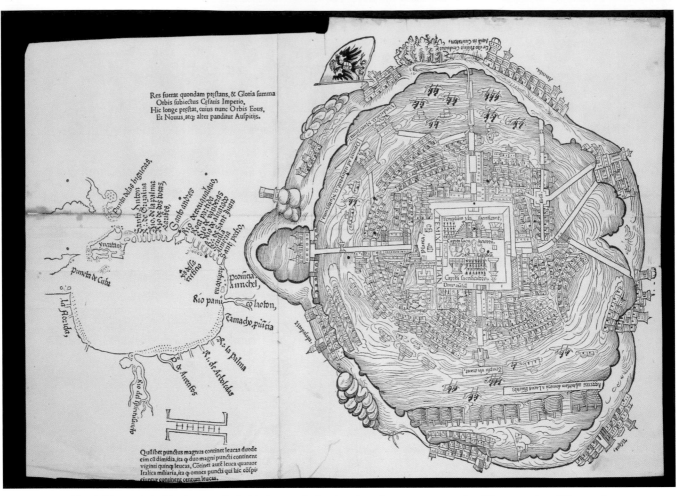

*Tenochtitlan, capital of the Aztec empire in Mexico, was the first American city to appear on a printed European plan. This example illustrated Hernán Cortés'*Praeclara Ferdinädi Cortesii de Noua Maris Oceani Hyspania *(Nuremburg, 1524). A map of the Gulf of Mexico is inset at left. Peter Martyr chronicled Cortés' conquest of Tenochtitlan in his fifth decade.*

Martyr's narrative of Columbus' first voyage continues, recording contacts with the indigenous people ("a greate multitude of them came runnynge to the shore to behold this new nation, whom they thought to have discended from heauen") and the immediate human impulse to barter with the Spanish sailors (they "came swimming to the shyppes, bryngyng gold with them, which they changed with owre men for erthen pots, drinking glasses, poyntes, pynnes, hawkes bells, lokinge glasses, and suche other trifles"). Throughout his decades, Martyr describes the people of the New World in equally vivid terms.

The land and its animals and plants are introduced in similar fashion, such as the first mention in the book of parrots:

> *They brought from this Iland vii Popingayes, bygger than phesantes, muche differing from other in coloure: hauyng theyr backes, brestes, and bealies of purple coloure and theyre wynges of other variable coloures. In all these Ilandes is no lesse plenty of popingayes then with vs of sparrows or starlings.*

Martyr described coconuts by relating an incident when natives brought to the ships:

> *gourdes full of water offeringe theym vnto our men. . . . In all these Ilandes is a certeyne kynde of trees as bygge as elmes, whiche bear gourdes in the steade of fruites. These they vse*

only as drinkynge pottes, and to fetche water in, but not for meate, for the inner substance of them, is sowrer then gaule, and the barke as harde as any shell.

Martyr's accounts of the natural wonders of the New World continue throughout the four decades translated and published by Richard Eden, and they are interspersed with the other events of Columbus' voyages and some of those who followed him. Much of this is a tale of violence as the Spanish explorers became settlers and conquistadors. Martyr respected Columbus and thought him a wonderful man, but he also realized that it was nearly impossible for him or any other leader to control the sailors and colonists once they were at a distance from Spain. Although violence against the native peoples was officially prohibited by the Council of the Indies and by Columbus when he was viceroy of the Indies, it became a prominent part of the tale told by Peter Martyr in his eight decades.

Richard Eden's translation of Peter Martyr's tales of the exploration of the New World revealed to Englishmen for the first time a huge area of opportunity that had not previously been a part of their national vision. It was unlikely that this would long go unnoticed. By the 1570s, English navigators were competing with those of Spain and other nations in both exploration and trade. This development was particularly galling to Spain and helped lead to open conflict at sea by the 1580s. By that time England was beginning to embark on its own colonial enterprises, which would result in the establishment of short-lived enclaves at Roanoke in the late 1580s and, by 1607, a permanent settlement in Virginia.

For William L. Clements, the importance of books such as Richard Eden's translation of Peter Martyr was obvious and too much to resist. He was able to purchase a copy from New York rare book collector Grenville Kane and add *The Decades of the Newe Worlde or West India* to the personal collection that would form the nucleus of the Clements Library. It remains today one of the jewels of the Library's extensive holdings of books on the earliest explorations of the Americas.

A gilded national eagle hangs above the door to the Rare Book Room.

MAMVSSE
WUNNEETUPANATAMWE
UP-BIBLUM GOD
NANEESWE
NUKKONE TESTAMENT
KAH WONK
WUSKU TESTAMENT.

Ne quoſhkinnumuk naſhpe Wuttinneumoh *CHRIST*
noh aſoowesit

JOHN ELIOT·

CAMBRIDGE:

Printeuoop naſhpe *Samuel Green* kah *Marmaduke Johnſon.*

1 6 6 3.

THE BIBLE IN MASSACHUSETT

— Emiko Hastings

The Eliot Indian Bible is one of the great landmarks of early American printing. When Cambridge, Massachusetts, printers Samuel Green and Marmaduke Johnson completed four years of work on the project in 1663, *Mamusse Wunnestupanatamwe Up-Biblum God naneeswe Nukkone Testament kah wonk Wusku Testament* was the first Bible printed in North America. Principal credit for translating the Bible into the language of the Massachusett Indians went to missionary John Eliot, although he drew on the expertise of several others. Given the translation and technical challenges of this ambitious initiative, it was a remarkable achievement for the first printing press in what would become the United States. As a high point in American book history, the Eliot Indian Bible has long been a focus for collectors of Americana, who have coveted it despite its linguistic inaccessibility.

Although John Eliot intended his Indian Bible for the use of Christian Indians in New England, he and his collaborators were also conscious of its reception by the English-speaking world. It was the first time American missionaries had attempted to translate the entire text of the Bible into a Native American language. This massive undertaking, if successful, would raise the profile of missionary endeavors in the New World, and bring prestige to the New England colonies. Eliot's supporters and contemporaries recognized the importance of this project to the Massachusetts Bay Colony. Writing in 1702, Cotton Mather proclaimed: "Behold, ye Americans, the greatest honor that ever you were partakers of! This Bible was printed here at our Cambridge; and it is the only Bible that ever was printed in all America, from the very foundation of the world."

Translating the Bible into Massachusett came during a turbulent period in English history. The efforts of New England missionaries like John Eliot to convert the American Indians paralleled the outbreak of civil war in England. Determined to complete church reform and establish godly rule in England, the Puritan faction led by Oliver Cromwell regarded Christian missionary work with Native Americans as a worthwhile colonial extension of their religious principles. In 1649, after the execution of King Charles I and the formation of the Commonwealth of England, Parliament established the Corporation for the Propagation of the Gospel in New England. The legislation authorized the Corporation to collect charitable subscriptions from all the parishes of England and Wales for disbursement in New England by the Commissioners of the United Colonies (leaders of the four settlements in Boston, Plymouth, New Haven, and Hartford). These revenues funded the printing of the Indian Bible from 1659 to 1663.

With the restoration of Charles II to the British throne in 1660, the corporation was in a precarious position. The charter issued by Parliament was no longer valid, placing the corporation's lands and funds in jeopardy, and it had already invested considerable resources in the Bible printing project. The members of the corporation decided to continue with the work, and when the New Testament was completed in 1661, 40 copies intended for presentation to the king went to England with a dedication inserted by the commissioners. Diplomatically, they took the opportunity to "congratulate Your majesties happy Restitution, after Your long suffering" and assure him that the translation "will be a perpetual monument, that by your majesties Favour the Gospel of our Lord and Saviour Jesus Christ was first made known to the Indians." During this period of uncertainty, the members of the Corporation did not meet openly or record entries in their record book; in writing, they carefully referred to themselves as the "late pretended corporation." Fortunately for the fate of the Indian Bible, the king issued a new charter for the corporation in 1662, and it was able to recover its lands and complete the printing of the Bible.

In recognition of the Indian Bible's transatlantic audience, copies intended for presentation had English-language materials inserted in the front. Those intended for the use of Indians, including the one now owned by the Clements Library, lacked these English pages. The English title page read: "The Holy Bible: containing the Old Testament and the New. Translated into the Indian language and ordered to be printed by the Commissioners of the United Colonies in New-England, at the charge, and with the consent of the Corporation in England for the Propagation of the Gospel amongst the Indians in New-England." When the entire Bible was completed in 1663, the Corporation sent 20 presentation copies, bound in dark blue morocco with the English title page and special dedication to the king, to notables and universities in England. Significantly, the English title pages and dedications made no mention of John Eliot, although he was prominently listed on the Indian title page. After the restoration of the monarchy, the Bible's supporters may have thought it prudent not to remind the new king about Eliot's association with the work, since he was also the author of a controversial anti-monarchy book, *The Christian Commonwealth,* banned in Massachusetts. Nevertheless, Eliot's name became firmly attached to the Indian Bible in popular usage.

The idea to translate the Bible into a native language emerged from John Eliot's decades of missionary work in New England. He came to Massachusetts Bay as a teenager in 1631, reportedly bringing 23 barrels of books with him. In 1646 Eliot began to learn the Massachusett language and preach sermons to Indians. His first teacher was an Indian named Cockenoe who had been taken captive during the Pequot War of 1637, and who could speak and read English. Five years later Eliot established a Christian Indian village at Natick to educate the "praying Indians." At one point, there were 14 such praying towns in New England, although most were disbanded after King Philip's War.

The Natick residents learned the written Massachusett language from translations of religious works, produced by Eliot and printed at the Cambridge press. The primers, catechisms and religious

NEGONNE OOSUKKUHWHONK *MOSES,*

Ne aſoweetamuk

GENESIS.

CHAP. I.

Pſal.
33.6.
& 136.
5.
Act.14.
15.
& 17.
24.
Hebr.
11.3.
b 2Cor.
4.6.

Eſke kutchiſſik *a* ayum God 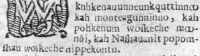 Keſuk kah Ohke.

2 Kah Ohke mô matta knhkenauunneunkquttinnœ kah monteagunninnœ, kah pohkenum woikeche mœnôi, kah Naſhauanit popomſhau woikeche nippekontu.

3 Onk nœwau God *b* wequaiaj, káh mô wequai.

4 Kah wunnaumun God wequai ne en wunnegen : Kah wutchadchaûbe-ponumun God noeu wequai kah noeu pohkenum.

e Pſal.
136.5.
Jer.10.
12. &
51.15.

5 Kah wutuiloweetamun God wequai Keſukod, kah pohkenum wutuiſoweetamun Nukon : kah mô wunnonkœœk kah mo mohtompog negonne keſuk.

6 Kah nœwau God *c* ſepakehtamœudj nôeu nippekontu, kah chadchapemœudj naſhauweit nippe wutch nippekóntu.

7 Kah ayimup God ſepakehtamóonk, kah wutchadchabeponumunnap naſhàueu nippe agwu, uttiyeu agwu ſepakehtamóonk, kah naſhàueu nippekontu uttiyeu ongkouwe ſepakehtamóonk, kah mônkó n nih.

d Jer.
51.15.

8 Kah wuttiſoweétamun God *d* ſepakehtamóonk Keſukquaſh, kah mô wunnonkœœk, kah mô mohtompog nahohtôeu keſukok.

e Pſal.
33.7.
& 136.
5.
Job 38.
8

9 Kah nœwau God moémœuidj *e* nippe ut agwu keſukquaſh kah paſukqunnu, kah pahkemoidj nanabpeu, kah mônkó n nih.

10 Kah wuttiſoweétam un God nanabpi ohke, kah môeémœ nippe wuttiſoweetamun Kehtoh, & wunnaumun God ne en wunnegen.

11 Kah nœwau God dtanuéej ohke moſkeht, moiket ikannémunéœk ikannémunaſh, & meechummue mahtugquaſh meechummi-œok meechummuonk niſh noh paſuk neane wuttinnuſuonk , ubbuhkummininûœk et woikeche ohke, kah mônko n niſh.

12 Kah ohke dtannegeaup moiket, kah moiket ikannenennûœk ikannemunaſh, niſh noh paſuk neane wuttinnu-ſiſh, kah mahtug meechu ımùtœk , ubbuhkammininûœk wu ıhogkut niſh noh paſuk neane wuttinnuſuonk, kah wunnaumun b ne en wunnegen.

13 Kah mo wunnonkœœk, kah mo mohtompog ſhwekeſukod.

14 Kah nœwau God, *f* Wequanantégiſ nmôhettich ut wuſſepakentamœonganit keſukquaſh, & pohſhéhettich ut naſhⁱuwe keſukod, kah ut naſhⁱuwe nukkonut, kah kukkineatuonganûhhettich , kah uttœcheyeûhettich , kah keſukodtuœwuſhettich , kah kodtumnœœwuhhettich.

f Deut.
4.19.
Pſal.
136.7.

15 Kah n nag wequanantéganûôhetticla ut ſepakehtamœwonganit wequaiumóhettich ohke, onk mô n nih.

16 Kah ayum God neeſunaſh miſſiyeuaſh wequananteganaſh, wequananteg môiag nanánumœomœ keſukod, wequananteg peaſik nanáni nœmœ nukon, kah anogqlog.

17 Kah uppónuh God wuſſepakentamœonganit keſukquaſh , woh wequohſumwog ohke.

18 Onk woh *g* wunnananumunneau keſukod kah nûkon , kah pohſhémœ naſhaueu wequai, kah pohkenum, kah wunnaumun God ne en wunnegen.

g Jer.
31.23.

19 Kah mô wunnonkœœk kah mo mohtompog yaou quinukok.

20 Kah nœwau God, mœonahettich nippekóntu pomómutcheg pomantamwae, kah puppinſhaûuſſog pumunahettich ongkouwe ohket woikeche wuſſepahkehtamœonganit keſukquaſh.

21 Kah kezheau God matikkeñunutche'n Pœtâbpoh, kah niſh noh pomanta nôe ôáas noh pompámayit uttiyeug mœnacheg nippekóntu, niſh noh paſuk neane wuttinnuſuonk, kah niſh noh œnuppohwhunin puppinſhaaſh, niſh noh paſuk neane wuttinnuſuonk, kah wunnau nu u God ne en wunnegen.

22 Kah œninu noh nhhóg God nœwau, Miſſéneetuónittegk, *b* kah muttaanœk, kah nu nwapezk nippeut kehtohhannit, kah puppin ſhitog mattáaⁱahettich ohket.

b Gen.
8.17.
& 9.1.

23 Kah mo wınonk o'ok kah mo mohtompog napanna audtaſhıkquinukok.

24 Kah nœwau God, Paſœwaheonⁱh ohke oſas pomanta nwᵘeu, niſh noh paſuk neane wuttinnuſin, neetaſſiog, pamayéch 'j kah

A

The beginning of the Book of Genesis as it appears printed in the Massachusett language.

tracts that Eliot translated into the Massachusett language have become known as the "Indian Library." Like other Puritans, Eliot believed that literacy was essential for conversion to Christianity. Individual study of the Bible was a central tenet of Puritan belief and thus an important goal for Indian converts. Eliot wrote in 1653, "I have had a great longing desire (if it were the will of God) that our Indian Language might be sanctified by the Translation of the Holy Scriptures into it . . . but I fear it will not be obtained in my days. . . . While I live, if God please to assist me, I resolve to follow the work of translating the Scriptures."

ELLIOT, THE FIRST MISSIONARY AMONG THE INDIANS.

A romanticized nineteenth-century interpretation of John Eliot as missionary. From J.A. Spencer, History of the United States from the Earliest Period to the Administration of James Buchanan *(New York, 1858).*

The language of the Eliot Indian Bible was spoken by the Massachusett and Wampanoag nations of Native Americans, who lived in what is now southeastern Massachusetts. The language itself, part of the Algonquian language family, is one of a related group variously known as Massachusett, Pokanoket or Wampanoag (for which the modern spelling is Wôpanâak). It has also been called the Natick dialect, after the Christian Indian village founded by John Eliot in 1651. Since there was no written form of the language at that time, Eliot rendered the spelling phonetically. Translating the Bible presented a number of challenges, not least the problem of finding equivalents for concepts that did not exist in native culture. In some cases Eliot chose to insert the English word with an appropriate suffix, such as "cherubim*lab*." Eliot's translation choices also reflected his desire to have Native Americans convert to Christianity and adopt European ways. For example, bias against native customs emerges through his use of the Massachusett term for "pipe carrier" (a person in charge of indigenous religious ceremonies) as the translation for "witch." Careful study of the text also reveals some errors that may be the result of misunderstandings between Eliot and the Christian Indians with whom he worked. Linguist James Hammond Trumbull observed one curious mistake in a passage in 2 Kings ii. 23, where the bad boys say to the prophet, "Go up, thou bald head." In the translation, the last word is *pompasuhkonkanontup*, literally, "*ball*-head," as in "a ball to play with," probably because a translator misheard Eliot's pronunciation.

Cotton Mather praised John Eliot as solely responsible for the Indian Bible, claiming, "The whole translation he writ with but one pen." However, one biographer of Eliot noted in 1840 that "Mather is sometimes so loose in his statements, that one scarcely knows how much they mean. In this instance, however, his story seems more precise than credible." Although Eliot was the guiding force behind the production of this Bible, he relied extensively on the help of native translators and assistants to complete the project. In 1654 Eliot himself referred to an Indian helper "whom I have used in Translating a good part of the holy Scriptures."

Several of Eliot's Indian associates are known by name, including Cockenoe, Job Nesutan, John Sassamon, and James Printer. Job Nesutan was a scholar and preacher, and according to a contemporary was "a very good linguist in the English tongue, and was Mr. Eliot's assistant and interpreter in his translation of the Bible, and other books of the Indian language." John Sassamon was a Christian Indian minister who helped to build the town of Natick and attended Harvard College in 1653. Increase Mather wrote that "being of very excellent parts," Sassamon had "translated some part of the bible into the Indian language." Sassamon also worked occasionally as an advisor and translator for King Philip, and his death in 1675 precipitated King Philip's War. James Printer, a former student of Eliot, became an apprentice to the Harvard printer Samuel Green in 1659 and may have assisted with proofreading the first edition of the Bible. In 1683, during production of the second edition, Eliot said of Printer, "We have but one man (viz. the Indian printer) that is able to compose the sheets, and correct the press, with understanding."

The process of printing the first Bible in North America was well documented by a steady stream of instructions flowing from England and reports sent back from the colony. As George Parker

Winship observed in *The Cambridge Press, 1638–1692*, "There are few books of any period whose progress through the intricacies of bookmaking can be followed with as documental detail as can that of the Eliot Indian Bible." Eliot and his supporters in New England made a persuasive case for the necessity of an Indian-language Bible, and in 1659 the corporation approved the decision to print the translation: "As to the printing of the bible in the Indian language . . . we conceive it will not onely bee acceptable unto god, but very profitable to the poor heathen and will much tend to the promotion of the sperituall parte of this worke amongst them."

Once the support of the corporation was assured, printing the Bible required considerable preparation and planning. Eliot's first Indian-language pamphlets had been printed on Massachusetts' only press at Harvard College, but printing the entire Bible was a challenge for this small shop. With a skilled typesetter needed for the process of setting well over a million individual characters in type, the corporation brought Marmaduke Johnson from London to assist Samuel Green. Eliot arranged to have a new printing press and type sent from England, and the corporation provided the necessary reams of paper. A custom font, later described as a "full faced bourgeois on a brevier body," was ordered from a type foundry. It included a specially cast character (a linked "oo" for a particular sound in the Native language) and a larger proportion than usual of the letters "k," "m," "q," and "w" to accommodate their frequent use in Massachusett. This type was smaller than the fonts previously used at the Cambridge press, undoubtedly to save paper costs for printing the whole Bible.

Printing of the Bible proceeded at a steady pace from 1660 to 1663, at a rate of about one sheet per week. In 1662 printing faltered for a time when Samuel Green accused Marmaduke Johnson of "obtaining the affections" of Green's daughter. During the trial, it was revealed that Johnson already had an estranged wife in England and therefore could not marry Elizabeth Green. Johnson sat in jail for six months, then returned to work and to his previous lodgings in the Green home. Printing slowed considerably in his absence, and Winship noted several errors from the sheets printed during that period, attributing them to disruption from the ongoing social drama at the press.

By 1661 Green and Johnson had completed 1,500 copies of the New Testament, binding some of them separately for distribution. Two years later with more than 1,000 copies of the Old Testament ready, they bound the two parts together to make up the full Indian Bible. The entire Bible consisted of 149 sheets, printed in quarto with eight pages per sheet. All told, approximately 368 reams of paper went into the Indian Bible, more than the entire printed output of the English colonies in North America to that point.

John Ratcliff came from England in 1663 to bind copies of the Eliot Indian Bible. His instructions were to "take care of the binding of 200 of them strongly and as speedily as may bee with leather, or as may bee most serviceable for the Indians." In correspondence with the Commissioners, Ratcliff objected to the payment of two shillings sixpence to bind a copy of the Indian Bible, since the work took him a whole day to complete, and he had to furnish his own leather and clasps. It is likely that Ratcliff bound the Clements Library copy of the Eliot Bible.

Little is known of the initial dissemination or reception of the translated Bible, particularly among its primary audience of Christian Indians. With over a thousand copies printed, or approximately one for every 2.5 Christian Indians in New England, supply considerably exceeded demand. However, most of the copies were unbound, and the majority may have remained in storage until their destruction during King Philip's War. What is known about the subsequent history of the Bible has come mostly from annotations by native readers in surviving copies. These marginalia serve to illustrate the role of the Indian Bible in the lives of native Christians, who often passed copies from hand to hand within a community. Their notes include commentaries on the text, religious sentiments, warnings and reminders, and announcements to the community. Some writers used bare spaces to practice their penmanship or copy out whole passages from the Bible.

A dozen years after the first printing of the Indian Bible, King Philip's War erupted as the culmination of bitter tensions between Native Americans and English colonists. John Eliot and his Christian Indian converts were caught in the middle of this cultural collision. Eliot had previously attempted to convert King Philip to Christianity by using John Sassamon's connection to him, without success. In one memorable confrontation recorded by Cotton Mather, King Philip ripped a button off Eliot's coat and said that, "he cared for his Gospel just as much as he cared for that Button." When Sassamon's corpse was discovered in a frozen pond and three Wampanoags were executed for his murder, hostility turned into violent attacks by both sides. Most Christian Indians sided with the English colonists, but others, including Eliot's assistant James Printer, allied themselves with the Wampanoags.

King Philip's War marked the decline of John Eliot's missionary program. Many of the Christian Indians from "praying towns" were imprisoned for the duration of the war on Deer Island in Boston Harbor. Eliot recorded in his diary, "When the Indians were hurried away to an iland at half an hours warning, pore soules in terror thei left theire goods, books, bibles, only some few caryed their bibles, the rest were spoyled & lost." Three years later, when Dutch traders asked Eliot for a copy of the Indian Bible, he told them that, "in the late Indian War all the Bibles and Testaments were carried away and burned or destroyed, so that he had not been able to save any for himself." It is entirely possible that King Philip's forces deliberately sought out the Indian Bible for destruction, viewing it as a symbol of English influence over Indian culture.

By the end of the war, the Native American population in New England was a fraction of its previous numbers. Few of the "praying towns" survived into the eighteenth century; in 1698, church membership at Natick was down to seven men and three women. Eliot's ambition to establish self-governing Christian Indian societies gave way to a new missionary goal of assimilation into English-speaking society. Although Eliot printed a second edition of the translated Bible in 1685, his death in 1690 marked the end of that endeavor. When the corporation proposed a third edition of the Indian Bible in 1710, Cotton Mather discouraged the idea and concluded, "The best thing we can do for our Indians is to Anglicise them in all agreeable Instances." By the nineteenth century, the Massachusett language had ceased to be widely spoken and was generally viewed as a "dead language." Once a vital part of John Eliot's missionary program in the New World, the Indian Bible was now a "typographical curiosity" for collectors of Americana. As the twentieth century began, linguists like James Hammond Trumbull and Wilberforce Eames were the only living people who could read the Eliot Bible in the original language. Trumbull was the author of the *Natick Dictionary* (1903), a compilation he based on the vocabulary of the Indian Bible. Eames was an influential bibliographer and librarian whose 1890 survey of extant copies of both editions of the Eliot Indian Bible is still the most complete census available. William L. Clements adopted the classification system Eames developed for the Americana collection of James Lenox, and it is still in use at the Clements Library.

The exact number and whereabouts of extant Indian Bibles is uncertain. Of the thousand copies originally printed in 1663, many apparently perished during King Philip's War. Eames' 1890 census identified 39 copies of the 1663 edition owned by institutions or private collectors, although the Clements Library copy does not appear on his listing. Of the 39 copies Eames found, 19 contained the English title page, even though many more of the Indian variant had been printed. The survival rate indicates that the presentation copies sent to England were more likely to survive in universities and private collections than the copies intended for use by Indians, making the Clements Library copy of even greater interest. Eames listed 55 copies of the 1685 edition, including the one now owned by the Clements Library.

The Clements Library acquired its copy of the first edition Eliot Indian Bible in 1949, during the directorship of Randolph G. Adams. The Library already had a copy of the 1685 edition that William L. Clements had bought in 1914 at the auction of the library of Houghton, Michigan, collector Lucius L. Hubbard. The Merwin Sales Company of New York devoted 10 auction sessions to selling 2,451 lots from Hubbard's collection for "a grand total of $21,849.10." Lot 688 in the Hubbard sales was the "large and perfect copy of the 1685 Bible, a very handsome and desirable copy of this exceedingly rare volume." Hubbard was on the University of Michigan board of regents with Clements in 1914, and it must have pleased the older collector to see one of his treasures go to a fellow enthusiast of antiquarian Americana. In an elaborate late-nineteenth-century red morocco binding by Francis Bedford, the Hubbard copy of the Eliot Bible features two 1748 manuscript signatures of noted Native American Presbyterian clergyman Samson Occom (1723–92), the first Native American to publish his writings in English. The back of the book also contains a manuscript note, "Purchased of the Revd. Samson Occom by Thomas Shaw Esquire of New London & by him presented to Yale College Library A.D. 1790."

The prized first edition came to the Library as a purchase from Dr. Otto Oren Fisher of Detroit, who agreed to sell his copy after effective cultivation by Dr. Adams. Dr. Fisher's copy of the Bible had long been the property of Queen's College at Oxford University. It carries the Queen's College book-plate, with the college motto and founder's arms, inside the front cover. The provenance of the Clements Library copy before its appearance in the Queen's College Library is unknown. Use of the college bookplate found in the Clements copy began in the late seventeenth century, offering little evidence for the date of the book's arrival at Oxford. The 1890 census by Eames recorded only one copy of the 1663 Bible at Oxford, in the Bodleian Library. That the Queen's College copy was not listed then might indicate either that it was not in the library's possession at that time or that it had not been catalogued. Also unanswered is how the college acquired one of the copies intended for use by Indians, since most copies Eames found in England were presentation copies with the English title page.

The story of the Clements copy's return to America is dramatic. During World War II, England's Antiquarian Booksellers Association raised money for British munitions by selling duplicate copies of rare books from British libraries and museums. Since the Bodleian Library at Oxford had two copies of the Eliot Indian Bible, the University selected the Queen's College copy for sale. In 1941 Lionel Robertson, president of the ABA, took a number of books to the United States to sell. The most valuable book he carried was the Queen's College copy of the first edition Indian Bible. The voyage from Liverpool on the Holland America freighter *Blommersdijk* put the Eliot Bible and Robertson's other rarities at risk. German planes followed the convoy 1,000 miles out to sea and subjected the ships to daily attacks. Passengers on the *Blommersdijk* reported that German bombers came within 100 feet of the ship to spray the decks with machine-gun fire, and a bomb struck a ship from another nearby convoy and sank it immediately. Upon Robertson's arrival in the United States, a *New York Times* article on the German air attacks quoted him as saying that the Antiquarian Booksellers Association had raised $20 million in American exchange since the start of the war to pay for British munitions. He discussed the Queen's College copy of the Indian Bible he was carrying and hinted that he already had a purchaser for it.

Dr. Adams filled a large gap in the Clements Library's early Americana holdings when he purchased the 1663 Eliot Bible from Dr. Fisher. The Clements copy of the Bible is the version issued for use by the Indians, as distinguished by the absence of the English titles and dedications. It contains the Old Testament, New Testament and Psalms of David in the original American binding of blind-tooled calf, probably by John Ratcliff. The spine has been repaired with new leather at some point, with the original leather glued over it. Although the book currently lacks clasps, there are traces of a clasp on the upper front cover. The endpapers have a large motif of a vase and stylized flowers in blue, and the printed end sheets consist of waste sheets from a different book bound in horizontally. "Biblia Americana" is written in black ink along the fore-edge of the book, and "Biblia sacra / Indo-Americana / Eliot / Cambridge 1663 & 1661" is stamped in gold on the book's spine, possibly added as a form of cataloging while the book was in the Queen's College Library. While there is some wear to the exterior of the book, the inner pages are crisp and clean, with no apparent annotations or other markings.

Despite its reputation as "the book no one can read," the Indian Bible has experienced a cultural revival in the past two decades. The Native American cultures of New England, once assumed to be disappearing, have instead reemerged with considerable strength in the modern era. In 1993, spear-headed by Jessie Little Doe Baird, the Mashpee and Aquinnah tribes of the Wampanoag Nation launched the Wôpanâak Language Reclamation Project. One of the primary sources for the project was the Massachusetts Institute of Technology's copy of the 1685 Eliot Indian Bible, which provided a detailed source for pronunciation, vocabulary and grammar of the language. Partly because of the efforts of missionaries like John Eliot, Massachusett is one of the best-documented native languages in the region. Using the Indian Bible in combination with such other sources as the writings of Wampanoag Indians of the 1600s and 1700s enables modern scholars to reconstruct the Massachusett and Wampanoag vocabulary and speech patterns. The dictionary created by this project now contains over 10,000 words, and Baird has taught Wôpanâak language classes and written a number of books in Wôpanâak. An estimated 200 Wampanoags now speak at least some of the language, and Baird's daughter, raised to be bilingual, is the first native speaker of Wôpanâak in seven generations. The Indian Bible's transformative use by modern native communities to revive a lost language is an unanticipated result of the work that John Eliot and his colleagues did more than three centuries ago.

The creation of the Eliot Indian Bible was a significant achievement in 1663, as the first Bible printed in North America and the first to be translated into a Native American language for missionary purposes. Even more than a monument of American printing, however, the Indian Bible represents a moment in the history of European-Native American encounters. Once regarded as the sole product of John Eliot's pen, the book known as "the Eliot Indian Bible" is now recognized as the result of a dynamic collaboration between Eliot and Native Americans. Tracing its production and dissemination reveals a complex intersection of shifting alliances and negotiations that sometimes placed John Eliot and his fellow missionaries in opposition to the Native Americans they worked with and sought to convert. In the aftermath of King Philip's War and the long history of oppression of Native American peoples, the Bible's symbolic value has undergone a significant transformation. As both an artifact of the past and a living document in the present, the Indian Bible continues to occupy a significant place in collections of early Americana.

*Detail from one of the
Library's bronze front doors.*

GOOD NEWS FROM A FAR COUNTRY
A MAP OF NEW-ENGLAND

— *Mary Sponberg Pedley*

"Being the first that ever was here cut, And done by / the best Pattern that could be had, which being in / some places defective, it made the other less exact: / yet doth it sufficiently shew the Scituation of / the Country, and conveniently well the / distances of Places. / The figures that are joined with the Name of Places / are to distinguish such as have been assaulted / by the Indians from others."

This small map, measuring a mere 31 by 40 centimeters, does not draw attention to itself for its beauty. Carved upon and printed from a block of wood, its unprepossessing features are relieved neither by color nor elegant lettering. Nonetheless, the map is not shy; its title boasts that it is "the first that ever was here cut." Indeed, it is the first map to be printed in the British colonies of North America and, as Randolph G. Adams maintained, is perhaps the first map to be printed in all of North America. It appeared in 1677, issued from the press of the printer John Foster in Boston. It was designed to be tipped into the Reverend William Hubbard's book, *A Narrative of the Troubles with the Indians;* more specifically, it was meant to be bound in the text opposite page 132, where "A Table of Events" begins. Hubbard's *Narrative* was an account of King Philip's War (1675–77), a conflict between English settlers in Massachusetts and Native Americans led by "King Philip," the name given by the English to the sachem Metacom, leader of the Wampanoag confederacy and Narragansett groups in New England. The violence and carnage inflicted on both sides had deeply shaken the young English colony in North America, whose settlers had left behind the violence of England's civil war to seek a more peaceful promised land in the New World.

Hubbard's *Narrative* was nearly the last in a queue of many works that appeared over the three years of this "war." Most were short publications, some no more than a few pages, based on reports sent from Massachusetts and printed in London. Only a few were printed in New England, either in Cambridge or in Boston. Of these, two stand out for their length and purpose: influential New England preacher Increase Mather's *A Brief History of the War with the Indians in New England* (Boston, 1676), at about 50 pages, and William Hubbard's *Narrative,* with a substantial 132 pages

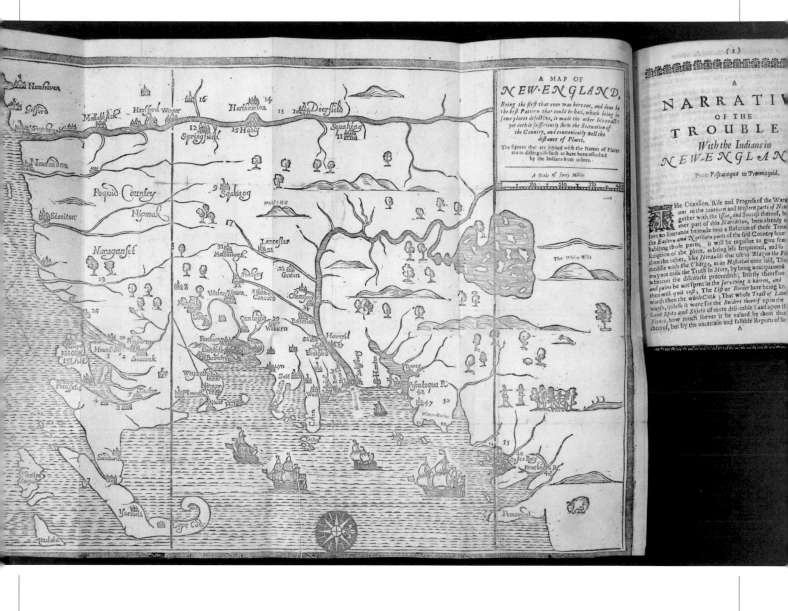

(1)

A
NARRATIVE
OF THE
TROUBLE
With the Indians in
NEW-ENGLAN
From Pescataqua to Pemmaquid.

HE Occasion, Rise and Progress of the War
ans in the *Southern* and *Western* parts of New-
gether with the Issue, and Success thereof, h
mer part of this *Narrative*, been already
fore an Entrance be made into a Relation of those Trou
the *Eastern* and *Northern* parts of the said Country from
habiting those parts; it will be requisite to give son
scription of the place, as being less frequented, and so
meddle with the *Charge*, as an *Historian* once said, Th
may not miss the Truth in Story, by being unacquainted
whereon the discourse proceedeth; Briefly therefore
then will *quit cost*, The *List* or *Border* here being kn
worth then the *whole Cloth* ; That whole *Tract of Lan*
worth, unless it were for the *Borders* thereof upon the
some *Spots* and *Skirts* of more desireable Land upon th
Rivers, how much soever it be valued by them that
thereof, but by the uncertain and fallible Reports of su

A

A NARRATIVE

OF THE TROUBLES WITH THE

INDIANS

In *NEW-ENGLAND*, from the first planting thereof in the year 1607. to this present year 1677. But chiefly of the late Troubles in the two last years, 1675. and 1676.

To which is added a Discourse about the *Warre* with the

PEQUODS

In the year 1637.

By W. Hubbard, *Minister of* Ipswich.

And the Lord said unto Moses, write this for a Memoriall in a Book, and rehearse it in the ears of Joshua; for I will utterly put out the Remembrance of Amalek from under heaven Exod. 17.14.
Wherefore it is said in the book of the Warrs of the Lord, what he did in the red sea, and in the Brooks of Arnon. Numb.21.14
As cold waters to a thirsty soul, so is good news from a far Country. Prov. 25.25.

Expressa Imago, et quasi speculum quoddam viæ humanæ est historia, quia talia vel similia semper possunt in mundo accidere. *Thucyd.*
Historia tradit quæ facta sint, et quæ semper sint futura, donec eadem manet hominum natura idem.
Historiæ cognitio utilissima institutio, et præparatio est ad actiones politicas, et illustris Magistra ad perferendas fortunæ vices. *Polyb.*

Published by Authority.

B O S T O N;
Printed by *John Foster*, in the year 1677.

of text to which Hubbard had added his table listing the events of the war, keyed to places clearly marked on the map. Of all the accounts of King Philip's war, only Hubbard's *Narrative* was illustrated, and more significantly, illustrated with a map.

Born in Ipswich, England, around 1621, William Hubbard came to Ipswich, Massachusetts, with his father and three siblings when he was about 14. He studied medicine and was a member of the first Harvard College graduating class. He did not turn to the ministry until he was 35 and was ordained in 1658. Hardly a retiring type, Hubbard joined other elders to protest what they felt were unjust actions by the General Court in Massachusetts; he adopted a moderate line on witchcraft, even helping a woman escape charges by testifying to her good character. Hubbard's contrarian approach to topical issues emerges in his interpretation of King Philip's War as found in the *Narrative*. He dedicated his book to the governors of Massachusetts Bay, Plymouth and Connecticut, clearly a local audience, even though a later printing in London, under a different title and with a different copy of the map, certainly argues for a broader interest in these events in North America. Nonetheless, Hubbard wrote with a local audience in mind: the people of Massachusetts who had survived this war. In order to make sense of a brutal conflict, Hubbard offered an alternative view to that set forth by Increase Mather. Mather's *Brief History,* based on his sermons and published shortly before Hubbard's work, maintained that the violence perpetrated by the Indians was God's punishment of the Puritan colonists for their own degeneracy: they had become lax in sobriety and seriousness, decadent in their morals. Mather's subtitle explains: *Wherein the grounds, beginning, and Progress of the Warr, Is summarily Expressed; Together with a Serious Exhortation to the Inhabitants of That Land.*

Hubbard avoids the word "war" by titling his book *A Narrative of the* Troubles *with the Indians in New England.* Indeed, Hubbard does not place the blame for the conflict, if blame were to be ascribed, on the decadence of the colonists, but rather attempts to assemble facts and eyewitness accounts in a dispassionate way in order to produce a "narrative" from which the reader may draw his or her own conclusions. To create a convincing and trustworthy narrative, Hubbard needed to establish a trustworthy context. To this end, his map provided the needed illustration.

Hubbard's use of a map as his only illustration reflected a seventeenth-century interest and trust in cartography, which could seem to be an objective and impartial purveyor of a "situation." Maps are often based on measurement and can provide an image of space upon which viewers from different backgrounds may agree. Hubbard lays claim to such truthfulness in the title of his map: it is "done by the best Pattern that could be had, which being in / some places defective, it made the other less exact: yet doth it sufficiently shew the Scituation of the Country, and conveniently well the distances of Places." "Sufficiently shew" and "conveniently well" assure the viewer that care has been taken to produce a reliable image; the map's scale of miles and compass bearing in the sea in the foreground are further indications of a claim to veracity. The numbers on the map link each place to Hubbard's "Table of Events," which lists towns and sites, number by number, with brief descriptions of the Indian attacks on the colonial settlers, and references to more detailed descriptions elsewhere in the text. On the map, symbols of towns indicate English settlements; clumps of trees or single trees represent

Indian lairs. Signs like these were standard on seventeenth-century maps of the New World and New England in particular.

Two strong vertical printed lines run down the map, from top to bottom, cutting it almost into thirds. These lines provide a clue as to the source of the map's geography. William Reed of Boston prepared a large map of New England in 1665, in response to the request of four commissioners sent to North America by King Charles II. Their mission was to seize New Amsterdam from the Dutch and additionally to visit the New England colonies to report on boundary disputes, one of which concerned the boundary between Massachusetts, New York and New Hampshire. The commissioners employed Reed "to draw up an exact map of his majesties colonie of Massachusetts" for which they paid him the large sum of 10 pounds. Reed's map, or a copy of it, was sent to England but was lost at sea, although the original may have remained in Boston. Some years later, in 1676, as the boundary disputes remained unresolved, two agents from Massachusetts paid 10 shillings for a surveyor to copy a map which was "a Draft or plott of ye country wch ye Commissioners sent to his majtje." This version, copied from the map in Boston and sent to London, survives in an atlas assembled by William Blathwayt, Secretary to the Lords of Trade and Plantations. Considerably larger (55.7 x 65.7cm) than the Hubbard map, it nonetheless bears a remarkable resemblance to his with its prominent boundary lines drawn along two latitudes. These latitudinal boundaries reflected the terms of the Massachusetts charter (1629), which defined the territory of the colony; subsequent surveys would determine that latitude lines north of the Merrimack and south of the Charles River would form the boundaries of New England. The Reed map also shows a very large Lake Winnepesaukee, which, though unnamed on the Hubbard map, is clearly marked as the source of the unidentified Merrimack River.

Yet Hubbard did not use the Reed map in order to show boundaries; his bold latitude lines are neither labeled as boundaries nor identified as geographical lines of latitude. Their function seems rather to frame and separate an area, which would be known to readers as Massachusetts, and to display this area as the region of New England particularly affected by the Indian attacks described in his *Narrative.* The orientation of the map to the west also provides a framing device within which to understand the war. The colonists of Massachusetts are hemmed in by land and water; the Atlantic Ocean prevents escape to the east; the Connecticut River forms a line of demarcation to the west, beyond which lie more Indians and another enemy, the French; the south is equally bounded by ocean; and the north, by impassable hills and thick woods. Not only are the colonists beset by the godless Indians, they are also suffering from their isolation from England and any hope of worldly help.

By orienting his map to the west, with the Atlantic Ocean filling the foreground, Hubbard echoed a well-known cartographic image of the Holy Land. This would not surprise his Bible-reading audience. For Puritan households, the Bible formed an integral part of daily communion, and an illustrated Bible, especially with maps, would not have been an unusual possession. The Protestant Bible, whether published in Germany, the Netherlands, Switzerland, or London, was often illustrated with maps. The general map of the Holy Land in such Bibles often displayed the region as oriented to the east, with the Mediterranean forming the foreground. Such an orientation had been used to portray the Promised Land from the time of Claudius Ptolemy in the first century A.D. and continued well into the seventeenth century.

The role of such a cartographic image was to allow the reader to "well read the Bible," in the words of the English printer Reyner Wolfe, who in 1549 printed the first New Testament to contain maps. With a map the reader would learn more than just the location of places; the scale of miles which would instruct him as to "the distance of the miles [by which] thou mayest easily perceive what painful travail" the holy fathers and early saints had endured. Thus maps in Bibles were first and foremost explanatory devices, supporting the primacy of scripture over theological doctrine. They emphasized historical reality and illustrated the Bible's geographical setting. They also helped the reader to understand "dark" places in the text in order to experience its truth. And of course, maps could help sell Bibles.

An engraver's error distinguishes the London edition of Hubbard's map (right) from that produced earlier in Boston. The "White Hills" of the latter became "Wine Hills" on the former.

KING PHILIP.

Metacom or "King Philip," adversary of the Massachusetts colonists in the war of 1675–76. This conjectural portrait appeared in Henry Trumbull, History of the Indian Wars *(Boston, 1846).*

Hubbard connected his audience to the Bible on the title page of the *Narrative*, on which he provides quotations from Exodus, Numbers and Proverbs:

And the Lord said unto Moses, write this for a Memoriall in a Book, and rehearse it in the ears of Joshua, for I will utterly put out the Remembrance of Amalek from under heaven. (Exodus 17.14)

wherefore it is said in the book of the Warrs of the Lord, what he did in the red Sea, and in the Brooks of Arnon. (Numbers 21.4)

As cold waters to a thirsty soul, so is good news from a far Country." (Proverbs 25.25)

In these three quotations, Hubbard evokes the role of the printed word in explicating the troubles of a "chosen people," as the Puritans certainly regarded themselves. By writing his "Memoriall in a Book," a book of the "Warrs of the Lord," he casts his account of King Philip's war as "good news from a far Country." Hubbard's map shows a New England constrained on all sides by geographical boundaries and hostile enemies, unable to expand. Like the Israelites, the colonists are surrounded by hostile elements, whether human, animal or geographical. The Indians are not the only peoples who are inimical to the English: "We are hemm'd in on both sides and almost round about with people of foreign nations, whose design is neither religion nor yet planting colonies of civil people so much as present emolument by commerce and traffic with the Indians" (pp. 74–75). Hubbard refers here, of course, to the Dutch and French traders who pursued their own colonial aspirations and who had supplied arms to the Indians, exacerbating the war. New England, both in Hubbard's book and his map, is a coherent place, but one that is surrounded and embattled. It is not a land for God's punishment, as Increase Mather maintained, but a land of martyrs, the long-suffering colonists who had died because they believed themselves to be in a promised land. Hubbard uses a map to demonstrate the truth of this interpretation: the map portrays a real place, whose landmarks may be measured in scaled distances, and whose shape may be seen in the same configuration as the Holy Land. His account is based on eyewitness reports, another bulwark of truth telling. Yet for all of Hubbard's claims to truth and trustworthiness, we still must note that his narrative only lists the sites of Indian attacks on the Puritans, not the equally deadly and vicious colonial attacks on the Indians.

Hubbard's book was printed again a few months later in London by Thomas Parkhurst under a new title, *The present state of New-England. Being a narrative of the troubles with the Indians in New-England, from the First Planting Thereof in the year 1607, to This Present Year 1677: But Chiefly of the Late Troubles in the Two Last Years 1675, and 1676: To which is added a discourse about the war with the Peqvods in the year 1637.* The map was also re-cut in London, with several changes to the place names, including the most easily recognized: the alteration of the name of the hills to the north of Massachusetts Bay from the "White Hills" of the Boston map to the "Wine Hills" of the London map, a clear copyist's error.

While the map had been bound into the original Boston edition of the book at a significant location opposite page 132, where "A Table" explains the numbers on the map, in the London edition the map usually appears opposite page 1. In this location it functions only as a general geographical indicator, without any clear purpose or explanation for the numbers on it. The placement of the map in the text, opposite the table which it accompanies, and the linkage between the numbers on the map and the numbers on the table, have often been missed in early scholarship surrounding the map.

Throughout the twentieth century, Hubbard's map attracted interest and attention from bibliographers and print historians, largely because of its "first" status: it is the first map produced in North America, and it is an early graphic image of New England. The nature of its publication from woodcut is also unusual in a century during which engraving on copper plate replaced woodcut as the preferred medium for map reproduction. For these reasons, collectors of Americana, such as William L. Clements, were eager to acquire both the *Narrative* and the map. Building on a desire to have a complete collection of geography and history of North America, Clements acquired the London edition *(The Present State of New England)* before his library was turned over to the University of Michigan in 1923. He would have been pleased, had he lived long enough, with Randolph Adams' purchase of the Boston edition in 1935, which provided the Clements Library with the means to compare the two books and their maps.

Randolph G. Adams, the first director and curator of books of the Clements Library, was the first scholar to look critically at the Boston and London editions of Hubbard's work. In a paper read to the 1938 Chicago meeting of the Bibliographical Society of America, he noted that only half of the 50 Boston editions he examined contained the original map in its original place in the book (and, of these 25, a dozen contained facsimiles instead of the original map). Of the 50 London editions he analyzed, only seven copies lacked a map, while five had facsimiles inserted. These numbers suggest that the map was either occasionally left out of the Boston edition or removed. No one has undertaken a census of separate copies of the Hubbard New England map. For identification purposes, Adams and subsequently David Woodward, who studied the Boston and London woodcuts for all possible variants, proved conclusively that the version with the hills in northern Massachusetts labeled the "White Hills" was cut in Boston; the variant with the hills labeled the "Wine Hills" was cut in London by a copyist who presumably did not know the region and thus made the spelling error.

Yet, to focus on the details of the copying process is to neglect a larger understanding of Hubbard's purpose. Historians Matthew Edney and Susan Cimburek have provided the fullest context for understanding the map's role as a device to persuade the audience of a truth about the war and as a means to help the sufferer make some sense of it, by giving "comfort and encouragement to the surviving Generation." As Hubbard himself said on the page facing the map: "The more pains hath been taken to search out the broken pieces of that Story and thus put them together before the memory thereof was buried in the ruins of time, and past the recovery and knowledge of the present age, the which though it be here in the last place recorded, should in the first be remembered."

Decorative panels from the vaulted ceiling of the Great Room.

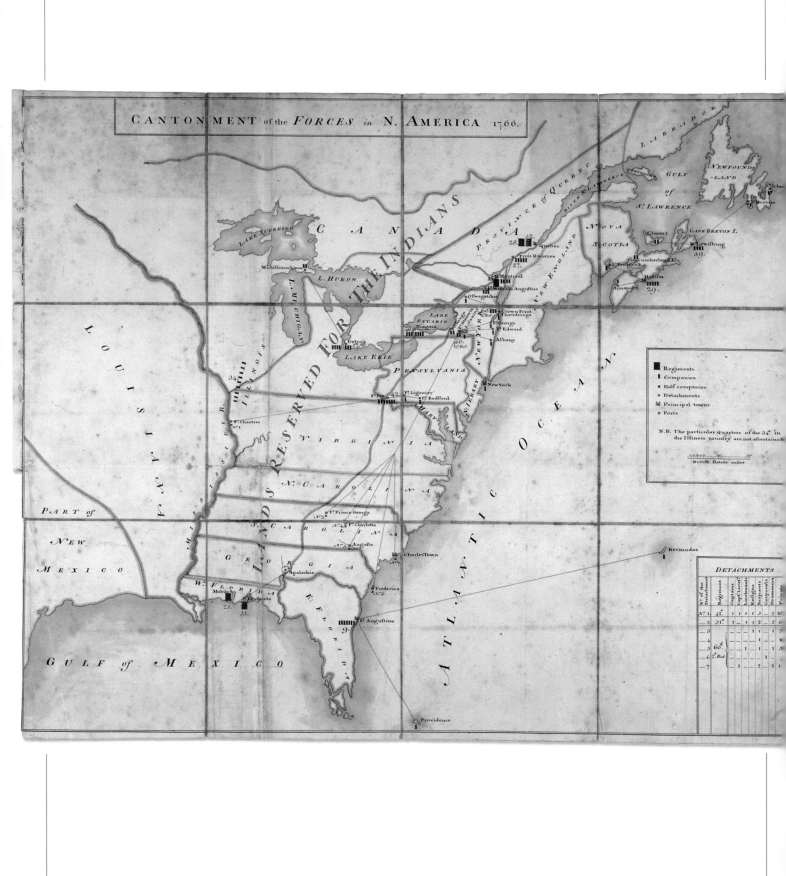

CANTONMENT of the FORCES in N. AMERICA 1766.

MAPPING AN ARMY IN NORTH AMERICA

— Brian Leigh Dunnigan

The title of the map is brief and straightforward: "Cantonment of the Forces in N. America 1766." Neatly laid out below is a rough but colorful outline of the eastern part of the continent, from the Mississippi River to the Atlantic Ocean. Its simplified geography lacks mountains, rivers, towns, and other physical features that one would expect in a rendering of the region. Instead, clusters of small, red rectangles punctuate its space and identify, virtually at a glance, the quarters or "cantonments" of every significant unit of the British army stationed in the American colonies at the beginning of 1766. To an administrator or government minister in far-off London, this map provided a snapshot of how Britain's forces were deployed in America three years after the conclusion of the Seven Years' War. It is unique among the thousands of maps and plans in the collections of the Clements Library in its clear and concise depiction of military demographics on a continental scale.

The map was drawn during a watershed time in the American colonies. The peace treaty of 1763 had ended the Seven Years' War (the North American component of which is known in the United States as the "French and Indian War") and left Great Britain with a much-expanded empire, a depleted treasury, and the responsibility for administering and protecting colonial territories taken from France and Spain. The growth of the empire was most apparent in North America, where large parts of the former New France—Canada, the Maritimes, the Great Lakes, and the Ohio Valley—were confirmed as British possessions. To the south, the Floridas—parts of modern Alabama, Mississippi and Florida—were given up by France and Spain. Britain's old colonial rivals were thus eliminated from the map of eastern North America, and the western boundaries of the British colonies could be projected to the banks of the Mississippi River.

It was one thing to win these vast areas at the negotiating table but quite another to exercise effective control over them. Aside from the sheer scale of the acquisition of territory, the former Spanish and French areas had potentially hostile, non-English-speaking colonial populations whose allegiances were suspect to many British officers and administrators. Beyond the bounds of European settlement, much of the interior of the continent was a wilderness peopled by diverse and scattered groups of Native Americans. Many were former allies of France, who certainly did not consider the decisions of a few men in Paris to have placed their homelands within the British Empire. Their long-term loyalty was questioned as well.

The new regime manifested its authority by placing military garrisons in strategic towns and settlements and in the forts that guarded communications or served as centers of the western fur trade. From these posts the troops could watch for rebellious behavior and guard against external threats from a resurgent France or Spain. Although the colonial populations made the transition without difficulty, in 1763–64 the British faced a widespread uprising of the Native American groups of the Great Lakes and Ohio Valley. Many smaller forts were lost to the Indians, but the British were ultimately able to concentrate sufficient forces to undertake punitive expeditions and end the rebellion. The 1766 map of the cantonments reflects the situation as it was following the Indian uprising after most of the smaller posts had been abandoned as indefensible and the troops were concentrated in the larger and stronger forts such as Niagara, Detroit, Michilimackinac, and Pittsburgh. A look at the map will show that in 1766 the former French and Spanish colonies and the Indian country claimed the lion's share of the army. Not until 1768 would the British begin to shift troop strength to the "old" English colonies with their increasingly restive populations.

The cantonment map was intended to record the deployment of Britain's forces in America to accomplish the task at hand. It is simple and uncluttered in its composition, allowing the reader to focus on the information it was intended to convey. Based on its scale and the size and shape of certain geographical features, particularly the Great Lakes, it appears to have been copied directly from Thomas Kitchin's *A New and Accurate map of the British Dominions in America, according to the Treaty of 1763* (London, [1763]). Although Kitchin's map provided the template for the shape of eastern North America, virtually all of its other details have been omitted. All that remains of the topography are a few of the major lakes and rivers. Provincial boundaries have been retained, with those of colonies from Virginia southward extended to the Mississippi River. Boldly drawn along the crest of the Appalachian Mountains is the line established by the Proclamation of 1763 to exclude American settlers from the "Lands Reserved for the Indians." Important towns and forts are identified as well, for they were the locations of the quarters housing Britain's military forces in America. The finished map was sectioned and affixed to durable linen to allow it to be more easily folded for filing or for transport.

This basic map served as a canvas on which to project a simple but effective schematic system for identifying the locations and composition of garrisons and other bodies of troops. The British forces in America in 1766 consisted primarily of infantry organized into numbered regiments of about five hundred officers and men. Regiments were divided into nine companies. As revealed by the map's key, each complete regiment stationed in one place is represented by a large rectangle, while individual companies or groupings of companies of less than nine are shown by smaller rectangles. Tiny squares indicate half companies, while detachments of troops are shown by "x"es with their size and composition given in a table on the right of the map. Each large rectangle or group of nine smaller rectangles is associated with the number of a particular regiment, and separate elements are linked to their regimental numbers by delicate lines so the complete distribution of the unit is revealed. Thus, for example, the nine companies divided between Detroit and Michilimackinac are readily identified as

In 1765 the British constructed officers' quarters (depicted here in a ca. 1790 watercolor by David W. Smith) and soldiers' barracks at Detroit. Similar structures, usually of a single story, were to be found at most of the posts identified on the 1766 map of cantonments.

comprising the whole of the 17th Regiment of Foot. The convenient format of the 1766 cantonment map suggests that it was designed to be revised annually to reflect the shifting of units from post to post.

No author is attributed for the cantonment map. Nor is there any clear indication of whether it was drawn in America or in Britain. William L. Clements acquired it in 1921 with the papers of William Petty, second earl of Shelburne. In 1766–67 Shelburne held the appointment of secretary of state for the Southern Department with responsibility for formulating policy for colonial areas, including North America. Although there is no documentation in Shelburne's papers, the information shown on the map was surely directed to him (or to his immediate predecessor) by General Thomas Gage, commander-in-chief in North America. Gage's papers, which Mr. Clements purchased in 1930, are also in the Clements Library, but unfortunately they too are silent on the subject of the map of the cantonments. During Shelburne's administration, he and Gage carried on a regular correspondence about the distribution of military units and the justification for maintaining certain posts. The map of the cantonments could have supported their discussion by illustrating for Shelburne the current locations of all the forces available in North America.

The author and place of production of the 1766 map can be deduced with reasonable certainty through comparison with a very similar one in the collections of the Library of Congress. Titled "Cantonment of His Majesty's forces in N. America according to the disposition now made & to be compleated as soon as practicable, taken from the general distribution dated at New York 29th March 1766," it is identical in style and format to the map from the Shelburne Papers. The Library of Congress example appears, in fact, to be the immediate successor to the Clements map, illustrating quartering changes that were to be accomplished during the summer of 1766. Further amendments

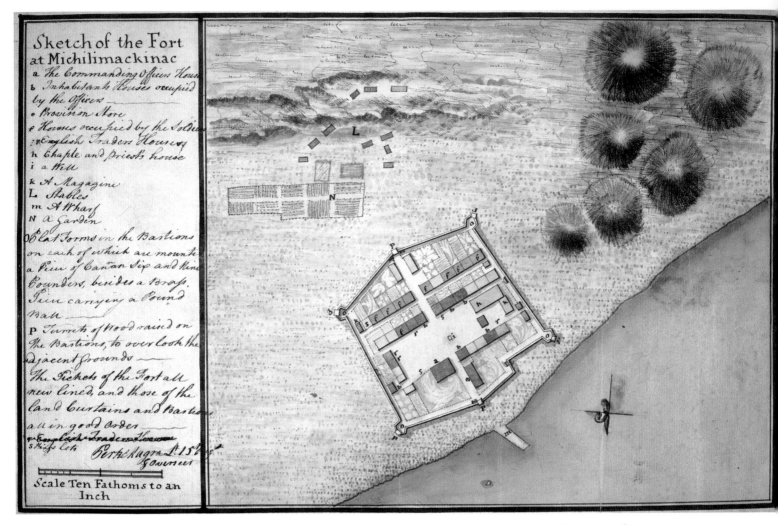

Lieutenant Perkins Magra drafted this detailed plan of the fortified village of Michilimackinac in the late summer of 1765. The isolated post lacked barracks to accommodate its garrison, so the soldiers lived in vacant houses rented from their absentee, fur-trader owners. The plan is from the Gage Papers.

reflect troop movements in 1767 as well, for a crude addition to the title, written in cursive, states, "with the alterations to summer 1767 done in yellow. By Dan Paterson, Asst. Qr. Mr. Genl." Rather than produce a completely new map for 1767, Paterson updated that of 1766 by scratching out obsolete information and inserting changes with yellow ink.

Daniel Paterson (1738–1825) was very likely the author of both maps, though his name does not appear formally on either one. Commissioned an ensign in the 30th Regiment of Foot in 1765, he did not follow his unit to Gibraltar but rather obtained an appointment as assistant deputy quartermaster general and remained in London on duty at Horse Guards, the headquarters of the British Army. He held that position for many years and did not serve in America during the eighteenth century. Paterson also had cartographic talents. In 1771 he published a compilation and description of the crossroads of Great Britain, a book that went through 18 editions by 1829. He also produced works on the roads of Scotland and the topography of the Caribbean island of Grenada. Paterson could easily have copied the Kitchin map and added the information on the postings of the troops in North America.

General Gage's New York headquarters provided the details of the actual or intended disposition of the American forces in the form of a "general distribution" as noted in the title of the Library of Congress map. Although the document of March 1766 has not been found, the Shelburne Papers at the Clements Library do include a "General Distribution of His Majesty's Forces in North America" sent from New York by Gage on February 22, 1767. Organized in tabular form, this document identifies military units and their postings in great detail. In fact, it appears to have provided much of the information used by Paterson to make his 1767 alterations to the Library of Congress map. Despite its convenient format, Paterson's crude update appears to signal the end of this genre of cantonment map, as no further examples are known.

The presence in the Shelburne Papers of the 1766 map of the cantonments demonstrates that the administration of military forces in America was a major concern. Only a dozen years earlier this would not have been the case as there were few British regular soldiers in North America, their numbers being limited to some neglected independent companies in New York and South Carolina and a pair of regiments posted in Nova Scotia to watch over the population of the former French colony of Acadia. This situation changed in 1754 with the outbreak of the French and Indian War. Britain was soon sending regular units to America to fight the French. By the climactic campaign years of 1759–60, twenty-five British regiments were serving in the colonies. Although these numbers would shrink following the conquest of Canada in 1760 and the end of the Seven Years' War in 1763, there would be no return to the tiny garrisons of the pre-war era. At least 15 regiments, roughly 7,500 soldiers, would remain to provide security for North America. That is the number accounted for on the 1766 map of the cantonments.

Their distribution is revealing. Virtually all of the British soldiers are to be found outside the 13 "old" or English-speaking colonies, far from their major centers of population. Despite civil unrest during the Stamp Act crisis of 1765, not a red coat was to be seen in New England, Philadelphia or the Jerseys, while only a single company was stationed in the city of New York where General Gage kept his headquarters. Instead, the major concentrations of troops were still to be found in the newly acquired or recently threatened territories: Canada and its communication with New York (five regiments); the Great Lakes and the line of communication to Albany (three regiments); and the Floridas (three regiments). Another full regiment was posted in the far-off Illinois country, formerly a part of New France. One more guarded Fort Pitt and the road from Philadelphia to the Ohio River, the route by which land seekers might attempt to defy the proclamation line and slip into the Indian country. Two others were scattered between posts in Nova Scotia and Newfoundland, including the ruined and depopulated former French maritime fortress town of Louisbourg. The British garrisons were posted to fight the French or Spanish or to contend with another Indian uprising but not to police the old colonies.

The Clements Library is a rich source for documentary material revealing the administration of British military forces in America from the French and Indian War through the American Revolution. For the period between the wars, nothing compares with the papers of General Thomas Gage (1721–87), who arrived in America in 1755 and served as commander-in-chief from 1763 until 1775. Working mostly from New York City, and later Boston, with a small staff and deputy commanders in Canada and Florida, Gage regularly dealt with matters as diverse as personnel, Indian relations and the construction and maintenance of forts and barracks. A particularly useful aspect of his papers is the regular correspondence he kept up with post commandants, many of them captains or junior officers. His correspondence is full of news and detail from all of the locations shown on the 1766 cantonment map. The Gage Papers, like Shelburne's, also include maps—nearly ninety of them. Most are manuscripts, and many depict forts and barracks at places such as Michilimackinac, Niagara, Québec, St. Augustine, Pittsburgh, Pensacola, and elsewhere.

The quartering of troops was a subject of considerable importance in Gage's correspondence at the time the map of the cantonments was drafted. The influx of regular soldiers during the French

St. Augustine's British garrison inherited barracks originally constructed by the Spanish. This plan from the Gage Papers was drawn about 1767 to show the arrangement of soldiers' bunks in the crowded rooms of the building.

and Indian War had required facilities for housing them. Few barracks were to be found in England in the 1750s and '60s, so the normal practice there was to quarter troops in "public houses" or inns. The relatively undeveloped state of the American colonies meant that public houses were few, and so, from the beginning, purpose-built barracks were constructed for the accommodation of troops. Large barracks were erected during the war in New York, Philadelphia, Albany, several locations in New Jersey, and other places where soldiers could be housed in transit and for winter quarters. The forts built during the course of the war all included barracks and housing for the officers, while the posts taken from the French and Spanish had them as well.

The smaller number of troops assigned to America following the peace of 1763 lessened the strain on quarters, but barracks and their furniture still had to be managed for the sake of economy and efficiency. One of Gage's priorities early in his command was to regularize the way barracks were managed. At his urging, a Barrack Master General's Department was created in the American command in 1765, and barrack masters were appointed to oversee buildings and their contents at most of the posts where soldiers could be housed. In 1765 Parliament extended the Mutiny Act to the American colonies with a provision for quartering troops in private homes. This deeply resented action was quickly amended by the Quartering Act of the same year. It prohibited accommodation in private houses, but provincial governments were required to fund certain expenses—firewood, barracks furniture, and some other supplies—for maintaining troops in local barracks. Although viewed by many colonists as another form of taxation, this requirement was almost a moot point when the majority of soldiers were stationed in areas such as Florida, Canada and the Great Lakes that were beyond provincial boundaries and where the expenses of maintaining troops were borne directly by the army as they were in other less-developed areas of the empire, particularly Ireland. At none of the places shown on the 1766 cantonment map, it should be noted, would it have been necessary to quarter troops upon the inhabitants or in the few existing public houses.

The Clements Library holds an unequalled collection of maps charting the history of the Americas from European discovery through the end of the nineteenth century. Although most of them depict geography, topography or man-made features, "Cantonment of the Forces in N. America 1766" is unique for what it reveals about the British Army in the colonies during the mid-1760s. It graphically represents the British military position at a time when the focus was still on consolidating the gains of 1763 and before the army was called upon to become an instrument for dealing with civil disorder and, eventually, civil war. It shows that the army was largely quartered far from the English-speaking population, where its soldiers could be segregated in purpose-built barracks. And it works in conjunction with other elements of the Clements collection—books, manuscripts and graphics— to inform scholars as to how the British Army functioned in America during the eventful years between the French and Indian War and the coming of the American Revolution.

CONSIDERING THE STATE OF THE COLONIES

— Christine Walker

In 1769 Anthony Bacon, like many people on both sides of the Atlantic Ocean, voiced increasing alarm as he watched relations between the North American colonists and the British government deteriorate. As a member of the House of Commons in Parliament, Bacon was caught in the cross hairs of this political crisis. Yet, he also had access to the most influential men in Britain. Bacon published 20 copies of a pamphlet, *Considerations on the Present State of the North American Colonies,* to air his views to key government officials, including the First Lord of the Treasury, the principle secretary of state for the North American colonies, and the Chancellor of the Exchequer. In his *Considerations,* Bacon criticized members of Parliament for instituting ill-conceived policies in America, starting with the Stamp Act. He argued that government officials had callously ignored the colonists, and chided them for their lack of knowledge about the colonies, writing that North America was "of so little Estimation in the Eyes of our great Men, 'till of late, that they did not think it worth their while to enquire, whether it was a Continent or an Island?"

In his pamphlet, Bacon claimed an insider's perspective on British-North American relations. He characterized himself as a social chameleon who might comfortably inhabit London or Philadelphia. Having spent most of his childhood in America, Bacon capitalized on his knowledge of the colonies throughout his life. As he wrote, he was "bred up" in Maryland, and had "been engaged in extensive Commerce with them ever since." Bacon parlayed his ties in both places into lucrative trade relationships among North America, Britain and Africa. Reading Bacon's 39-page text opens up the character of a man who embodied the complex and often contradictory currents of the eighteenth century. He was a gifted entrepreneur who navigated a commercial world in the midst of seismic economic growth and few financial regulations. Despite his lack of a noble pedigree, Bacon gained a seat in Parliament. His political success attests to the increasing importance of money over bloodlines in British politics. And he made his money as a military contractor, slave trader and weapons manufacturer who participated in the destructive projects of slavery, colonization and international warfare that defined his era.

Bacon published his *Considerations* when many people in Great Britain believed that the colonists planned to disregard the rule of law and engage in nefarious plots to overthrow the British government. On the other side of the Atlantic, the colonists suspected that the British government

CONSIDERATIONS

ON THE

PRESENT STATE

OF THE

NORTH AMERICAN COLONIES.

LONDON:

Printed in the YEAR MDCCLXIX.

intended to strangle them with unconstitutional taxation policies and to install a permanent standing army in North America. In his pamphlet Bacon identified the mutual misunderstandings that caused tensions to escalate between colonists and their government. Though Parliament repealed the detested Stamp Act, England instituted the Townshend duties in 1767 as an attempt to assert the government's right to collect taxes from the colonies. By printing his pamphlet, Bacon joined the ranks of hundreds of other writers who felt compelled to debate the nature of the relationships among the colonies, Parliament and the Crown. What rights did the colonists have as British subjects? How much power could the British government exert in North America? What, if any, financial obligations did the colonists have to pay for the government's military activities in North America? Could the colonists legally refuse to pay the taxes that Parliament legislated?

The pamphlet offered Revolutionary writers the perfect venue to outline and debate these urgent issues. In the eighteenth century the pamphlet was *the* most immediate and effective way to circulate ideas to the largest audience possible. One did not have to be an author to write a pamphlet, nor wealthy to buy one and read it. Pamphlets expressed an immediacy that lengthier newspapers and magazines did not. Ranging from a few pages to nearly 100, pamphlets had the flexibility to accommodate a variety of print forms. People published sermons, state papers, correspondence, and poems in pamphlets. Pamphlets were also cheap, usually costing no more than a few shillings. The pamphlet addressed the rich and the poor, the erudite and the illiterate. In an era before reading meant silence, people read broadsides, newspapers, novels, and pamphlets to each other at home, in taverns and at coffee houses. On street corners, news criers attempted to lure customers by yelling out the juiciest headlines. The printed pages of pamphlets in the archives leave us the skeletal remains of a boisterous, noisy, newsy culture, where information traveled fluidly between the printed page and the spoken word.

In Great Britain pamphlet writing had developed into high art. Two of the most renowned authors of the century, Jonathan Swift and Daniel Defoe, perfected the searing satirical pamphlet in the early 1700s. Along with these famous writers, scores of hack pamphleteers formed a cadre of professional writers in London's "Grub Street." The colonies did not afford the same opportunities to professional writers, and the authors of political pamphlets in North America often imitated the works of their British counterparts. However, this did not stop the colonists from participating in the print world. In North America people published pamphlets wherever there were printers. During the crisis of the 1760s and 1770s more than 400 pamphlets were printed in the colonies, and over 1,500 had been printed by 1783. As Bernard Bailyn writes in his classic work, *The Ideological Origins of the America Revolution,* "the pamphlets are the distinctive literature of the Revolution. They reveal, more clearly than any other single group of documents, the contemporary meaning of that transforming event."

Though Bacon's *Considerations* is a pamphlet, he was not a professional writer, nor did he intend his work for widespread publication and sale. He printed only 20 copies for an exclusive, highly educated, and politically powerful audience. However, in 1775, Bacon reiterated many of the points

View of CHARLES TOWN the Capital of South Carolina in North America. Vue de CHARLES TOWN Capitale de la Carolina du Sud dans l'Amérique Septentrionale.
Engraved by C. Canot from an Original Painting of T. Mellish, in the Collection of Mr. John Bowles.

LONDON, Printed for John Bowles at Nº 13, in Cornhill, Robt Sayer at Nº 53, in Fleet Street, Thos Jefferys at the Corner of St Martins Lane in the Strand, & Carington Bowles at Nº 69, in St Pauls Church Yard.

The bustling harbor of Charleston, South Carolina, suggests the extent of maritime commercial activity in seaports of the American colonies. This view is from the collection of prints presented in Scenographia Americana *(London, 1768).*

that he made in *Considerations* in a pamphlet entitled, *A Short Address to the Government, the Merchants, Manufacturers, and the Colonists in America and the Sugar Islands, on the present State of Affairs.* This pamphlet was reprinted many times, attesting to the popularity of the views Bacon first laid out in the 1769 *Considerations.* In this text Bacon casts himself as a pragmatic merchant, not an erudite and aristocratic politician. He claims that he had unsuccessfully attempted to convince the chancellor of the exchequer that the Stamp Act was a foolhardy piece of legislation before it was passed. He urges Parliament not to make the same mistake by passing more tax acts that would further alienate the colonists and generate little revenue for the Crown. Bacon's involvement in overseas trade made him acutely aware of how valuable the colonies were to the British economy. Great Britain, he argues, "already has from the Colonies all it possibly *can* have, and on the most advantageous terms likewise to itself." The colonists exported raw materials—grain, lumber, beef, flax, and hemp—across the ocean in return for manufactured goods from Great Britain. As Bacon stated, Great Britain benefited enormously from this unequal trading partnership with the colonies, receiving revenues of five to six million pounds per year. Taxing the colonists had only heightened their awareness of this inequality and asymmetry that Bacon wanted to maintain.

North America's economic and legal dependency upon Great Britain had made Bacon a rich man, and he knew it. He was one of the thousands of merchants, customs house employees and sailors who facilitated the classic "triangle trade" among Great Britain, Africa and America in the eighteenth century. Like his father and grandfather, both of whom had been ship captains, Bacon left land for the sea. At age twenty-one he became master of his first ship, owned by the leading tobacco importer in London. During the Seven Years' War, he expanded his business ventures into government contracting by supplying vessels to the navy and shipping food and pay to British soldiers who were

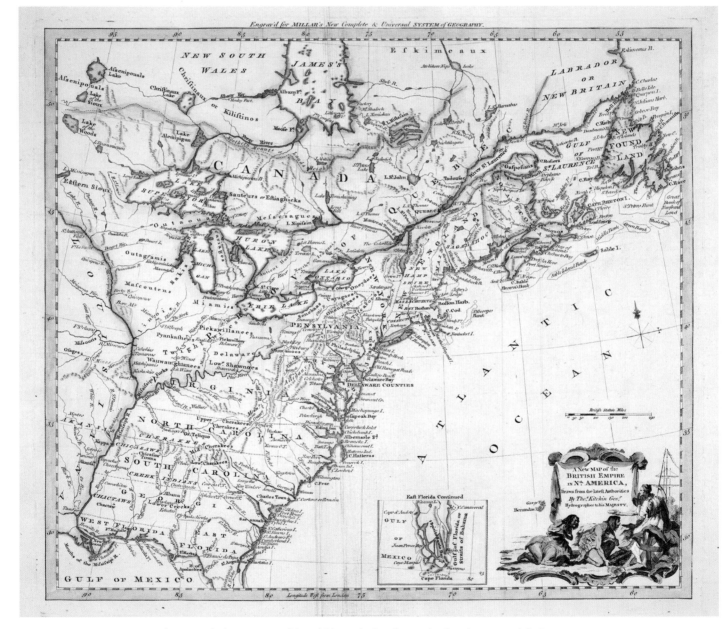

Thomas Kitchin's A New Map of the British Empire in Nth. America *(London, ca. 1763) depicts the American colonies following victory in the Seven Years' War.*

stationed in Africa. After the war Bacon became involved in the slave trade, purchasing slaves in Africa and selling them in the Caribbean. He also leased slaves to the army as laborers.

Merchants like Bacon grew wealthy from the slave trade. They sold slaves to planters in America and the Caribbean who often amassed fabulous fortunes by selling the products of slave labor—sugar, cotton, indigo, coffee, cacao—in Britain. The influx of goods produced by slaves stimulated the economies in America and Britain. New manufacturing facilities provided employment opportunities to thousands of people. Increased overseas trade also created new jobs for merchants and government employees who constituted the emerging "middling" class. Bacon's involvement in the slave trade exemplifies how slavery enriched both individuals and the British government and transformed the Atlantic economy in the eighteenth century. It also explains why Bacon believed that the government's taxation policies in North America were so misguided.

Bacon contended that making the goods that the colonists bought from British manufacturers prohibitively expensive would drive Americans to develop their own manufacturing operations. He also predicted that the more the colonies began to resemble Great Britain the likelier they were to defy the "mother-country." In his *Considerations* Bacon suggests a series of draconian restrictions to prevent colonists from trading either unfinished or manufactured goods with each other or with any country except Great Britain. According to Bacon's plan, each colony was to export any hemp, flax, cotton, silk, wool, beaver, fur of beasts, leather, iron, copper, lead, or brass that it produced immediately to British ports. Likewise, no manufactured goods that the colonists imported from British merchants could be traded among the colonies. Bacon asked government officials to imagine how these restrictions would have impacted Great Britain if they had been imposed on the country a century ago: "the most wealthy and populous towns in Britain would never have rose to their eminence: Manchester, Birmingham, Leeds and Hallifax would be but little Country Villages." Bacon prescribed a financial plan for the colonies that directly contradicted the principles that governed his own business activities. He had used his contacts in both America and Great Britain to launch his career, benefited from the flourishing Atlantic trade, and capitalized on the British government's military endeavors in North America, but the colonists in his eyes should have no such economic freedom.

Bacon's approach toward the North American colonists makes sense within the framework of how people thought about authority and power relations in the eighteenth century. Like most people, he described political and economic relationships as personal and sentimental, and he characterized North America and Britain as a "family." Bacon cast the colonies as dependent children who were behaving badly towards their "mother" country. His portrayal of the soured relations between the colonists and Great Britain as a series of family intrigues resonated with the plots of the most popular novels of the time, Samuel Richardson's *Clarissa* and *Pamela*. The colonists, Bacon declared, had been "affectionate" and loyal subjects until Parliament issued the Stamp Act. Bacon's pamphlet is steeped in the universalizing language of his age: a sentimentality that collapsed the distance between the personal and political and sought to affect the heart.

Yet, though Bacon used sentimental language to describe the political situation, he did not believe that the colonies had any right to challenge British authority. In the eighteenth century, neither the personal nor the political family consisted of equals. Obedience and submission to authority shaped relations between children and parents, wives and husbands, servants, slaves, and masters. Likewise, the colonists owed loyalty and obedience to Great Britain in return for military protection and trading opportunities, according to this belief about how society should be ordered. Like a stern parent, Bacon recommended an economic policy that would first punish the colonists for their wayward behavior and then encourage them to remain dependent upon Great Britain. In his *Considerations,* Bacon outlined a series of maxims that he believed would clarify the relationship between colony and Crown. He asserted that Britain had an absolute Parliament. According to Bacon, the colonies had no right to pass their own laws. Even if the colonists disagreed with a law issued from Britain, they should dispute it through the proper channels. In return for their submission, the colonists, like familial dependents, were entitled to the same protection from the government as people in Britain. In Bacon's *Considerations,* he envisioned North America as stuck in a perpetual state of agrarian adolescence. Great Britain, and in turn Bacon, would reap the rewards of this stunted growth.

But Bacon's portrayal of the relationship was not entirely one-sided. He argued that the colonists had been well-behaved and obedient children. In return for their submission the "great men" in Britain had neglected them and then instituted the hated Stamp Act. He urged government officials to assuage the concerns of the colonists, do "the utmost to recover their affection," and let them "see you have their interest still at Heart." The heightening tensions between America and Great Britain may have been particularly poignant for Bacon, who like so many people in the eighteenth century had lost both his parents early in life. An orphan by age eight, Bacon was sent from Britain to Maryland to be raised by two of his uncles. The loss of parental protection figured prominently in his pamphlet. Bacon also fathered five illegitimate children with his mistress, but unlike the "mother" country, he did not neglect his offspring. Upon his death Bacon left enough money to support the needs of his extramarital family.

Though he was a man of trade most interested in taxation policies, Bacon's vision of reconciliation went far beyond finance. Centuries before the United States government established the Fulbright Program, Bacon recommended in his pamphlet that the British government implement a similar soft-diplomacy program. Perhaps inspired by his own experiences of living in North America and Great Britain, Bacon suggested that the government establish scholarships at universities for colonial boys who would not otherwise be able to afford to be educated abroad. While it was common for elite children in America to be sent to England to be educated, Bacon proposed that ordinary men benefit from the same opportunities. American boys who spent several years in Great Britain would develop a strong loyalty and affection for the country and be less likely to disregard its laws.

Unlike pamphlets printed in the hundreds and thousands, the tiny print-run of Bacon's *Considerations* affords the reader a rare look at the inner workings of the world's most powerful eighteenth-century empire. The Clements Library owns one of two copies of this pamphlet that still

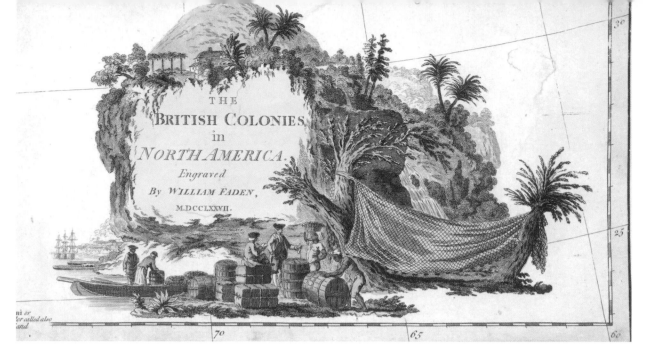

Colonial merchants watch as slaves load cargo bound for England in this cartouche illustration from William Faden's map,
The British Colonies in North America *(London, 1777)*

exist. Bacon's text exhibits the thought process of one British politician attempting to make sense of how formerly "affectionate" relations between North America and Great Britain had grown so fractious. It captures a man at the prime of his life and his career, a self-made success who rose from colonial backwaters to attain wealth and a seat in Parliament from 1764 to 1784, the twenty-year span book-ended by the passage of the Stamp Act and American independence.

In his pamphlet Bacon proposed plans to instill a combination of emotional attachment and respect for authority in North American colonists. But Parliament seems to have either disregarded his *Considerations* or he was too late with them. At the outbreak of the American Revolution Bacon's business ventures had expanded into iron foundries, where he had started to employ a new method for manufacturing "bore" cannon. Always the consummate businessman, Bacon maximized his profits during the Revolution by convincing the government of the superiority of this new technology. He obtained lucrative military contracts for large orders of these weapons, exploiting the very opportunity for manufacturing innovations in Britain that he sought to deny the colonists in North America. By selling artillery to the British Army, moreover, he was literally turning the inhabitants of his former home into cannon fodder. The land that had nurtured him in his youth and provided him with his first opportunities to trade overseas was now in a state of open rebellion against the Crown. Bacon's *Considerations* make clear that he would not tolerate this defiance of government authority. When he published the pamphlet in 1769, Bacon still believed that the disaffected members of Britain's growing colonial family could be mollified, but his message to Parliament did not result in the sentimental reunion of estranged parent and child. Instead, his darkest predictions became reality as the British "family" tore itself apart.

"[I]F THEY MEAN TO HAVE A WAR"

UNDERSTANDING THE AMERICAN REVOLUTION WITH THE HELP OF EYEWITNESS ACCOUNTS

— *David Hancock*

"Historians relate, not so much what is done, as what they would have believed."
Benjamin Franklin, Poor Richard's Almanack, *1758*

Major John Pitcairn commanded the British troops on Lexington Common. The second page of his April 26 letter to General Gage describes the skirmishes at Lexington and Concord and the long retreat to Boston.

Wednesday, April 19, 1775, saw the first hostile confrontations between armed British and colonial forces in the American Revolutionary War. Skirmishes occurred in a string of towns between Boston and Concord, and the import of that day's "battles" are deeply ingrained in the collective American psyche. But what do we—can we—know about what happened?

Nested in boxes and volumes of the manuscripts collection of the William L. Clements Library lie over a dozen eyewitness accounts of participants and bystanders and a few near-contemporary engravings of Ralph Earl's sketches of the engagements that drew from interviews the artist had with the same. Curiously, the reports tell us less than we want to know about the military events, even though they provide interesting insights into the mindsets of the participants. Surprisingly, they are more revealing about participants' positions and attitudes than they are about simpler matters of fact like how many people participated and who did what to whom.

Eyewitness accounts are a mixed blessing. They provide rich details from multiple perspectives, not only those of British regulars and colonial "Patriots," but also American Loyalists and middle-of-the-road men who were simply observers. As is common in the case of armed conflict, eyewitness accounts are often the only evidence available for determining what happened. Yet, they pose huge interpretative problems for historians.

Characteristics of the event, the witnesses and the form of testimony affect the evidence, as cognitive and social psychologists tell us. The length of time an event is experienced and the quality of attention during it affect subsequent reporting. If an observer has time to make abstract inferences during observation, for instance, he or she is more likely to recount the event accurately. At Lexington, the engagement was brief—a matter of minutes. The viewing conditions also influence reporting. The battle at Lexington occurred a half-hour before or just at the moment of sunrise. Smoke from the muskets reduced

Lieutenant Colonel Francis Smith, commander of the Concord expedition, wrote his report to General Gage on April 22. Smith's account of the first shots was based on information obtained from Major Pitcairn and other British participants. Gage forwarded Smith's original letter to Secretary of State the Earl of Dartmouth and retained this copy.

visibility. A distinctive visage or dress of participants can mitigate these handicaps. But in this early revolutionary encounter, only a basic distinction between the uniforms of regulars and the work clothes of Minutemen could have been made. While the distinction in form of dress was stark enough between Redcoats and Minutemen, it was almost insignificant between Minutemen and their neighbor-observers.

People under stress have special difficulty remembering events, and battle is among the most stressful situations. Military actions are full of "noise." The presence of weapons and the possibility of wounds or death diverts attention from details such as how many opposed you and who shot first. Confusion, shouting, pushing, and especially huzzas and rushes would have heightened anxiety. The strain was compounded when the act might be construed a crime, even treason, as some Minutemen would have felt. As a result, there was considerable disagreement as to who was involved, what happened and when it occurred.

Witnesses' age, health, physical position during the event, psychological state, and personal biases affect their accounts. While psychologists have shown that the quality of evidence is not affected by gender, race or intelligence, extremely old and young eyewitnesses, like physically impaired observers, are less trustworthy than most adults. That is not so much an issue in the April 1775 encounters, for those who gave testimony ranged between young adult ("of lawful age") and late middle age. If health problems—such as poor eyesight or hearing—impeded their reconstitution of events, it is not obvious from their testimony.

Different vantage points cause people to perceive causation and participation quite differently. Lieutenant Edward Gould stood at the heart of the fighting. Thomas Fessenden was not on Lexington Common but in a pasture near the meetinghouse, and "ran off as fast as I could." Thomas Willard looked out from "the house of Daniel Harrington"; others did the same from behind stone walls. The captive Simon Winship who had lectured the regulars on liberty stood with other prisoners inside the British vanguard. The townsman Timothy Smith stood upon the Common and then fled from a volley, while his neighbor Bryan Tidd viewed from his house. Some officers like Lieutenant William Sutherland sat on an unruly horse. Nathaniel Mulliken and Israel Parker mustered on the Common, engulfed by smoke. While their accounts agree on many important points, could they have actually seen what they thought they saw from their different vantage points on and off the battlefields? The fact of the matter is very few could have seen very well what they later purported to see with such clarity.

Perceptions of events are also shaped by observers' attitudes towards difference and biases attaching to them. People are more accurate when reporting on their own national, ethnic or racial group, and less accurate on those of other groups, especially when the latter oppose them. Clashes between Britons and Americans invoked long-standing cultural biases held by metropolitans of provincials, and vice versa, and these inclinations would have distorted reporting of the clash. Throughout the war, Britons were particularly intolerant of colonists who for decades had held minimal allegiance or outright antipathy to the Crown, such as the Scots, Irish and Germans.

No. 4.   Lexington April 25th 1775

I John Parker, of Lawfull Age, and commander of the Militia in Lexington, do testify and declare, that on the 19th instant in the morning, about one of the clock, being informed that there were a number of regular officers riding up and down the road, stoping and insulting people as they passed the road, and also was informed that a number of the regular troops were on their march from Boston, in order to take the province Stores at Concord, ordered our Militia to meet on the common in said Lexington, to consult what to do, and concluded not to be discovered, nor meddle or make with said regular troops (if they should approach) unless they should insult or molest us — and upon their sudden approach I immediately ordered our militia to disperse and not to fire — immediately said troops made their appearance and rushed furiously, fired upon and killed eight of our party, without reciving any provocation therefor from us. ——

                                                              John Parker

On April 25 Captain John Parker, leader of the militia assembled on Lexington Common, gave his version of the encounter in a deposition to the Massachusetts Provincial Congress.

Another dimension of difference that affected perception and reporting was the presence or absence of professional training. Britons could imagine little coming from the crudely trained Americans; Americans would slight the formality and lack of local knowledge of the British soldiers. Each side embodied propriety and virtue, in contrast to the other side. In a classic attack on the "other," the Cambridge Committee attacked "the Corrupt Administration of a British Minister of State" on the one hand and praised the "one indissoluble Bond of Union in the Common Cause of the American Colonies" on the other. Eyewitness reports were never free from such distortion.

Related to problems of perception are problems of memory. According to the psychologist Elizabeth Loftus, "memory traces can actually undergo distortion. With the passage of time, with proper motivation, with the introduction of special kinds of interfering facts, the memory traces seem sometime to change or become transformed." The speed with which an eyewitness makes a report is critical to its accuracy. The earlier eyewitness reporters have much less time to make significant revisions to their observations, while the later have much more. The accounts of the April 19 battles are variable in this regard: one statement was made the same day, and another the next day; three more issued forth three days later; thirty-one between four and six days later; and two a week later. The last Clements account was penned almost six months after the battles. Participants and onlookers who reported after the ensuing forty-eight hours had more time and comfort to narrate and interpret the events with others—they were not still marching or addressing the immediate needs imposed by injury and destruction—and thereby to refine, amplify or change their accounts, such reworking

The Battle of Lexington, April 19th, 1775, *drawn by Ralph Earl (1751–1801) and engraved by Amos Doolittle (1754–1832), is one in a series of four prints depicting the events of April 19. The artist visited the scene just a few days after the fighting, and his generally accurate rendering provides the best visual documentation of the affair. The Clements Library copy of this extremely rare series of prints was struck from plates re-engraved in 1903.*

introducing a greater degree of uniformity than that which prevailed in the reports made in the immediate aftermath of battle.

Some of the most serious memory distortions are introduced as a result of post-event interrogation and reporting, which smooth out the narrative, eliminating discordant detail. A soldier reporting what happened to a colonel responds to his superior's questions, as well as the soldier's perceptions of what information the colonel already has and whether the colonel has already established a version he wants to confirm. In addition, there operates the soldier's natural desire to justify his command, or lapse in it, and extol the virtue of compatriots, while accentuating the failures of opponents. In their eyewitness reports, Lieutenant Colonel Francis Smith and his second, Major John Pitcairn, reported to their superior General Thomas Gage, as did Lieutenant General Hugh Percy, while Gage in turn reported to his commander the colonial secretary in London. Likewise, Captain John Parker tendered his account to the Massachusetts Provincial Congress, and, between peers, the Committee of Safety for Cambridge reported to the Committee of Safety for Albany. Distortion, often unwitting, is endemic in such situations, and would have been so in 1775. In a similar vein, complicated relationships existed between captors and captives; almost certainly, this would alter the latters' narratives, perhaps their very memories, as captives crafted an account to more likely please their captors and ensure their release.

If observation is flawed and memory distorted, what can we believe in an eyewitness account? We have what participants and observers thought happened, at least retrospectively. If there is enough congruence, we can be confident we have an approximation of what transpired.

Specifically, what light does eyewitness testimony, such as that housed in the Clements, shed on some of the more provocative questions about the first firing on Lexington Common? Historians have returned to three again and again: 1) How many combatants were involved on the two sides? 2) Who fired the first shot? And 3) did the Minutemen disperse or stand their ground?

As to the numbers, we are remarkably uncertain. The estimates of the regulars' strength show the distortions in eyewitness accounts: one American officer reckoned there were between 1,200 and 1,500 Britons, and Revere's friend Joseph Palmer estimated slightly fewer, "about 1000 or 1200." In fact, we know from painstaking combing of British Army records that there were only about 238 in Pitcairn's companies that day, although many Americans imagined more than six times that number. Much variance pervades eyewitness reports about the strength of Patriots, and for it we have no registers to consult. Paul Revere, when intercepted, told the British that 500 men were assembled. Hours before the Battle of Lexington, in the dim light of dawn, Lieutenant William Sutherland heard there were 600 men at Lexington, with "a vast number of the Country Militias going over the Hill with their arms" to join them. On April 25, Pitcairn told Gage that "Near three in the morning ... Intelligence was received that about 500 men were assembled, determined to oppose the King's troops and retard them in their March," although the next day he recalled seeing only "200 rebels." The young British Lieutenant John Barker recalled encountering between 200 and 300. Another onlooker remembered half that: "about 100 company of militia." Officer Edward Gould counted the provincial ranks to contain only "about 60 or 70." Somewhere between 600 and 60 is not very precise!

Just as divergent were the reports that the Americans scattered or stood their ground when asked by the British to disperse and that they received or fired the first shot. The reports agree that Major Pitcairn ordered the men from Lexington to disperse and, to the surprise of many, the Patriots' Captain Parker ordered the same. Then a gun fired. Minutemen and colonial advocates averred that the provincials were dispersing when the regulars fired on them. John Robbins reported that one of "the three officers ordered their men saying fire by God fire"; Thomas Willard noted that "not a gun [was] fired till the militia of Lexington were dispersed"; Nathaniel Mulliken claimed that they "were fired on . . . whilst our backs were turned."

But who fired the first shot? The British were quick to deny having made the first move—a hugely important claim in eighteenth-century warfare. Colonel Smith informed General Gage that the regulars approached the Minutemen "without an intention of injuring them further than to inquire the reason of their being assembled." Smith and Pitcairn "took all possible pains to convince [them] that we meant them no injury" at Lexington (as well as at Concord). As Lieutenant Sutherland put it, "Some of the villains were got over the hedge, fired at us, and it was then and not before that the soldiers fired." Pitcairn added more detail: "Some of the Rebels who had jumped over the wall, fired 4 or 5 shott at the soldiers"; at this, "without any order or regularity, the Light Infantry began a scattered fire." Until he died, Pitcairn insisted he had not fired and had ordered his men not to fire. Sutherland confirmed his superior's version: "I heard Major Pitcairn's voice call out, 'Soldiers, don't fire, keep your ranks, and surround them." Curiously, none of the eyewitnesses explicitly stated a soldier (whether regular or Minuteman) fired the first shot. Perhaps a bystander—the "villains" and "rebels" singled out by the army officers—hidden behind a wall or home, fired the first shot, or, as the historian David Hackett Fischer surmises, several onlookers let go "several shots . . . close together," the first being entirely accidental. Sadly, Lieutenant Gould's own conclusion proved prophetic: "which party fired first I cannot exactly say."

Thus, on many material matters, often extremely significant ones in the minds of historians, we remain tentative. Little can be concluded.

Distorted though they are, we can make use of the Lexington and Concord battles' eyewitness reports to gain insight into other matters. For some questions, they provide sufficient evidence to draw some conclusions. The British sent out too few soldiers and guns and too little ammunition for what turned out to be an exceptionally hostile and bloody action. Had they brought greater manpower and weaponry, they still might have come up short, for they were handicapped by their lack of preparation and rampant disorganization. On April 19, 1775, neither the officers nor their men were prepared for a long, wet march at night. The British soldiers were fatigued and frightened. From Boston, they were forced to march fifteen miles to Lexington through wet marshes on a bone-chilling New England morning. Then they marched another seven miles to Concord after the skirmish on Lexington Common. Their shoes and uniforms were soaked, their hands and faces chapped, their stomachs growling, and their muscles aching long before they approached the Lexington parade

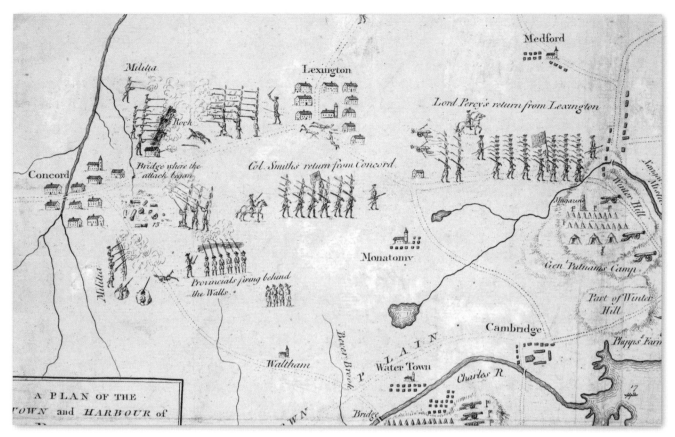

J. De Costa animated his map of the vicinity of Boston and the events of April 1775 with naïve illustrations of soldiers and buildings. Detail from A Plan of the Town and Harbour of Boston . . . Shewing the Place of the Late Engagement Between the King's Troops & the Provincials *(London, 1775).*

ground. Smith's men "were so very much fatigued." Heading home from Lexington in the afternoon, Percy's tired, hungry, and thirsty men—running a guerilla gauntlet along what became 21 very slow miles—were similarly "very much fatigued." Percy, ignoring the advice of subordinates, had brought no extra food or ammunition for his solders or their charges, Pitcairn's men.

Compounding the difficulties that they endured was their inexperience. Colonel Smith's junior officers were green. His soldiers were largely unused to battle. None but the officers had seen battle during the Seven Years' or French and Indian War. Regulars were famous worldwide for their technical skills, yet the young soldiers at Lexington and Concord could not even fire in the same direction. Eyewitness accounts hint at a lack of *esprit de corps* in the units—among fellow commanders, as well as between commanders and companies. Career officers generally did not know their troops, who were by and large new to the army. Given the high number of new recruits, fellow soldiers were often strangers.

Despite the lack of any pronounced bond, in principle the loyalties of regulars would flow to their immediate commander, and here they did. In an attempt to put "a stop to all further slaughter of those deluded people" and impose some order after the skirmish at Lexington, when Smith commanded all regulars to form a line, some obeyed, albeit begrudgingly, but others did not, at least at first. More tellingly, the loyalties of the regulars were to their *immediate* commander. When Laurie of the 43rd Foot ordered his companies to arrange for "street fighting" behind the North Bridge—a fairly tricky maneuver given the terrain—the result was confusion. The companies tumbled upon themselves. Sutherland of the 38th Foot tried to get Laurie's men in the 43rd to flank, but they largely refused; only three did as he ordered, for Sutherland was not their commander.

The speed with which the march was launched and executed also plagued the British. Too speedy a dispatch had left them ill equipped for the fighting that ensued. Advance intelligence was hopelessly partial, if not faulty. While spies' reports on Patriot political activity and thinking was fairly full and more-or-less accurate, that on its military preparedness was not, for the Americans had been moving or hiding what gunnery, cannon, and powder they had for over a week. The intelligence that General Gage received and acted upon was days and in some cases weeks old. To prevent the leakage of his own secrets to the Americans, Gage obsessively refused to reveal the march's route or objective even to its commander Colonel Smith until the afternoon of April 18. When he did inform Smith, Gage enjoined him to keep the target of the march and its details from junior officers and their troops, allowing the soldiers to think it would be a routine training exercise. As a deadly result, they were less on their guard than they might otherwise have been. Not until *after* the skirmish on Lexington Common did the junior officers and their men learn the truth from Smith about where they were going and what they would be doing.

The general's obsession with secrecy had the unintended effect of actually broadcasting his intentions. On the morning of the eighteenth, before he mustered the troops, Gage ordered mounted patrols to intercept Patriot messengers and gain intelligence. After he revealed the plan to Colonel Smith later that day, he ordered a different "small party on Horseback . . . to stop all advice of your march getting to Concord." A party on horseback was a sight, and more colonists noticed it than were stopped by it. Patrols and riders put the militias in Lexington and Concord on notice of an impending action. Accordingly, while the British regulars did not know what they would be doing, the Patriots, whose arms they were to seize, did know at least a day in advance.

Mentally, both sides were at war, and this significantly accelerated the hostilities. Historians focus too much attention on the first shot of the conflict, masking the fact that the colonies and mother country had already adopted the language and posture of war. The British confiscated carriages and horses and took captives, such as Simon Winship, to prevent advance warning. Solomon Brown, Jonathan Loving and Elijah Sanders told how British soldiers harried them by holding "pistols to our breasts" and grilling them for hours. The British objectives for the long march, mentioned in Gage's letter to Smith and then the official orders of April 18, were military: "march with all expedition," "secure the two Bridges" and "seize" and destroy all war materiel— ammunition, small arms, cannon, mortars, and provisions. The tone of the orders' official instructions was combative: Smith was to

march with the Corps of Grenadiers and Light Infantry put under your Command with
the utmost expedition and secrecy to Concord, where you will seize and destroy all the
artillery and ammunition, provisions, tents, small arms & all other military stores you
can find. You will knock off the trunnions at least of each of the iron guns, and destroy
the carriages, and beat in the muzzles of the brass ones so as to render them useless. The
powder & — may be shaken out of the Barrels into the water, the tents burnt, and the men
may put the balls & lead into their pockets, throwing them away by degrees into the fields,
ditches, ponds &c. You have a plan on which is marked off the places where the artillery &
ammunition &c is reported to be lodged, and after destroying the same you will return . . .
If any body of men dares to attack oppose you with arms, you will warn them to disperse
or attack them.

Gage's message was infused with the language of entrance into the territory of an enemy. The British would be taking possession. Significantly, Percy referred to the Americans not as "His Majesty's humble servants," but as "the Rebels." In their minds, the British were already at war when they left Boston.

The Americans too already felt themselves at war, and under siege. Harassed by the regulars since the preceding autumn and feeling the British had played too freely with their property and propriety, men and women in the Boston area then found themselves "rudely insulted" over the course of the evening of the eighteenth as they moved along their own community's roads, some in the course of everyday work and others, of course, in the course of resistance. According to Captain Parker, "a number of regular officers [were] riding up and down the road, stopping and insulting people," confiscating colonial conveyances and weapons, while "regular troops were on the march behind them." The colonists responded to these British insults with sticks and rocks. Several miles before Lexington, as militiamen looked down from the hills, Pitcairn ordered his companies to load and prepare for action.

Like the British, the Provincials' warlike mindset preceded April 19. They had been collecting war supplies for months: "a quantity of ammunition, provisions, artillery, tents, and small arms." They hardly needed these to satisfy Concord's daily needs. On hearing around April 7 of a possible march, the Americans hid their supplies—burying them underground at Colonel Barrett's and sending them to places like Sudbury and Stow—and reinforced their ranks with relatively well-trained bands of men drawn from neighboring towns and counties. Committees of Safety were charged with spreading the news, seizing military stores and mobilizing available men. Individuals were "charged to alarm" particular counties. All were in place when Colonel Joseph Palmer wrote to Philip Mortimer on the day of the battle, seeking to enlist support for the cause of Massachusetts: "Pray let the Delegates from this Colony to Connecticut see this" report.

Spies had informed the Americans several weeks before that the seizure of their supplies at Concord was imminent, and the night before that an expedition to Concord was planned for the following day. The colonists possessed an early warning system, operative for at least six months, that disseminated spies' reports and general correspondence among the Patriot colonial and inter-colonial committees. Famously, at mid-evening on the eighteenth, Joseph Warren told William Dawes and Paul Revere that the troops would soon land in Cambridge. Dawes followed the southerly route to Lexington on horseback, while Revere took the northerly one, warning their allies as they passed by. In Lexington, John Hancock and Samuel Adams dispatched other riders to notify neighboring communities. They knew what the British were doing almost as soon as, indeed well before, most of the British knew it. The effectiveness of the American reportage was apparent even to the British officers. In writing to General Gage three days after the battles, Colonel Smith admitted that he and his men "found the Country had Intelligence or Strong Suspicion of our Coming." Gun signals, alarm bells from meetinghouses, and supply removals all spoke of the strength of their opponent's communications.

On the early morning march to Lexington, the Patriots certainly fired on the regulars, even if they killed no one. Several miles before Lexington, "a Countryman snappt his piece at Lieutenants Adair and Sutherland but it Flash'd and did not go off." Armed men stood along the road to Lexington, staging silent armed menace. As the regulars approached that town, an American military drum beat out a call to arms, after which Captain Parker's men moved into line. On the Common itself, the Minutemen stood as "a Body of Country People drawn up in Military Order with Arms and Accoutrement and, as appeared after, Loaded." They adopted the posture of conflict, not exercise.

The colonists described their actions in warlike terms. They referred to themselves as "a Company of our Colony Militia at Arms" or "the Lexington Company." They used rank to differentiate their fighters. They marched against the regulars in formation as "formal military units." Theirs was undoubtedly a well-trained warring party, even if at times it looked ill equipped and resorted to non-traditional guerilla tactics. To them, the British were "enemies," who fired on them "without the least Provocation," or so they reported. They too felt it was important to declare that their opponent fired the first shot, for the same exculpatory reasons that Smith declared the opposite.

Confirming the warlike position was their response to the British retreat. Had they not been at war, they would not have been ready to pursue the regulars on their way back to Boston so aggressively. They could have accepted retreat as victory; in the words of William Grapen, they could have merely made "them escape by dispersing." But the Americans "endeavoured to surround us" on the return home, Lord Percy noted, and there "was not a Stone wall or house from whence the Rebels did not fire." They "attacked from all quarters where cover was to be found." The British were forced to retire under their "incessant fire," which would have been incommensurate with a peaceable posture, or a retributive tit-for-tat for the eight lives lost on Lexington's central common and the two more at Concord's North Bridge. While the Americans did their best to present their actions in the most defensible light, it was hard to escape the taint of warlike "Cruelty and Barberity" when some of their men "scalped and cut off the Ears of some of the Wounded" regulars. The Patriots were ready and eager for full-fledged warfare.

The importance of the Clements' eyewitness accounts is not so much in telling who fired at whom and when. Rather, by showing the participants' attitudes and presuppositions, they reveal some of the important factors contributing to war. It would be interesting to compare these findings with similar reports of other battles in the Clements—of the Civil War and the First World War—and to discern whether these conclusions are generally true. Certainly in the case of the Revolution, the British army regarded the Patriots as rebels, to be dealt with summarily. The Americans were ready for conflict and, indeed, already engaged in it. While the clash was not inevitable, it was also not spontaneous: the Americans were perpetrators, active, guileful participants from the earliest imaginable moment. Still today, American historians would have us believe that American revolutionaries were both innocent in their motives and spontaneous in their responses. Such was not the case. Eyewitness accounts give us deep insight into the early stage of the war, and the mental state of the respective combatants. By mid-April 1775, the Americans did mean to have a war, and the British did not, or at least not as much as the Americans did.

*Carving from the
porch ceiling.*

FIRST MAP OF THE NORTHWEST TERRITORY

— Brian Leigh Dunnigan

The area was truly vast, encompassing some 260,000 square miles of undeveloped land and water with the promise of abundant timber, rich soil and plentiful mineral resources. And it had all been added to the new United States by drawing a line on a map in Paris in 1783. The land between the Ohio River and the Great Lakes and from the Mississippi River to western Pennsylvania had few European Americans living within its boundaries in 1783 and had not been conquered by the United States through military action during the War for Independence. In fact, at the conclusion of hostilities, British garrisons still held its most important settlements and military posts, from which they would not finally withdraw until 1796. Most of the land itself was thinly populated by diverse groups of Native Americans, many of which had fought as allies of the British during the war and were sure to resist should American soldiers and settlers encroach on their homelands. Yet, under the Treaty of Paris in 1783 this had become the northwestern part of the United States of America and, by several acts of Congress from 1784 to 1787, the Northwest Territory.

The Northwest Territory—the "Old Northwest"—would be the first area of significant expansion and settlement by Americans beyond the bounds of the 13 original states. It would also be one of the earliest areas of expansion of the Clements Library's collecting scope beyond the age of European exploration, the colonial era and the American Revolution, all topics particularly favored by William L. Clements. After the death of the Library's founder in 1934, Randolph G. Adams, its first director, began to collect seriously in the subject area of westward expansion, especially the Old Northwest. Since that time, the Clements has grown to become one of the most important research collections for the study of the history of the region. The strength of its holdings range from both rare and common imprints to flagship manuscript collections such as the Josiah Harmar Papers, the Anthony Wayne Papers, the Northwest Territory Collection, and many others. The Library also has a wealth of maps, both manuscript and printed, that chart the development of the region and the growth of its forts and towns.

Given the strength of the Clements holdings relating to the Old Northwest, it is not surprising that one of the items long sought for the collection was the first published map to document the region, its resources and the new states of the Union that might be established there. John Fitch's *A Map of the north west parts of the United States of America* (Philadelphia, 1785) had eluded Clements Library map curators since Randolph Adams' day. It is, in fact, one of the rarest American maps. In

1969, when J. Clements Wheat and Christian F. Brun produced their *Maps and Charts Published in the Americas Before 1800,* they could identify only five institutions holding copies of Fitch's map, and that count represented just six individual examples. One or two others were known to be in private hands. A few more have surfaced since that time, but currently the best estimate is that perhaps only nine or 10 copies survive. As Library of Congress map division head P. Lee Phillips wrote in 1916, "when a copy of Fitch's map is discovered, it becomes a matter of great interest to cartographers."

Such an event occurred in 2006, when the Clements Library successfully bid on a unique copy of Fitch's map that had recently become available. The Clements Library Associates undertook to support this significant purchase as a gift in recognition of the 30 years of service of John C. Dann, only the third director of the institution, who was then poised to retire. A rapid-fire fund-raising effort ensued, and the map was presented to the Clements Library at the formal retirement dinner given for Dr. Dann in the summer of 2007. It is the only copy of the Fitch map currently held by an institution located within the Old Northwest.

The Fitch map not only represents the first published cartography of the Northwest Territory, it also reflects the solution for a dilemma posed by the addition of so much land to the United States. Here was the first opportunity for the new country to expand beyond the Appalachian Mountains and into the interior of the continent. The Treaty of Paris established a boundary between the United States and the remaining British possessions in Canada. This line generally followed the center of the Great Lakes to the supposed source of the Mississippi River. The area between that boundary and the Ohio River would eventually be divided into five modern states and part of a sixth, but in 1783 parts of the region were already claimed by some of the original thirteen. The first step was to convince those states to relinquish their claims and allow the central government to administer the area, systematically purchase and extinguish the claims of Native American groups, survey the land, and offer it for sale to prospective settlers.

This seemingly difficult task was achieved in the land ordinance of 1784, much influenced by the ideas of Thomas Jefferson. Looking forward to a time when sufficient settlement would allow the division of the territory into new states, Jefferson projected 14 jurisdictions in the area between the existing states and the Mississippi River. Nine of these were located in the Old Northwest. Their roughly rectangular shapes were based on parallels of latitude and longitude that ignored natural boundaries. Jefferson proposed grand names for these new states—Assenisipia, Metropotamia, and Polypotamia, for example—most of which Congress disregarded. His general concept for division was a part of the Northwest Ordinance of 1784, and an interpretation of his proposed boundaries appears on the Fitch map.

Maps have a way of reflecting the personalities of their creators, both in the style of their execution and in the nature of the information they present. John Fitch's map of the Northwest Territory was the product of an inventive, brilliant but troubled individual, whose many endeavors always seemed to fall short of their initial promise. Fitch (1743–98) is best known for his successful but experimental application of steam power to river navigation. Born on a farm in Connecticut, he showed early promise in his education and an equivalent distaste for agricultural work. Early attempts to learn the trade of shopkeeper and merchant seaman were unsuccessful, and subsequent apprenticeships as a clockmaker did not take him permanently into that occupation, though it appealed to his mechanical nature and taught him the rudiments of brass founding and the workings of fine machinery. Fitch eventually enjoyed some success as a brass-founder, gun maker, and silversmith, but these did not prove to be lasting vocations.

In 1780, as the American Revolution neared its climax, Fitch invested in Virginia land warrants

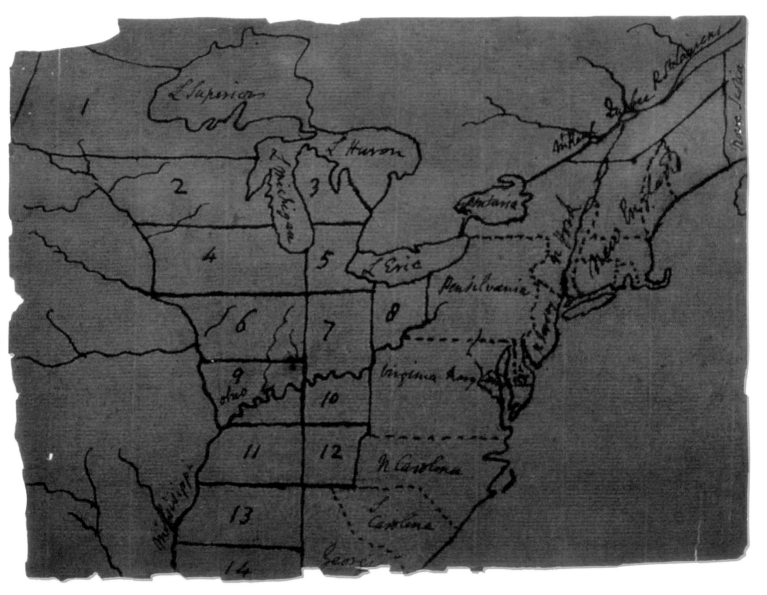

British politician David Hartley (ca. 1731–1813) recorded Thomas Jefferson's concept for the division of territory between the Appalachians and the Mississippi River into new states. Jefferson's original map has been lost, but Hartley's copy of it was enclosed in a January 9, 1785, letter to Lord Carmarthen. A second manuscript version of this map, traced on tissue, was acquired with the Charles Townshend Papers. Both are now in the Clements Library collection.

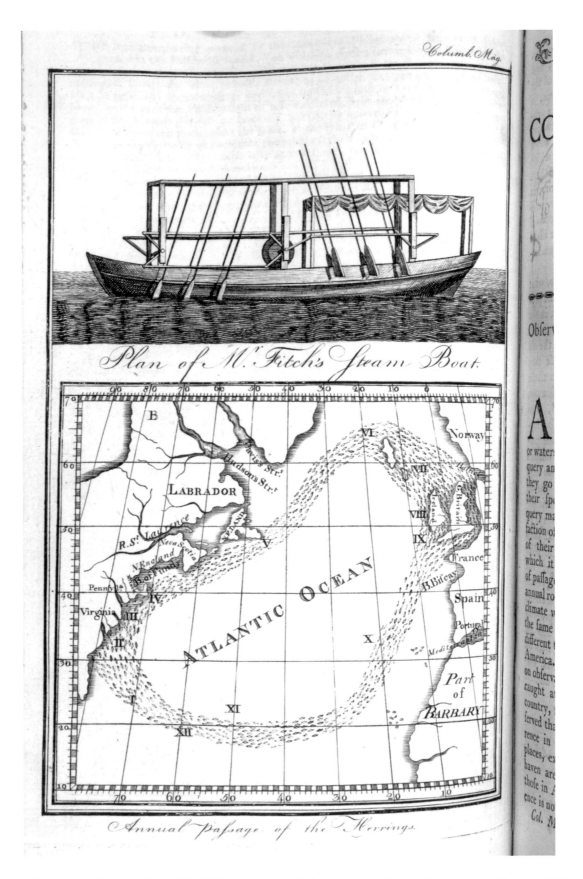

Plan of Mr. Fitch's Steam Boat.

Annual Passage of the Herrings.

An illustration and description of one of John Fitch's novel steamboat designs appeared in the Columbian Magazine *of December 1786.*

and obtained a surveyor's commission. This led him to his first experience with the Old Northwest and undoubtedly provided the kernel of the idea for his map of the region. He began by surveying in Kentucky in 1780, where he recorded some lands on his own behalf. An attempt to continue this work in 1782 resulted in his capture by Indians. As was so often the case with frontier captivities, Fitch was carried as a prisoner to Detroit, ransomed by the British and taken by way of Fort Niagara to Canada and repatriation. Although his captivity did not provide an opportunity for any real surveying, he was at least able to observe some significant portions of the Old Northwest. Back in Pennsylvania as a free man, Fitch focused on land acquisition and surveyed again in the Old Northwest between 1783 and 1785. It was certainly during this time that he gathered much of the information that would be put forward in his map in the latter year.

Publication of Fitch's map, for which he served as cartographer, engraver and printer, was intended to raise revenue to support a new and ambitious project, the development of a practical steam-powered vessel. Much of the balance of his life was spent in trying to obtain official support and funding for his invention, efforts that proved largely futile. His actual design and construction of steamboats showed more promise, and by 1787 Fitch was able to test successfully a paddle-driven vessel. Three further prototypes followed, one of which was actually put into commercial service on the Delaware River. Finances always proved to be the stumbling block, however, and, Fitch's attempt to obtain support from the French proved as unsuccessful as had his efforts in America. Eventually giving up his dream to build a working steamboat, Fitch gravitated to Kentucky in 1796 to claim the lands he had recorded for himself there in 1780. He lived in a tavern in Bardstown for the next two years before ending his own life in 1798. John Fitch died having never been able to exploit his own genius, and public recognition of the invention of the steamboat went to others.

The production of John Fitch's map of the Northwest was as eclectic as his varied career and life experiences. It certainly was published at an opportune time, coming in the aftermath of the Revolution and as public interest was shifting to the new lands north and west of the Ohio River. As the author put it in his advertisements for the map in the Philadelphia newspapers, this new addition to the country opened "immense sources of wealth and advantageous speculation to the citizens of the United States" and was thus an object of "general attention." Having compiled and engraved the map, Fitch then reputedly printed it on a converted cider press! Unlike the large, multi-sheet maps from which he derived much of his information, Fitch's effort on one sheet (at roughly 72 by 54 centimeters in dimensions) was of a practical size for popular consumption. Dissected and affixed to linen backing, the map could be easily folded to fit into the pocket of a traveler or land speculator. The Clements example was treated in that way and was further provided with a crudely constructed and labeled slipcase to protect it when folded.

A Map of the north west parts of the United States of America is by no means the most sophisti-cated cartography of the Old Northwest, and parts of it are heavily dependent on other representations of the region produced in the 1770s and '80s. Fitch was straightforward in crediting his three chief sources. The first of these was Thomas Hutchins' *A New Map of the Western Parts of Virginia,*

Pennsylvania, Maryland and North Carolina Comprehending the River Ohio and all the Rivers, which fall into it (London, 1778), which provided some of the cartography and information on the area between the Ohio and the lower portions of Lakes Michigan and Huron. The more northerly parts, including Lake Superior (complete with three imaginary islands that were often a feature of maps of the day), owed much to William McMurray's *The United States Based on the Definitive Treaty of Peace Signed at Paris Septr 3d 1783* (Philadelphia, 1784), which displayed the official border with British Canada and an interpretation of the proposed boundaries for new states as laid out in the ordinance of 1784. The third major source was Fitch himself. According to his introduction to the map, "his own Surveys and observations" had resulted in "considerable improvements on those [Hutchins' and McMurray's] and all that had gone before him." Fitch's map was dedicated to Hutchins (1730–89), a gentleman, the author wrote, who "knows how to distinguish between form and substance in all things," and whom he hoped would approve of his efforts.

Scattered across the map in a format reminiscent of Hutchins' 1778 work is a potpourri of snippets of information about the resources, people and topography of the area. Some of these are clearly derivative (such as his comments on the copper deposits known to exist by the shores of Lake Superior) as they pertain to parts of the Old Northwest that Fitch had not visited. Others, notably his description of Niagara Falls, are convincing bits of personal observation. The cartographer was clearly impressed by the magnificent cataracts and awesome gorge, which he would have seen while en route to Fort Niagara following his brief Indian captivity. Equally convincing are Fitch's notations on Kentucky, where he had extensively surveyed in 1780.

A prominent feature of the Fitch map are the lines delineating nine states (plus Kentucky) proposed to be carved out of the Old Northwest. These are similar to the borders shown on McMurray's map, although they differ enough that they probably represent Fitch's own interpretation of the intent of Congress. All of the north-south and east-west boundaries correspond with specific parallels of latitude and longitude displayed in the border of the map. None of the projected states are named, and most appear to be situated somewhat farther south than those shown by McMurray. A sentence at the top of the map states that "the several divisions on the N.W. of the Ohio is the form which that country is to be laid off into states according to an ordinance of Congress of May the 20th 1785," the second of the acts that would finalize the form and government of the Northwest Territory.

All of these printed features are found in common on the known surviving examples of the Fitch map. The Clements copy is unique, however, in the presence of seven manuscript additions written in the style of the printed notations before the map was dissected. The reason for these addenda is not known, though one might speculate that they were included as the basis for changes to the copper plate to produce a second edition of the map. They might also represent the musings of an interested owner who decided to supplement his copy of the map with additional information. Four of the seven notations are credited to "Fitch," whose input might have been obtained either through his writings or by conversation with the map's owner. A comment about the discovery of prehistoric mammoth bones, written near Bluestone Creek in western Virginia, is credited to "Jefferson page 71," a reference

and provided for that purpose.   (6w.1w.)

Philad. 28 July, 1785.   THOS. PRICHETT, } Inspect-or.

JOHN FITCH,

HAVING traversed the country N. W. of the Ohio, in the several capacities of a captive, a surveyor and a traveller——as the result of his labors and remarks, has completed, and now wishes to sell, a new, accurate MAP of that country, generally distinguished by the Ten New States, including Kentucky, which opens immense sources of wealth and advantageous speculation to the citizens of the United States, and therefore is an object of general attention. And having performed the engraving and printing himself, is enabled to sell at the very small price of a French crown.

   To be sold by WILLIAM PRICHARD, on the north side of Market-street, opposite Lætitia court.   July 30.

Fresh Raisins, Smirna Figs,

almonds, filberts, walnuts, olives, capers, anchovies

Fitch's advertisement for his map ran in Philadelphia newspapers during July 1785.

to a passage in Thomas Jefferson's *Notes on the State of Virginia* (Paris, 1784–85).

Most of the manuscript notations pertain to resources of the region, such as the presence of coal in eastern Ohio. Fitch knew enough about the area for another of the comments to state, "There is No Coal West of Kanhawa [sic: Kanawha] River or West of a line drawn North from it." Most useful of the annotations is a large block of text that stretches across the northern parts of Illinois, Indiana and Ohio that reveals a bit about the sources of information used by Fitch for his map. "North of a Line drawn from the Illinois [River] to Detroit," it states, "Fitch has laid down this Map from other Maps or Information of others. He surveyed the Ohio from its Source to the Muskingum River."

This extended paragraph then goes on to discuss evidences of sophisticated, prehistoric Native American construction that were a source of fascination for the first Americans moving into the Old Northwest—the fortification, burial and effigy mounds found throughout much of what would become Ohio. The annotator inked in squares at Licking Creek, Hockhocking Creek, and Mingo Town to show the location of some of the largest of these "fortification" complexes further noting, *"Burying*

Mounts are always near them." Fitch had explored some of these sites and reported that one was so large as to be "more than a Days journey round." These were, of course, the constructions of a people who came to be called the "Mound Builders" and who were considered to have been much more advanced than the contemporary Native American hunters and farmers who were about to be displaced by the American settlers flooding into the Old Northwest.

The region depicted in the cartography of John Fitch would take a particularly prominent place in the history of the United States during the 30 years following the publication of his map. A decade of violence in the Old Northwest would pit the U.S. Army against Native Americans defending their homelands until concluded by the Battle of Fallen Timbers (1794) and the Treaty of Greenville (1795). Jay's Treaty of 1794 would clear the way for British troops to retire two years later from the posts of Detroit, Michilimackinac and Fort Miamis, all located within the bounds of the United States as established in 1783. Ohio would join the Union in 1803, the first state to be created from the Northwest Territory. The years 1811 to 1815 would see another war between the United States and the Indians of the region, supported by their British allies during the War of 1812. The subsequent decades would witness settlement of the land, removal of many of its remaining Native American occupants and the formation of the states of Indiana, Illinois, Michigan, Wisconsin, and Minnesota. Primary source material documenting all these events is plentiful in the map, manuscript, book, and graphics collections of the Clements Library. John Fitch's map serves as the crowning jewel of these magnificent holdings on the Old Northwest.

*Bronze maquette by
Daniel Chester French
(1850–1931) of his statue
for the Lincoln Memorial.*

EDWARD CLAY'S
LIFE IN PHILADELPHIA

— *Martha S. Jones*

White Americans increasingly encountered black people in new and provocative places in the early nineteenth century. It was the era of gradual abolition, with former slaves and their descendents migrating to urban centers and making northern cities such as Boston, New York and Philadelphia their homes. An African American public culture emerged through the founding of churches, political organizations, fraternal orders, and schools. Visual culture documents this presence. Painters, lithographers, illustrators, portrait makers, and caricaturists incorporated black subjects into their representations of cityscapes. Few of these artists are more remembered than Philadelphia's Edward Williams Clay (1799–1857). His late-1820s print series, *Life in Philadelphia,* queried who African Americans might be in the new republic. In a world that relied upon race and slavery to structure inequality, Clay's answers were pointedly racist. African Americans who took on the trappings of bourgeois urban life were portrayed as essentially overreaching and out of place. This critique came in the form of 14 engraved plates that combined observation, artistry, imagination, and contempt.

Life in Philadelphia reflected the tensions of a post-emancipation society, while it also drew upon notions of racial inferiority that had been developing since Europeans' earliest encounters with Africans. Beliefs about African physicality, intellectual and moral capacities, and sexuality were building blocks in the construction of a racial ideology that justified the transatlantic slave trade and the exploitation of enslaved laborers in the Americas. As gradual emancipation expanded, the number of free persons of African descent in northern U.S. cities increased, and notions of racial difference were central to the construction of a social order. In this context, a new brand of racism justified the economic, social and political subordination of black Americans. Racism remade itself in the 1820s in part through caricature. No longer slaves, free African Americans found themselves subject to pernicious ideas about racialized difference.

Clay's *Life in Philadelphia* entered an on-going debate about the parameters of freedom. In churches, there were questions about ordaining black men to the ministry. In politics, African Americans lost the franchise and faced the proposition that they be colonized to Africa. In Clay's images, the debate over freedom turned on the right to adopt the manners, dress, leisure habits, and associational life that had been reserved for whites. Clay, like many, doubted black Americans'

Miss Chloe and Mr. Caesar engage in social banter in plate 4 of Clay's original Life in Philadelphia. *The exaggerated proportions of Miss Chloe's hat and the awkward posture of Mr. Caesar suggest how ill suited this couple is to the bucolic setting of a city park. Clay's point of view is underscored by the text. A faux black dialect and Miss Chloe's malapropism further suggest that these figures are over-reaching; they "aspire too much."*

capacities to inhabit such roles. His caricatures depicted fatally flawed attempts to appear as "ladies" and "gentlemen" and thereby fixed lines of inequality.

Pictures—vivid, engaging and accessible—influenced the climate in which free African Americans entered public culture. These were cruel portrayals of black figures that uttered malapropisms, dressed in clothing of exaggerated proportions, struck ungraceful poses, and thereby failed to measure up to the demands of freedom and citizenship. We find Clay's characters strolling in parks, taking tea in parlors, exchanging banter at dances, and generally inhabiting a black social world that most white Americans might not otherwise glimpse. Blackness marked his subjects as misguided aspirants, always constrained by inassimilable difference. They might imitate middle-class manners and habits, but they always over-reached. Or as one of Clay's characters, a perspiring Miss Chloe, puts it, "I aspire too much." Despite carefully arranged adornments and the refinements of the setting, Clay's "Miss Chloe" betrayed her innate inferiority through subtle word usage— "aspire" versus "perspire"—and ostentatious dress. Clay's capacity to tap into whites' fascinations and fears about the problem of slavery and its abolition was the key to his popularity.

Edward Clay appears here in a paper silhouette made at the Peale Museum in Philadelphia about 1820–21. Many of the silhouettes cut there at the time were the work of Peale's former African slave, Moses Williams. The silhouette is inscribed "E.W.C. Ann Ætat 21."

Representations of blackness were a contested terrain, however, in antebellum Philadelphia. Free black leaders challenged their caricature, commissioning their own respectable renderings including portraits and images of their institutions. Abolition activists, including the African American engraver Patrick Reason, circulated their own images, making popular the fragile image of the kneeling enslaved supplicant pleading, "Am I Not a Man and a Brother?" Among white artists were some who challenged Clay. Charles Willson Peale painted romantic portraits of black working-class figures. James Akin included rather ordinary black figures in his animated parodies of the city's sporting culture. Father and son William and Thomas Birch in their Philadelphia "views" included black figures as unremarkable aspects of the cityscape. There was no single answer to the question that these artists posed: Who were black Americans, and who might

Completed during Clay's visit to Paris, this watercolor portrait of Hercules De B. and his bride reflects the artist's growing interest in fashion as an element of caricature. Note his attention to detail in the hairstyles and the bride's dress. Clay brings humor to this pairing by the use of slightly overdrawn proportions. The formality of the scene is further disturbed as each character is caught casting a furtive glance at the other.

LIFE IN PHILADELPHIA.

Published by Tregear, at his humourous Print Shop, Cheapside, London.

Eng.d by Chas. Hunt.

"How you find yourself dis hot Weader Miss Chloe?"

"Pretty well I tank you Mr. Cesar only I aspire too much!"

Life in Philadelphia *appeared in London in a more exaggerated and vividly colored version. There is no evidence, however, that Clay himself had a hand in republishing the series. For British audiences, questions about slavery and emancipation were also highly contested as the empire went from abolishing the slave trade in 1807 to outlawing slavery itself in 1833.*

they be in urban settings like Philadelphia? Clay's images charged them with being misplaced aspirants. Still, other representations argued that black people were sympathetic, respectable and even unremarkable participants in the urban scene.

Clay's work has long served as a touchstone for scholars of the history of the color line in the United States. *Life in Philadelphia* was an early and influential episode in what would be an enduring contest over race and representation. The series circulated widely in print shops from Philadelphia and New York to Baltimore and New Orleans. It spawned a parallel series titled *Life in New York*. Clay's figures adorned sheet music and were mass-produced in miniatures. Across the Atlantic in London they were incorporated into book illustrations and sold in elaborate, full-color reproductions. In Paris, Clay's images made their way into elite homes when they were reproduced in fine French wallpaper. By the 1840s, Clay's subject matter expanded to antebellum American politics. Still, his interest in the problem of race endured. He parodied abolitionist objectives, lampooning sites of inter-racial intimacy—dinner parties, balls and parlor scenes. His argument: The anti-slavery cause was driven by cross-racial lust rather than by a commitment to freeing the enslaved. Others quickly took up Clay's ideas about race. Countless nineteenth-century engravers, lithographers, cartoonists, and illustrators adopted his visual strategies. They transformed what began as a local look at black life in Philadelphia into a national taxonomy of race. Clay's ideas, which interwove social, political and corporeal commentary on blackness, dominated nineteenth-century visual culture's contribution to U.S. debates over race and power.

Today we understand the origins of Clay's visual vocabulary, and they are trans-Atlantic in scope. Clay's ideas grew as much out of the artist's engagement with his peers in London and Paris as it did from his encounters with African Americans in Philadelphia. In 1826, just prior to producing *Life in Philadelphia*, Clay sailed for Europe. Once aboard ship, he began to draw fellow passengers and crew. Herein lies evidence of Clay's developing interest in the well-established conventions of "types" that were typical in British and French artistic circles. Clay learned to call a figure's social pretensions into question by subtle nuances of proportion—a hat too tall, a coat too small, or a rotund mid-section brought into relief by feet so petite that they would fail to take the subject very far. Clay continued in this vein when he reached Paris where he brushed watercolors and filled scrapbooks that detailed the trans-Atlantic influences that refined his capacity to caricature many sorts of social others. With ink and watercolors he rendered the city's people, parks, cafes, parties, and street gatherings. Clay shows us urban Paris teeming with figures that, by their manners, attire and customs, appeared to be unsettling Restoration France's social order.

Considering this European sojourn opens a door to new understanding of Clay's most notorious series. He began *Life in Philadelphia* shortly after returning from Europe, linking narratives about race in the United States to those in the Atlantic world. In the streets as well as the literature, theater and visual culture of Europe, Clay encountered influential peers. Copying and reinterpretation have long been part of the culture of caricature, and there is evidence of Clay's study of British artists including Thomas Rowlandson and the Cruikshank brothers. His work also reflects encounters

In the 1827 edition of Robert Cruikshank's "Monstrosities" series, we see the British artist's parody of London gentry. Like Clay, Cruikshank uses fashion—particularly women's oversized hats and pinched waists—to lampoon this snapshot of urban sociability. City parks can be provocative places, as evidenced by the couple at the far left. She exposes her calf, which he furtively glances down.

with France's visual culture. In his scrapbooks are examples from Edmé-Jean Pigal, Frédéric Bouchot, Achille Devéria, and popular journal and print serials including the *Petit Courrier des Dame* and *Le Bon Genre*. Parallels to his contemporary Honoré Daumier are evident. These well-remembered European social satirists also took up the black subject and incorporated black men and women into their commentaries on London and Paris in the 1820s. Set alongside his British and French peers, Clay and his *Life in Philadelphia* are but one chapter of a far-reaching story about an early-nineteenth-century Atlantic world view of the other.

The enduring importance of *Life in Philadelphia* reflects the coming together of scholarly interests in the history of race in the United States and the Atlantic world with an increasing attention to the history of visual culture. The Clements Library has acquired the exceedingly rare Philadelphia and London editions of *Life in Philadelphia* and many of Clay's political satires over the past two decades. More recently, the artist's watercolors, drawings and scrapbook fragments from his formative trip to France became part of the Library's collection. The growing presence of the work of Edward Williams Clay stands as an example of the evolving scope of both historical research and the Clements Library collection. *Life in Philadelphia* represents a key moment in the formation of a trans-Atlantic visual vocabulary of race. It also permits us to glimpse the lives of free African Americans in the generation after the American Revolution, particularly when set alongside other Clement Library holdings. The letters of black Philadelphian Sarah Mapps Douglass in the Weld-Grimké Papers, the works of African American engraver Patrick Henry Reason, and the memoir of the black female preacher Jarena Lee complete the picture. Black Americans had taken up the challenges of freedom through the politics of abolitionism, the proliferation of print culture and the pulpit. Upon returning from France, Edward Clay would have encountered them as he walked the city's streets. *Life in Philadelphia* was indeed one part observation of an actual community that lived, breathed and flourished in antebellum America.

Boudewyn DeKorne carved the decorative woodwork of the Great Room. This frieze is above the bookcases.

Wash. 29 Sept. 1835 –

My dear Jeremiah –

I avail myself of the frank under wh. I forward some matters of business to my father to drop you a line of acknow= ledgmᵗ ofyᵣ. last letter, in wh. I was pleased to find you coincided with me in the advice I gave old Matthew. I told him of it last night – I asked him the questions – He has three children now in bondage – Eldest a girl 17 or 18 yrs. price $300 – The next a girl also – 14 or 15 "   "   250 Last a boy just entering his teens ————   "   200 As the price of the two last will increase while that of the first will not be raised his first aim ought to be to buy the youngest & then the next youngest – Towards this he has so far only about $10 or 15 having been put to unusual expenses in his family's arrival & settlemᵗ here &c a visit he lately pd. Mrs Spence & his children, & in buying them clothes– He is however making very wise arrangements about putting the diffᵗ _____ so that nᵉˣᵗ a while he will be able for their

Francis Markoe discusses the monetary values of some of Matthew Matthews' children in this extract from his September 29, 1835, letter to Jeremiah Wilbur.

90

PRICES OF FREEDOM
MATTHEW MATTHEWS' STRUGGLE TO BUY HIS CHILDREN, 1834–1848

— Mary Hrones Parsons

The Matthews family saga begins with a slim packet of a dozen letters written in 1835, found within the Masters-Taylor-Wilbur Papers at the Clements Library. Although most of the collection consists of correspondence among family members or business associates, these 12 letters are decidedly different. They deal with the dilemma faced by a freed slave trying to buy the freedom of his six children. The letters document the attempts of Matthew Matthews, a black man freed in 1830, and two white men, Francis Markoe, Jr., of Washington, D.C., and Jeremiah Wilbur of New York City, to raise funds and to work out a strategy for buying Matthew's children as rapidly as possible. In addition to figuring out ways of obtaining money for Matthew, the men assessed which child to buy first, how to lower the asking price, and how to maximize Matthew's earning ability, so that he could earn more money to speed up the purchases.

Although Wilbur had clear abolitionist leanings, Markoe did not. However, Markoe knew Matthews from his frequent visits to the home of Matthews' former master, and wanted to help him. Fortunately, the documents allow us to compare Matthews' successful attempt to free three of his children in 1835, so well documented by the Markoe-Wilbur correspondence, with his much publicized and difficult attempt to purchase his last enslaved child in 1848. Some records from the intervening years—an 1844 land purchase, Matthew's 1854 will, newspaper articles, and census data—both raise and answer some interesting questions about how Matthews may have decided to use his resources in attempting to free his last three children.

Matthew Matthews was born a slave in Virginia about the year 1786. He was owned by the Rev. Thomas Harrison of Dumfries, Virginia, and raised with the Harrisons' eldest son, Philip (b. 1781). When Thomas died in 1811, his estate was split among his seven children and his widow. An inventory and appraisal of the estate made in 1812 included 19 slaves, of whom Matthew, listed as 24 years old, was valued at $383.33. By the terms of the will, Matthew was given to Walter, Philip Harrison's youngest brother. Walter was 16 years old when his father died, and 20 when the will was finally settled in 1815—at which time he inherited Matthew. That same year, Philip purchased Matthew from his brother: "In the year 1815 I promised the bearer of this paper, Mathew, who calls himself

Public Sale of Negroes,

By RICHARD CLAGETT.

On Tuesday, March 5th, 1833 at 1:00 P. M. the following Slaves will be sold at Potters Mart, in Charleston, S. C.

Miscellaneous Lots of Negroes, mostly house servants, some for field work.

Conditions: ½ **cash, balance by bond, bearing interest from date of sale. Payable in one to two years to be secured by a mortgage of the Negroes, and appraised personal security.** *Auctioneer will pay for the papers.*

A valuable Negro woman, accustomed to all kinds of house work. Is a good plain cook, and excellent dairy maid, washes and irons. She has four children, one a girl about 13 years of age, another 7, a boy about 5, and an infant 11 months old. 2 of the children will be sold with mother, the others separately, if it best suits the purchaser.

A very valuable Blacksmith, wife and daughters; the Smith is in the prime of life, and a perfect master at his trade. His wife about 27 years old, and his daughters 12 and 10 years old have been brought up as house servants, and as such are very valuable. Also for sale 2 likely young negro wenches, one of whom is 16 the other 13, both of whom have been taught and accustomed to the duties of house servants. The 16 year old wench has one eye.

A likely yellow girl about 17 or 18 years old, has been accustomed to all kinds of house and garden work. She is sold for no fault. Sound as a dollar.

House servants: The owner of a family described herein, would sell them for a good price only, they are offered for no fault whatever, but because they can be done without, and money is needed. He has been offered $1250. They consist of a man 30 to 33 years old, who has been raised in a genteel Virginia family as house servant, Carriage driver etc., in all which he excels. His wife a likely wench of 25 to 30 raised in like manner, as chamber maid, seamstress. nurse etc., their two children, girls of 12 and 4 or 5. They are bright mulattoes, of mild tractable dispositions, unassuming manners. and of genteel appearance and well worthy the notice of a gentleman of fortune needing such.

Also 14 Negro Wenches ranging from 16 to 25 years of age, all sound and capable of doing a good days work in the house or field.

Broadside advertising a sale of slaves in Charleston, South Carolina, in 1833. Matthews' children faced a similar fate unless their father could raise the money to buy them.

Mathew Mathews, in consideration that we had been raised together from childhood, and in consideration of his good conduct and uniform good character, and in consideration that he would serve me faithfully a good length of time, to purchase him of his then master, Walter Harrison, to whom he had been devised by my father, and after a good time to set him free." Fifteen years later Philip wrote of Matthew, "I have trusted him for years to make contracts for me to large amounts, and with money to large amounts; and on one occasion sent him alone to Philadelphia, to take charge of money and property to the amount of twelve hundred dollars."

During this time, Matthew had started a family with Mary, a slave owned by Dr. John Spence of Dumfries. They had six children: Maria (b. ca. 1817), Lavinia (b. ca. 1822), Henry (b. ca. 1824), John (b. ca. 1826), Simon (b. ca. 1828), and Mary Ann, (b. ca. 1830). Philip Harrison, a lawyer, tried to figure out a way to keep his promise of freeing Matthew without permanently separating him from his family: "I have been prevented heretofore and am prevented now from carrying into effect fully my intention and promise of fully emancipating, by executing to him a deed of emancipation, in consequence of his having a wife and children, and as an honest man will not leave behind him— slaves if emancipated being by the laws of Virginia compelled to leave the State forever."

Manumission papers for Matthew were filed in Washington, D.C., on January 22, 1830, and signed by a James Birth of that city. It seems likely that Philip Harrison had finally discovered a way to circumvent the "Black Laws of Virginia" by transferring ownership of Matthew to a friend who did not live in Virginia, and who could then free Matthew outside that state. Hence, since Matthew's manumission papers would be issued in the District of Columbia and not Virginia, he could visit his family whenever he liked.

Mrs. Mary F. Spence, who owned Matthew's wife and children, was widowed in 1829. Several years later, she agreed to sell Matthews his children when he was able to raise the money to buy them; she would not sell them elsewhere. Unfortunately, in February 1835, Mrs. Spence found herself in financial straits, and wrote Matthew that if he wanted to buy his eldest son Henry, he needed to do so very soon, as she could not afford to keep him. He would have to be sold, if not to Matthew, then at public auction. Matthew, who had been working in Washington, had managed to buy his youngest daughter Mary Ann for $50 in May 1834 and had saved almost $150 towards the purchase of his son Henry, who was 10 or 11 years old, but he was $75 short of Mrs. Spence's asking price of $225.

At this point, Matthew approached Francis Markoe, who had been a frequent guest in the Harrison household when Matthew was a slave there. Matthew "came to me in great distress, & sd. he did not want to beg but to borrow what wd. be sufft., if added to [approximately] 150 the sum he owned, to make $225, the sum wh. his mistress asked for Henry." Markoe set about contacting local friends in D.C. who knew Matthew from his slave days. Markoe also wrote to Jeremiah Wilbur in New York City to enlist his aid. Thus began the remarkable six-month correspondence between the two men, as they tried to help Matthews secure the freedom of his children. A letter about Matthews' plight written by a third man, G.R. Birch, had been published in a New York City newspaper, *The Emancipator,* on February 17, 1835, but Birch got his facts wrong. This was a stroke of luck for later

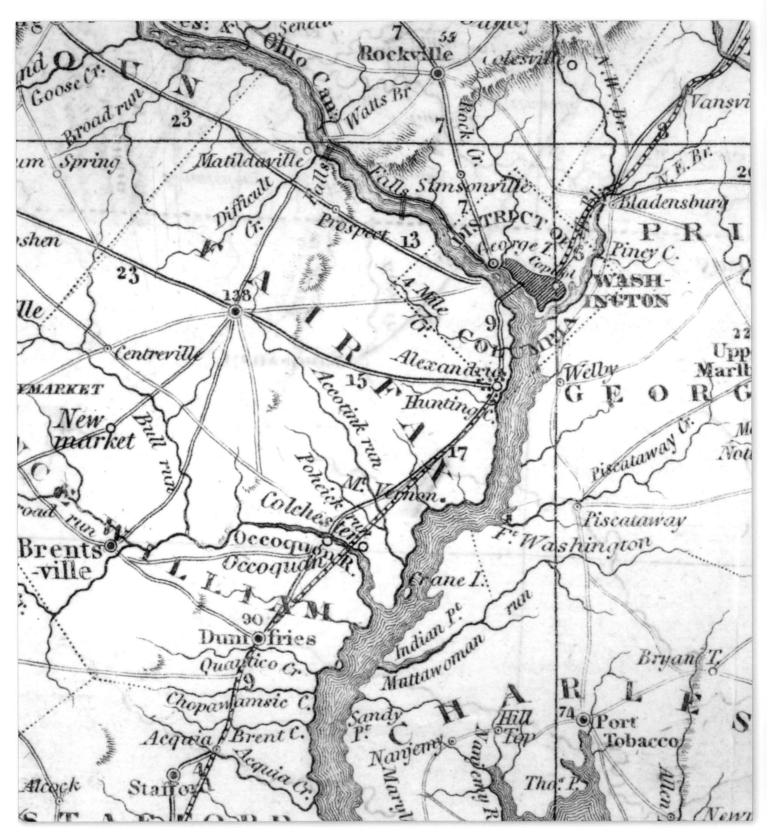

Matthews' frequently traveled route between Washington and Dumfries, Virginia, is shown in this detail from Virginia, Maryland, and Delaware *by Henry Schenck Tanner (Philadelphia, 1833).*

researchers, because Markoe went into great detail in his letters to Wilbur to correct the facts, listing the names, ages and prices of Matthew's children. We also know from this letter that Mrs. Spence threatened to put Henry up for public auction, that Matthew could have his wife Mary without having to pay for her, and much more. Markoe, the Southerner, and Wilbur, the abolitionist, bounced ideas back and forth regarding the best use of the money they were raising for Matthew.

Markoe succeeded in collecting about $25, which he gave to Matthew. Adding this money to his savings of almost $150, Matthew set out for Dumfries to offer it to Mrs. Spence for Henry. En route he stopped to see a friend in Dumfries named Luke Johnson, who loaned him $30, raising the amount to $200. Mrs. Spence had requested $225, but "after a little demur," she accepted his offer of cash. Henry now belonged to his father. When Masters and Markoe found out that Matthew had borrowed part of the money, they became concerned about Matthew's incurring any debts—if he were taken to court, Mary Ann and Henry could be sold to pay off his debts, as they were still slaves belonging to their father. They encouraged Matthew to free his children as quickly as possible. Only when the children had their manumission papers would they be safe.

Matthew had been told that his wife Mary could join him whenever she liked, without having to pay for her, but their children would remain slaves belonging to the Spence family. How the understanding to free Mary Matthews came about is unclear. The Spence and Harrison families were neighbors in Dumfries, and perhaps some sort of "gentlemen's agreement" was made to free both husband and wife. A character reference written in 1835 by Mrs. Mary F. Spence states, "Mary Matthews the bearer of this has been in my service as a slave for the last 25 years," which meant that Mary became Mrs. Spence's slave in 1810, the same year that Mrs. Spence married Dr. John Spence. Mary Matthews was probably in her early 20s then. The 1835 correspondence reveals that Francis Markoe and Jeremiah Wilbur urged Matthew to ask Mrs. Spence for his wife so that he could bring her to Washington, where her wages as a cook would help supplement Matthew's earnings and speed up the purchase of their children. They were also concerned that Mrs. Spence might change her mind about giving Mary to Matthew, especially given Mrs. Spence's financial problems. But Mary would not leave until her youngest son Simon was purchased and could leave with her.

Meanwhile, on February 21, 1835, Wilbur wrote that he had managed to raise $125 in New York, and that he could have raised the entire $225 to buy Henry, "had not your letter changed the aspect of things respecting him to me, from what Mr. Birch had stated." Mr. Birch's published letter stated that Matthews had freed three of his children "unaided," and now just needed help buying the last two, whereas in fact, Matthews had bought only one of his children, and five remained slaves. As a result of this misunderstanding, Wilbur felt he had solicited funds from personal friends under false pretenses, "in as much as I supposed the old man intended to liberate the girl with the $150 which he had saved & that the $225 which was demanded for the Boy Henry would entirely liberate all his *children*.... Those therefore who have contributed to this fund, have done so with the idea of making the old Man happy, before he goes to the grave, in seeing all his children free."

Wilbur decided to consult these friends, telling them the corrected facts. He did send $50 to be used immediately to cancel the $30 Matthew had borrowed from his friend Luke Johnson to purchase Henry; the other $20 was for Matthew to use as he saw fit. Now all efforts were focused on buying Simon. Once he was free, Mary Matthews would join Matthew in Washington, where their joint earnings would speed the accumulation of the money needed to free their other three children—John, Lavinia and Maria. On January 15, 1835, Mrs. Spence wrote Matthew "if you take Simon by paying as much down as you can, and the balance in 6 mos., by taking him directly, you shall have him for $150 . . . Simon in his 7th year as fine a Boy as I ever saw." Matthews hoped that in four months he might obtain the $30, which, added to Jeremiah Wilbur's $20, would give him the $50 down payment he needed to bring Simon (and thus also his wife Mary) to join Henry, Mary Ann and himself in Washington.

Although eager to help Matthews, Jeremiah Wilbur was worried that if they acted too fast, Mrs. Spence "might suppose some one was interested for him, & consequently be less likely to accept a low price for his children's liberty." In April, Wilbur offered to send whatever money Matthews lacked to meet Mrs. Spence's asking price of $150 for Simon. Markoe wrote back that Matthews planned a trip to Dumfries, Virginia, in a few weeks. On the strength of Wilbur's offered help, Markoe urged Matthews to offer Mrs. Spence $100 in cash for Simon, feeling that she would accept a lower price if cash were offered rather than having to wait six months for a slightly higher price. Wilbur sent the $100 needed to buy Simon, with the condition that Matthews obtain manumission papers for Mary, Henry, Simon, and Mary Ann as soon as possible.

Matthews made the trip to Dumfries and returned with Simon and Mary. A bill of sale from Mrs. Mary F. Spence to Matthew Matthews, dated June 13, 1835, records the legal transfer of ownership of Mary Matthews and her three children from Mary F. Spence to Matthew Matthews for the sum of $375. The combined prices of Henry ($200), Mary Ann ($50), and Simon ($125), add up to the $375 figure on the bill of sale. Clearly, Mrs. Spence kept her promise of giving Matthew his wife. Three days later, on June 16, 1835, Matthews signed manumission papers in Washington, D.C., for his wife and the three children living with them.

Three months later, in September 1835, Wilbur and Markoe exchanged three letters that mention a possible course of action for Matthew to take in attempting to free his three remaining enslaved children. Both Matthew and his wife could make higher wages in New York than in Washington—Mary could earn $5 per month as a cook in Washington, but would earn $7–8 per month in New York—so Matthew was considering making trips to Philadelphia and New York. Also, the possibility was good that Matthew might be able to locate sympathetic people in either city who would be willing to purchase the children still owned by Mrs. Spence, and let them work off their cost. Jeremiah Wilbur felt, "If they are *honest & faithful,* & willing to make themselves useful as house servants, they could *pay for their 'life time'* in the course of 5 or 10 years."

Markoe wrote the last letter in the Markoe-Wilbur correspondence on September 29, 1835. He described Matthews' situation, as he faced the challenge of trying to raise $750 to free his last three children:

Receipt signed by Luke Johnson, a black friend of Matthew Matthews, acknowledging that Matthews had repaid the $30 he had borrowed to buy his son, Henry.

> *He has three children now in bondage - Eldest a girl [Maria] 17 or 18 yrs. price $300*
> *the next a girl also [Lavinia] - 14 or 15   "   " $250*
> *last a boy just entering his teens [John]   " $200*
>
> *As the price of the last will increase while that of the first will not be raised his first aim ought to be to buy the youngest [John] & then the next youngest [Lavinia]. Towards this he has so far only about $10 or 15 having been put to unnatural expenses in his family's arrival & settle in here & in a visit he lately pd. Mrs. Spence & his children, & on buying them clothes. He is however making very wise arrangements about putting the difft. members out at service, so that after a while he will be able from their respective wages to appropriate portions of money to add to his own.*

The remarkable correspondence between Francis Markoe and Jeremiah Wilbur concerning Matthew Matthews and his children seems to have ended in late September 1835.

Maria Matthews, the eldest daughter, was not freed by her father, but she did not die a slave. Maria married Sandy Alexander, a slave on the large Hancock plantation between Dumfries and Occoquan. Eventually given his freedom, Alexander moved to Washington, where he worked at a number of jobs before becoming a prominent black minister and the founder of the First Baptist Church of Georgetown. The couple had two children born into slavery—Maria G. Alexander (b. ca. 1843) and Arthur Alexander (b. ca. 1844). Sometime before 1850, Maria Matthews Alexander and her two children were put up for sale at the old slave pen in Alexandria. Sandy Alexander, by using what money he had, and perhaps borrowing from friends, was able to purchase his family. Maria Matthews Alexander died before the 1850 Census.

The date of John Matthews' freedom is unknown. The original plan was to buy him before either Lavinia or Maria. Land records for the District of Columbia show that on July 5, 1844, Matthew Matthews paid $194.62 to buy about a tenth of an acre of land "together with buildings" on the south side of K Street, between 15th and 16th Streets, about two block north of Lafayette Park. Why was

Matthew buying land, instead of saving money to buy Lavinia's freedom? A possible explanation might be that Matthews had managed to buy and free his son John in the eight and a half years since the Markoe-Wilbur correspondence ended, and now Matthews' strategy was to increase the earning capacity of his freed family members (his wife, and his three sons) by eliminating the need to pay rent or to have room and board deducted from their earnings. Matthew had devoted himself to freeing his children, so he must have felt that the family's increased earnings would more than compensate for the $194.62 spent on the land and thus hasten the day of Lavinia's freedom.

In 1847 Matthews began his much-publicized attempt to free the last of his enslaved children, Lavinia. By this time, Lavinia was no longer owned by the Spence family; she belonged to Mrs. Robert J. Taylor of Alexandria. In the summer of 1847, she agreed to sell Lavinia to Matthew Matthews for $460. Matthew made a trip North to raise funds, returning in November with $350, which he hoped to give to Mrs. Taylor as security until he could raise the rest. She refused his money, and sold Lavinia to Joseph Bruin, a slave trader in Alexandria, for $425. Bruin raised Lavinia's price to $475 and set a date for her sale.

At this point abolitionist William L. Chaplin took Matthews' cause to the abolitionist press. In 1835, Jeremiah Wilbur had worried that publicity and the knowledge that others were willing to help Matthews buy his children might inflate their selling price. Chaplin's use of the abolitionist press in 1848 would prove Wilbur right. On February 28, 1848, *The Albany Patriot* carried Matthews' story under the bold headlines "Human Flesh Market." Gerrit Smith, the editor, proclaimed, "Read, ponder, and inwardly digest the following letter from Mr. Chaplin. Put your soul in the soul's stead of Mathew, and ACT!" Then followed a long article on Matthews, ending with an appeal that Matthews lacked only $100, "which he must have from the North, or at last after all his perseverance and toilsome effort, see his hopes dashed down forever by the loss of his daughter!"

On March 15, 1848, *The Albany Patriot* published a letter from Chaplin entitled, "Mathew Mathews," relating that the slave trader Bruin, "taking advantage of his [Matthews'] love for his daughter and his great anxiety to secure her freedom," had raised the price he was asking for Lavinia to $600. A more probable explanation for the increase in Lavinia's price would be that the slave trader Bruin was aware of the abolitionist newspaper's appeals to its readership to raise money for Matthew and saw a way to profit at their expense.

Chaplin had made it easy for Bruin to learn about his fund-raising activities by mentioning in print both Bruin's own name and also Lavinia's. Fortunately for Matthews, John W. Fairfax, a sympathetic "gentleman" in Alexandria, agreed to buy Lavinia, using Matthews' $350, plus $250 of his own money. Fairfax would keep Lavinia until Matthews could pay him the remaining $250. On March 25, 1848, Chaplin wrote to Gerrit Smith asking him for $200, which, added to the $50 Chaplin had raised, would give Matthews the money he needed to buy Lavinia. The money was sent, and on May 18, 1848, a deed of sale was signed transferring ownership of Lavinia Matthews from John W. Fairfax to Matthew Matthews of Washington, D.C. Lavinia was about 25 years old, and her father was about 60 or 62-years old. All of his children were free. Six years later, in 1854, Matthew Matthews died.

Matthews' wife Mary is not mentioned in his will and may have died before he did. She is listed with Matthew, Lavinia, Mary Ann, Henry, and granddaughter Maria Alexander in the 1850 Census of Washington. By his will, Matthew left "the property on which I now reside"—the same lot he purchased in 1844—to his daughter Mary Ann and his granddaughter Maria Alexander. Lavinia was given $25. None of his sons is mentioned in the will. John moved to Chelsea, Massachusetts, where three of his children were born between 1853 and 1858, and the family continued to live there until the mid 1860s. Lavinia joined her brother John's household in Chelsea and was working as a cook at the time of the 1860 Census. Sadly, on November 19, 1868, she was admitted to St. Elizabeth's Hospital for the insane in Washington, D.C., suffering from "mania—supposed cause: Typhoid fever," and died there on September 5, 1873. Mary Ann, Matthew's youngest child and the first he freed, inherited part of her father's land in 1854. A year later she married William H. Wheeler, and had five children, all born in Washington between the years 1859 and 1871.

The Matthew Matthews correspondence is just one of many African American resources related to slavery at the William L. Clements Library. The Tailyour Family Papers (1780–1840) include the records of a Scottish merchant who was active in the slave trade yet sent his own mixed-race Jamaican children to be educated in England, despite family opposition. The Jarvis Family Papers (1790–1884) and the Anne-Louis de Tousard Papers (1787–1855) provide the perspective of slave owners on plantations in the West Indies, while the Ruth N. Hastings Papers give a Northern governess' views of slaves and slavery on a plantation in South Carolina in 1852.

The Schoff Collection of Civil War letters and diaries includes numerous references to African Americans, both the runaway slaves (contrabands) who flocked to the Union lines, as well as the African Americans who served in Union regiments. Federal soldier Samuel F. Jayne's letters home are of particular note, because his written descriptions of contrabands and of an African American soldier include pencil sketches of them.

Legal documents are another useful source. The Dauphin County, Pennsylvania, Slave Register (1788–1825) is an interesting example, as it contains registration information on each African American child, as well as the owner's name, place of residence, and occupation. Other useful legal sources are wills and probate records, such as the Wilkes County, Georgia, Collection (1778–1849), which includes inventories of slaves, their ages, their value, and the names of those who inherited them. The John Fraser Estate Litigation Papers (1823–73) deal with the long, drawn-out court proceedings that followed Fraser's attempt to leave his large estate in Florida to the four children he fathered by one of his slaves.

Easily overlooked sources on slavery are the Henry Clinton Papers and the Shelburne Papers. Clinton was commander-in-chief of the British troops in America during the American Revolution, and his papers contain many references to an African American regiment (the Black Pioneers) and to African American civilians. Within the Shelburne Papers are the Assiento Papers, regarding the South Sea Company's monopoly of the Atlantic slave trade during the first half of the eighteenth century. Other Atlantic slave trade documents are two slave voyage account books for the late eighteenth century.

BLACK AND WHITE
SARAH FORTEN AND
THE IMPACT OF COLOR

— Barbara DeWolfe

The Clements Library is fortunate to own the papers of the well-known abolitionists Angelina and Sarah Grimké and Angelina's husband Theodore Weld; it is the Library's most important collection of manuscripts related to antislavery. The abolitionist movement came together in 1833 when William Lloyd Garrison and Theodore Weld formed the American Anti-Slavery Society in Philadelphia, and within the decade the organization had 2,000 branch societies and 150,000 to 200,000 members. At its convention in 1840, the group split when a woman was elected to a committee, with the radicals following William Lloyd Garrison, who allied with women's reform work, and the moderates supporting Lewis Tappan. The Weld-Grimké collection holds correspondence to and from most of the leading figures in the movement, including William Lloyd Garrison; James Birney; Catherine, Henry Ward, and Lyman Beecher; Lydia Maria Child; Thomas Clarkson; George Whitefield; Frederick Douglass; Lucretia Mott; Elizabeth Peabody; Sarah Mapps Douglass; Elizabeth Cady Stanton; Wendell Phillips; Gerrit Smith; Arthur and Lewis Tappan; John Greenleaf Whittier; and many others. It is one of the richest antislavery collections extant, especially for women.

The Grimké sisters' involvement with antislavery began about 1835, and by 1837 they were writing almost exclusively on this topic, as reflected in the collection's correspondence. As daughters of a wealthy South Carolina slave owner, they were surrounded by slaves and formed close relationships with some of them, even teaching them to read and write. They were sensitive to the punishments of slaves and developed extraordinary sympathy for them. Their hatred of the institution led them north to Philadelphia, where they converted to the Quaker faith and became active in the abolition movement after reading about a pro-slavery riot in Boston in 1835. Though their papers contain many outstanding letters from abolitionists, the single letter from Sarah Forten is one of the few in existence for the early nineteenth century regarding a black woman's perspective on racism.

Sarah Forten, whose background was quite different from that of the Grimké sisters, was born into one of the wealthiest black families in Philadelphia in 1814. Her stance against slavery and racial discrimination was influenced early by her family and her parents' friends, but her involvement in the cause began at age 19 when the founding of the all-male American Anti-Slavery Society and its

Philadelphia April 15th 1837

Esteemed Friend,

I have to thank you for the interest which has led you to address a letter to me on a subject which claims so large a share of your attention – in making a reply to the questions proposed by you I might truly advance the excuse of inability – but you will know how to compassionate the weakness of one who has written but little on the subject, and who has untill very lately lived and acted more for herself than for the good of others – I confess that I am wholly indebted to the Abolition cause for arousing me from apathy and indifference, shedding light into a mind which has been too long wrapt in selfish darkness – In reply to your question – of the "effect of Predjudice" on myself, I must acknowledge that it has often embittered my feelings, particularly when I recollect that we are the innocent victims of it – for you are well aware that it originates from dislike to the color of the skin, as much as from the degradation of Slavery – I am peculiarly sensitive on this point, and consequently seek to avoid as much as possible from mingling with those who exist under its influence, I must also own that it has often engendered feelings of discontent and mortification in my breast when I saw that many were preferred before me, who by education – birth – or wordly circumstances were no better than myself – their sole claim to notice depending on the superior advantage of being White – but I am striving to live above such heart burnings – and will learn to "bear and forbear" believing that a spirit of forbearance under such evils is all that we as a people can well exert –

Colonization is as you well know the Offspring of Predjudice – it has doubtless had a baneful influence on our People – I despise the aim of

Sarah Forten's letter of April 15, 1837, in which she responds to Angelina Grimké's query about prejudice.

The highly-charged antislavery image of a kneeling female slave appears on this silk purse once owned by Angelina Grimké.

passage of a resolution acknowledging the importance of women's participation inspired her to action.

Sarah's father, James Forten, was born free in 1766 to a family of modest means. As a child James attended the Friends' African School, for which abolitionist Anthony Benezet was one of the overseers and designers of the curriculum. The death of James' father and his family's subsequent financial difficulties forced James to leave school and work for a local storekeeper. After the Revolution he was apprenticed to Robert Bridges, who owned a sail-making business. James excelled at the trade, and when Bridges died he left his business to James, who invested the profits in real estate and stock, making him a wealthy man. As a man of high moral sensitivity, he participated in reform activities early, the first being a public protest against slavery in 1799, for which he signed a petition of black citizens for an end to the slave trade and for the prevention of kidnapping of free people. Among his later contributions, he provided funds for William Lloyd Garrison's *Liberator* and with other black activists founded the American Moral Reform Society, which advocated the rights of all Americans regardless of skin color.

After his first wife died, James Forten married Charlotte Vandine, who was also a proponent of the rights of blacks, slave and free. Of African American and Native American lineage, she was born about 1785 in Philadelphia and married James, 19 years her senior, on December 10, 1805. She moved into James' house on Shippen Street, but within a year they relocated to a more affluent neighborhood on Lombard Street and started raising a family. By 1823 Charlotte had given birth to nine children, at least five of whom—Harriet (1810–75), James Jr. (1811–?), Robert Bridges (1813–64), Sarah (1814–83), and Margaretta (1815–75)—became active abolitionists.

With such a strong underpinning of family support and encouragement, the Forten children adopted the reform zeal of their parents, though they expressed it in different ways. Harriet was an organizer, James Jr. and Robert Bridges were speakers, Margaretta was an educator, and Sarah wrote poetry. With Harriet's marriage to Robert Purvis, the Fortens united with another well-known Philadelphia family active in the drive to abolish slavery. In 1837 Robert Purvis formed a committee to help runaway slaves and set up his house as a station on the Underground Railroad, for which he was dubbed the "President of the Underground Railroad." Harriet and Robert's home, like that of the Fortens, also became a gathering place for reformers. Not just involved with abolition, the Forten and Purvis families were also active supporters of temperance, education, pacifism, and women's rights.

In 1835 the city and county of Philadelphia had 15,000 African Americans, the largest black population in the North, so the fact that it was a haven for runaway slaves and reform activities is not surprising. By the time Sarah was born the family was part of a wide network of abolitionists, both black and white, in America and Great Britain. They hosted prominent abolitionists at their home and with their collaborators and friends established at least six organizations dedicated to the elimination of slavery. One of their closest family friends was William Lloyd Garrison, a frequent visitor to the Forten home and one of James' staunchest associates. Other household names and acquaintances were the British abolitionists Granville Sharp, William Wilberforce and Thomas Clarkson; Benjamin Rush, the noted Philadelphia physician; Richard Peters, Jr., James Forten's lawyer; Gerrit Smith, a white politician; the Grimkés; and the Douglasses, a prominent black Philadelphia family.

During the 1830s and 1840s the female abolition movement in the North was active in forming local societies and groups for the purpose of raising money to support the antislavery cause. Many of the associations and close friendships of the Forten women were formed within these societies and organizations. In 1833 Charlotte and her daughters helped to found the Philadelphia Female Antislavery Society, the first interracial society of women abolitionists in the country, composed mostly of Quaker activists. Lucretia Mott organized the first meeting on December 9, when all interested women gathered to draft a constitution and elect officers. Mott intended this to be the auxiliary society to the all-male American Antislavery Society, which was established five days earlier. Margaretta Forten helped draft the society's constitution, Sarah served on the governing board, and Harriet co-chaired the society-sponsored fundraising fairs, which helped spread information and sold needlework and pottery displaying the antislavery emblem and inscriptions. The society petitioned

Congress to outlaw slavery and sold shares to build a meeting place for their reformist gatherings. Though open to all, membership consisted mostly of Quaker women from the middle class, including Abigail (Abba) Alcott, mother of Louisa May Alcott; Lydia White, who kept a store that sold freely produced goods not derived from slave labor; and the Grimké sisters. Through this society the Forten women kept in touch with a wide circle of friends in other American antislavery societies and in Great Britain.

The emblem that represented the female abolition movement, found on many goods produced for fairs and widely used on stationery, books, invitations, textiles, and other items, was the icon of the kneeling female slave with chained hands raised. The image was so ubiquitous that the Clements Library could mount an exhibit on this one topic, using materials from at least three manuscript collections, including the Weld-Grimké Papers, the Margaret Chandler Collection and the Birney Papers, as well as objects from the Graphics Division. Examples include Angelina Grimké's 1838 wedding invitation and silk purse, and an engraving in the Chandler collection. Sarah Forten herself sketched the kneeling female slave in a friend's album. This figure, adopted by the women's abolition community, was engraved in 1835 by Patrick Reason, "A Colored Young Man of the City of New York," but he did not introduce it. The female kneeling slave made its first appearance in England in 1826 as the symbol for the Ladies Negro's Friend Society of Birmingham, and in America in 1830 in the publication *The Genius of Universal Emancipation,* for which Elizabeth Margaret Chandler wrote a poem entitled "Kneeling Slave." The original, however, was a male slave rather than a female, kneeling in the same position. It was used as the seal of the Society for the Abolition of Slavery in England in the 1780s and appeared on antislavery publications and Wedgewood medallions.

In addition to her active involvement in antislavery activities, Sarah Forten used poetry to express her feelings. Todd Gernes has suggested that many of Sarah's poems are "verbal equivalents of antislavery emblems, which depicted African slaves, half naked, kneeling in supplication." Sarah wrote her first published poem, "The Grave of the Slave," at the age of 17 and sent it under the pen name Ada to the *Liberator.* The paper's editor, William Lloyd Garrison, printed it on January 22, 1831, not knowing his friend's daughter was the author. The black composer and bandleader Frank Johnson, whose band played at antislavery meetings, later set it to music. In this poem, Sarah sees death as the slave's answer to captivity.

> *Poor slave! Shall we sorrow that death was thy friend,*
> *The last, and the kindest, that heaven could send?*
> *The grave to the weary is welcomed and blest;*
> *And death, to the captive, is freedom and rest.*

Sarah continued to publish in *The Liberator, The Philanthropist,* the *National Enquirer,* and *The Pennsylvania Freeman* until 1839, with about 30 prose and poetry entries, some printed more than once. But as Sarah's poetry developed she also became a strong advocate against racial discrimination. To Sarah, the kneeling slave praying to be released from bondage was only half the picture; the other

Angelina Grimké (1805–79) photographed with her husband, Theodore Weld (1803–95), and their children.

half was acceptance and equality. Many of her white "sisters" were allied in their hatred of slavery, but most, the Grimké sisters being the leading exception, found it hard to abandon their prejudices against blacks and accept them as social equals. Sarah's most famous poem, "An Appeal to Women," was an impassioned plea to white women to accept their black sisters as social equals. It was originally published in the *Lowell Observer*, then reprinted by Garrison for *The Liberator* in 1834. It abandons the "freedom is death" motif of her first poem and adopts the more hopeful circumstance of true sisterhood. In the first verse, Sarah is challenging white women to overlook the color of skin:

> *Oh, woman, woman in thy brightest hour*
> *Of conscious worth, of pride, of conscious power*
> *Oh, nobly dare to act a Christian's part,*
> *That well befits a lovely woman's heart!*
> *Dare to be good, as thou canst dare be great;*
> *Despise the taunts of envy, scorn and hate;*
> *Our 'skins may differ,' but from thee we claim*
> *A sister's privilege, in a sister's name.*

This poem received widespread attention in 1837, when the first National Women's Antislavery Convention met in New York. Seventy-one delegates from seven states and 103 corresponding members met on May 9 at the Third Free Church, with the largest number of participants coming from Massachusetts, New York and Pennsylvania. This was the first attempt to gather all the different female antislavery groups in one place, and it included such leading figures as Lucretia Mott, Lydia Maria Child and Juliana Tappan, daughter of the abolitionist Lewis Tappan. Sarah Grimké stated that the purpose was to "establish a system of operations throughout every town and village in the free states, that would exert a powerful influence in the abolition of American slavery." The convention issued resolutions, formed committees, and pledged to petition Congress for the abolition of slavery— the only way women could "vote" their opinions. Angelina Grimké proposed a resolution, which was

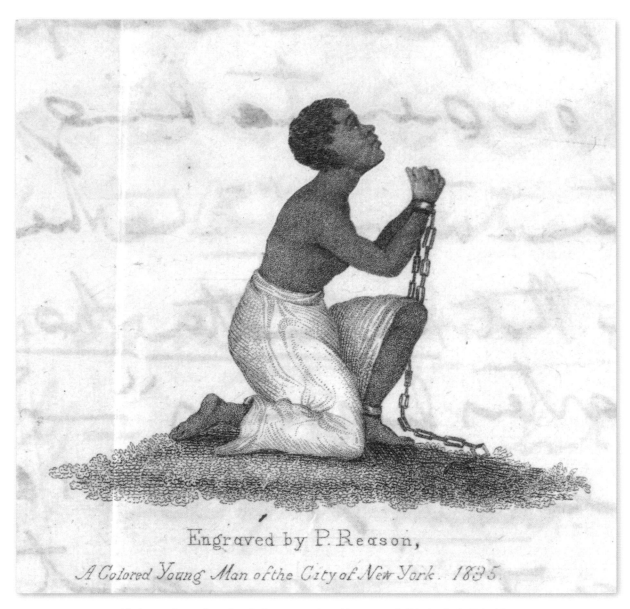

The image of a supplicant female slave was much used by women abolitionists in the United States. This example, engraved by Patrick Reason in 1835, was printed as a letterhead.

passed, stating that every woman had a duty to petition Congress annually for the abolition of slavery.

Though only four delegates at the New York convention and 14 corresponding members were black, they represented several other black abolitionist organizations, most notably the Colored Ladies' Literary Society of New York, the Rising Daughters of Abyssinia (of New York) and the female anti-slavery societies of Boston and Philadelphia. Angelina Grimké was especially eager for African American women like Sarah Forten and Grace and Sarah Douglass to attend and to lend their perspective, since she felt that white women delegates were primarily interested in achieving equal status with the men in the movement and would overlook the issue of racism. Sarah Forten informed Angelina that she and her sisters would be staying in New York with the Reverend Peter Williams, but the Fortens do not appear on the delegate list in the convention's minutes. Grace and her daughter Sarah Mapps Douglass, members of a well-known black family from Philadelphia, were very close friends of the Fortens and shared their feelings of social isolation. They both attended, and Grace was elected one of the six vice presidents.

Prior to the convention, Angelina Grimké had solicited information from her African American friends about what it was like to be black. Sarah Forten responded on April 15, 1837, shortly before the convention met on May 9. In her letter to Angelina, she was forthright in the way that she could not be in her published poems. Sarah was as well educated as the white women with whom she associated and had all the refinement and privileges associated with wealth, but because of the color of her skin she was excluded from much of what American society offered the middle and upper classes. She wrote, in part:

> I must acknowledge that it has often embittered my feelings, particularly when I recollect that we are the innocent victims of it; for you are well aware that it originates from dislike to the color of the skin, as much as from the degradation of Slavery. I am peculiarly sensitive on this point, and consequently seek to avoid as much as possible mingling with those who exist under its influence. I must also own that it has often engendered feelings of discontent and mortification in my breast when I saw that many were preferred before me, who by education, birth, of worldly circumstances were no better than myself. THEIR sole claim to notice depending on the superior advantage of being White ... [prejudice] can be seen in the exclusion of the colored people from their churches, or placing them in obscure corners. We see it in their being barred from a participation with others in acquiring any useful knowledge; public lectures are not usually free to the colored people; they may not avail themselves of the right to drink at the fountain of learning, or gain an insight into the arts and science of our favored land. All this and more do they feel acutely. . . . Even our professed friends have not yet rid themselves of it – to some of them it clings like a dark mantle obscuring their many virtues and choking up the avenues to higher and nobler sentiments.

In this letter, we get a look behind the poetry, so to speak, and can more clearly understand the effect of prejudice on the essence of Sarah's being: her mortification at being passed over; her embitterment; her isolation from the normal activities of white society; and her mistrust of professed friends. The color of one's skin becomes more clearly the demarcation point; on one side are social acceptance, an open path to education, liberty to enjoy museums and cultural events, and the right to attend the same church as a white person. On the other side are isolation, condescending glances, "no admission signs," and fear. Sarah's letter says what her poetry does not, that prejudice is cruel.

In her *Appeal to the Women of the Nominally Free States*, Angelina Grimké used this information and that sent in by others to persuade white women in the Northern free states to accept black women as equals: "here [in the North], too in profound deference to the South, we refuse to eat, or ride, or walk, or associate, or open our institutions of learning, or even our zoological institutions to people of color, unless they visit them in the capacity of *servants*, of menials in humble attendance upon the Anglo-American. Who ever heard of a more wicked absurdity in a Republican country?" The speech was one of 6 pamphlets published for the convention, with the third verse of Sarah's poem, "An Appeal to Women," added to the title page as a kind of poetic symbol that captured the essence of the address. The entreaty in the first verse has turned into a declaration in the third.

> *We are thy sisters. –God has truly said,*
> *That of one blood the nations He has made.*
> *Oh, Christian woman! In a Christian land,*
> *Canst thou unblushing read this great command?*
> *Suffer the wrongs which wring our inmost heart,*
> *To draw one throb of pity on thy part!*
> *Our 'skins may differ,' but from thee we claim*
> *A sister's privilege, and a sister's name.*

Though off to a brilliant start, Sarah's career as an activist was short-lived. In 1838, when she was about 24, she married her sister Harriet's brother-in-law Joseph Purvis, a wealthy man with whom she had little in common. Joseph certainly did not share Sarah's passion for antislavery causes. The couple moved up the Delaware River to Bensalem, away from her friends and family in Philadelphia, and too far for her to attend the Female Antislavery Society meetings. With her attention directed toward raising eight children and attending to the household, Sarah ceased writing poetry as well. In the remaining years of her life, she never returned to reform work.

Aside from the Weld-Grimké Papers, the Clements Library holds many other outstanding antislavery collections, such as the James Birney Papers. Birney was a Princeton-educated lawyer who closed his Alabama law practice in 1832 to devote himself to antislavery causes. In 1836 he established a newspaper in Cincinnati, Ohio, called *The Philanthropist*, the first of its kind in the Midwest. The following year he became corresponding secretary for the American Antislavery Society, where he campaigned for a more political approach to the cause, differing on this issue with his friend Theodore Weld and William Lloyd Garrison. In 1840, the year before Birney moved to Michigan, he founded the Liberty Party, with the singular platform of advocating the abolition of slavery, and in

1840 and 1844 he ran as its candidate for President. Of the approximately 1,700 items in the Birney collection, most are from 1834–44.

Other important Clements antislavery collections for the 1830s and 1840s are the Lydia Maria Child Papers, Maria Churchill Journals, Elizabeth Margaret Chandler Collection, and the Owen Lovejoy Papers. They all knew each other, or knew of each other, and all were associates in the widespread circle of Northern abolitionists. Since slavery and antislavery are collecting strengths of the Library, the Clements also owns many such collections from the eighteenth century to the Civil War, notably the Thomas Clarkson Papers and the Rochester Ladies' Antislavery Society Papers, which contain information about the Underground Railroad. The Library has over 300 printed titles on the subject and numerous prints, photographs, sheet music, and three-dimensional objects in the Graphics Division.

Though Sarah Forten's career as an antislavery advocate was short, she helped to give to the predominately white movement the critically important perspective of black women. Sarah's poetry and her April 15, 1837, letter stand as passionate expressions of early-nineteenth-century anti-discrimination and a reminder to whites sympathetic to the abolitionist cause that people are not truly free until they are accepted as social equals. Intended for a relatively narrow 1837 white audience, her writings have retained their significance for twenty-first-century America.

HMS Victory, *Admiral Horatio Lord Nelson's flagship at the Battle of Trafalgar. Scale model by Russell C. Aller. The Clements Library holds a small but important collection of Nelson's papers.*

TOUSSAINT L'OUVERTURE
HAITI'S GEORGE WASHINGTON

— Diana Sykes

In 1801 Napoleon Bonaparte sent General Charles Leclerc to the French colony of Saint-Domingue to quell a decade-long slave revolt there. Napoleon's goal was not only to reassert French control; he also wanted to reestablish slavery on the island. Then, to protect and nourish Saint-Domingue and France's other sugar colonies, he planned to build a military base and agricultural center in the vast Louisiana Territory to fortify France's presence in the Americas.

Toussaint L'Ouverture, former-slave-turned-commander-in-chief of Saint-Domingue, and his troops had fought long and hard for the abolition of slavery on the island. They responded vigorously to the new French incursion and in 1804 decisively defeated the invaders. The victors declared their independence and renamed their republic "Haiti" ("land of mountains"), the name given to the island by its original inhabitants. The repercussions of the successful slave revolt in Haiti extended far beyond the island's shores. After losing his most prosperous colony in the Caribbean, a frustrated Napoleon abandoned his ambitions to reestablish a great French presence in the Americas. Needing money to wage war with England, he offered to sell the Louisiana Territory to the United States, doubling the area owned by the young nation. Despite those results, few people in the United States today are familiar with the Haitian revolution and its close connection with American history or with Toussaint L'Ouverture, leader of the only successful slave revolt in the Americas.

European exploitation fertilized the ground in which the seeds of the Haitian revolution grew. In 1492 Christopher Columbus landed on the coast of present-day Haiti. He was so impressed by the island's topography and natural resources that he named it "Hispaniola," or "Little Spain." Motivated by the gold jewelry worn by the indigenous Taino people, the Spanish colonists established gold mines on the island and forced the native population to work them. The labor was so grueling and the diseases brought by the Europeans so fatal for the Taino people that their population went from more than one million to fewer than 300 in just four decades. Bartolomé de las Casas, a Dominican priest who went to Hispaniola as a colonist, recognized that if the Taino continued to work in the mines they would be wiped out completely. He and others suggested that African slaves might be better suited for the grueling labor of the mines, leading to the first importation of African slaves to the New World in 1501. Towards the end of his life, las Casas realized that the enslavement of Africans was just as detestable as the enslavement of the Tainos, and he became a champion of abolition. Unfortunately, it was too late; by then the African slave trade in the Americas was running strong.

TOUSSAINT L'OUVERTURE.

Eventually the Spaniards left the west coast of Hispaniola, deciding to search for gold elsewhere in the New World. French privateers settled on the coast, and under the Treaty of Ryswick in 1697 the western third of Hispaniola became a French possession. Called Saint-Domingue by the French, the colony developed a sugar and coffee plantation economy that greatly increased the number of African slaves brought to the island; as many as thirty thousand were imported to the colony every year.

François-Dominique Toussaint was born into slavery in approximately 1743 on the estate of Bréda near Cape François in Saint-Domingue. His father was Gaou-Guinou, chief of the Arrada tribe of Western Africa who was captured during a tribal battle and sent to the New World as a slave. Because Gaou-Guinou's heightened status was evident among his peers, the overseer of the Bréda estate treated his family favorably in comparison with the other slaves. Toussaint spent his early life working as a shepherd on the Bréda estate. He was greatly influenced by his godfather Pierre Baptiste, who passed on his love of knowledge and devout belief in Christianity to Toussaint. During his free time (which was ample compared with slaves working in the fields), Toussaint read the works of Abbé Guillaume Raynal. The following section of Raynal's *Philosophical and Political History of the Settlements and Trade of the Europeans in the East and West Indies* had a significant impact on Toussaint's perspective:

> *Already have two colonies of fugitive negroes been established,*
> *to whom treaties and power give a perfect security. . . . These*
> *enterprises are so many indications of the impending storm, and*
> *the negroes only want a chief, sufficiently courageous. . . . Where*
> *is this great man to be found, whom nature, perhaps, owes to the*
> *honour of the human species? Where is this new Spartacus?*

An able equestrian, as a young man Toussaint earned the reputation as a horse doctor and rose to coachman for the Bréda plantation. He learned to conduct himself in white society while remaining a respected and influential figure among his fellow slaves, developing skills that proved useful later in life. He was a staunch Roman Catholic and a member of the Masonic Lodge of Saint-Domingue. At 33, the year his master freed him, Toussaint married his godfather's daughter Suzanne. They had several children and lived quietly on the Bréda estate.

While Toussaint was starting family life, tensions were building between the different social castes on Saint-Domingue. The "large" whites—plantation owners and other wealthy colonists—were few but powerful. The "small" whites were less affluent and included the managers and stewards of the estates. People of mixed racial heritage and free blacks (often grouped together under the general term "free people of color") formed a segment of society almost as large as the white population. Many were free landowners and some became as wealthy as the white planters. Yet the free people of color—feared by the large whites and despised by the small—had no political power. No individual suspected to have any non-white blood in his ancestry could vote, hold political office or participate in any aspect of white public life. Slaves comprised the lowest class in the colony, but the economy of Saint-Domingue, which produced 40% of the world's sugar, rested on their backs. With slaves outnumbering the rest of the population by approximately eight to one, the possibility of a slave uprising was a constant worry to the white residents. In 1751 voodoo priest François Mackandal led a revolt that lasted until his execution in 1758 and left a legacy of armed bands of "maroons," or runaway slaves, living in the hills and conducting raids on plantations for decades afterwards.

When the French Revolution, with its rallying cry of *"Liberté, Egalité et Fraternité,"* broke out in 1789, the shaky social structure and the differing hopes and expectations that the Revolution instilled in Saint-Domingue's heterogeneous population led to great unrest. Wealthy colonists wanted greater independence from the mother country, or at least to be represented more fully in the French democratic government, and supported the Revolution. Small whites and free people of color hoped for

Two Bréda family plantations are recorded on René Phelipeau's Plan de la plaine du Cap François en l'Isle St. Domingue *(Paris, 1786). The main property, located south of the town of Cap François (today Cap Haitien), is most likely that with the large complex of buildings. Many are probably slave quarters.*

The harbor of Cap François is crammed with shipping in this view of the city from Nicolas Ponce, Recueil de vues des lieux principaux de la colonie françoise de Saint-Domingue, gravées par les soins de M. Ponce *(Paris, 1791).*

increased influence and rights, often at each other's expense. The slave population was initially apathetic toward events in distant France, but the Revolution lit a fuse in the minds of some black leaders. Allegiances changed as often as ships brought news from Europe. When authorities in France began to suggest that the Declaration of the Rights of Man should extend to free people of color, many whites in Saint-Domingue took up the cause of the counter-revolution. Gradually the free people of color, realizing that they could energize a formidable set of allies against the wealthy whites, urged the island's slaves to rebel.

The worst fears of the white colonists of Saint-Domingue were realized in the early 1790s. Vincent Oge, a wealthy free man of color, led a short-lived rebellion in 1790–91, when the colonial governor refused to extend full civil equality to non-whites. In August 1791, Saint-Domingue's slaves rose at the instigation of Dutty Boukman, a maroon and a voodoo high priest. Within 10 days the rebels took control of the Northern Province, and within weeks their numbers swelled to 100,000. By early 1792 slaves controlled a third of Saint-Domingue, at the cost of 4,000 white deaths and the destruction of several hundred sugar, coffee and indigo plantations. In March 1792 the French Legislative Assembly granted civil and political rights to free men of color in the colonies, but the same body also sent 6,000 soldiers to Saint-Domingue to crush the rebellion.

Toussaint did not participate in the slave revolt and white massacre of 1791. During the destruction of the early stages of the revolt he helped his master's family escape from the island.

After securing his own family's protection by sending them to the Spanish-held eastern portion of Hispaniola, Toussaint and some other slaves from the Bréda estate joined the insurrection. Toussaint became secretary to Georges Biassou, who along with Jean François Papillon and Jeannot Billet led the revolutionaries. Toussaint moved rapidly up the ranks to command a large section of the army. Maintaining his focus on freedom for Haiti's slaves but shifting political allegiance several times, he used guerrilla tactics effectively and turned his troops into a disciplined and deadly force that successfully battled French colonists, the Spanish Empire, British troops, and Haiti's free people of color. In 1793 Toussaint adopted the surname "L'Ouverture" because he regarded himself as "the opening" to independence for his people.

Toussaint's military success accelerated in the second half of the 1790s. By the end of 1795 the Spanish had withdrawn from fighting on the island, and the British fought only from the coastal towns. Aided by competent lieutenants Jean-Jacques Dessalines and Henri Christophe, Toussaint gained control of the northern and western portions of Saint-Domingue. In 1797 he became commander-in-chief of the French republican army on the island. When the British failed in a last-ditch attempt to dislodge Toussaint by attacking from the south, General Thomas Maitland signed a secret treaty with him and withdrew all British troops from the colony in October 1798. Toussaint defeated the army of André Rigaud, his principal remaining rival for control of Haiti, in October 1799, crushing all remaining internal resistance to his rule by allowing Dessalines to kill some 40,000 men, women and children of color. Toussaint's forces drove the remaining Spanish forces from Santo Domingo in January 1801, and he proclaimed the abolition of slavery on Saint-Domingue. Seven months later he approved a new constitution naming him governor for life.

Toussaint's constitution was a curious mix of revolutionary and reactionary provisions. Although his drafting committee included a number of protections against the reinstitution of slavery, the document also made Catholicism the state religion and granted Toussaint near-absolute powers. Concerned that Napoleon Bonaparte might try to reassert French control of the island, Toussaint worked to present himself as a loyal Frenchman. Napoleon denied any intention of overthrowing Toussaint or reinstituting slavery, but in January 1802 a French army under Charles Leclerc landed on Saint-Domingue. By May they forced Toussaint to sign a treaty at Cap-Haitien, and he retired to his farm at Ennery. Three weeks later French troops seized Toussaint and his family and deported them to France under charges of plotting an insurrection. Napoleon imprisoned Toussaint at Fort-de-Joux in Doubs, and he died there of pneumonia in April 1803. His body went to an unmarked grave in a cavern under the prison chapel.

Toussaint L'Ouverture created a significant legacy in his short military and political career. He played a key role in the first successful uprising by a slave population in the Americas. He defeated armies of Spain, Great Britain and France in making Haiti the second independent republic in the New World. The creation of Haiti rocked the institution of slavery in the Caribbean and sent shock waves through the southern half of the United States. When General Leclerc deported him to France in 1802, Toussaint warned his captors, "In overthrowing me you have cut down in Saint Domingue on the trunk of the tree of liberty. It will spring up again from the roots, for they are deep and many." On January 1, 1804, Jean-Jacques Dessalines declared Haiti a free republic again. In the following decades, as freedom came to the enslaved millions of the West Indies and the southern United States, the flame of Toussaint's accomplishments burned bright. More than two centuries after his death, he remains an emblem of resistance for oppressed peoples worldwide.

For years after the Haitian Revolution every unidentified portrait of an African American male was purported to be Toussaint L'Ouverture. Published in Paris in 1838 and acquired at auction by the Clements Library in 2009, this lithograph by Nicholas Eustache Maurin is one of the most widely reproduced nineteenth-century images of him. First issued by François-Seraphin Delpech in 1832, it depicts Toussaint in a general's cocked hat with the red, white and blue French Revolutionary cockade. Although the exaggerated facial features may strike modern viewers as racially stereotyped, in his 1850 biography of Toussaint historian Joseph Saint-Remy describes the lithograph as based on a painting that Toussaint himself gave to the family of Philippe-Rose Roume de Saint-Laurent, one of the commissioners France sent to Saint-Domingue in the early 1790s. Regardless of its origins, the portrait presents Toussaint as a proud and powerful figure worthy of his fine military attire.

The Clements Library owns a variety of valuable primary source material on Toussaint L'Ouverture and the West Indies, in which he lived, fought and attempted to govern. In the Manuscripts Division, the Oliver Hazard Perry Papers include correspondence between Captain Christopher R. Perry and Toussaint, while the Tailyour Papers contain a wealth of original information on the slave trade in the islands. The Map Division holds numerous maps of the West Indies, notably Rene Phelipeau's *Plan de la plaine du Cap Francois en l'Isle St. Domingue* that lists the names of northern property and plantation owners on the eve of the slave uprising that destroyed their world. The Book Division includes numerous eighteenth-century titles about Hispaniola that detail conditions on the island prior to the slave insurrection, events during it, and the establishment of Haiti as a free nation, from a wide range of perspectives and interpretations. There are also several biographies of Toussaint himself in the collection. An 1802 study by Louis Dubroca, *La vie de Toussaint-Louverture, chef des noirs insurges de Saint-Domingue,* portrays him in 74 pages as a savage and hypocritical traitor to France. Half a century later, English author J. R. Beard devoted 335 pages to memorializing Toussaint as the sacrificial liberator of his island in *The Life of Toussaint L'Ouverture, the Negro Patriot of Hayti.* Similarly, when Thomas Prosper Gragnon-Lacoste published *Toussaint Louverture, général en chef de l'armée de Saint-Domingue, surnommé le premier des noirs* in 1877, he prefaced his book with, *"Va, mon livre; va, au nom de Toussaint-Louverture; va, au nom de cet homme qu'une convention fit esclave; mais que Dieu fit grand! Va attester au Monde que les plus nobles qualites de l'esprit et du Coeur se recontrent chez le Noir civilize, tandis qu'elles ne sauraient etre le partage du blanc vaniteux et intolerant!"*

Once the most prosperous sugar colony in the West Indies, after two centuries of independence the Republic of Haiti is the poorest nation in the Americas. The first independent country in Latin America, a republic that provided refuge and aid to Simon Bolivar during the 1810s as he began his

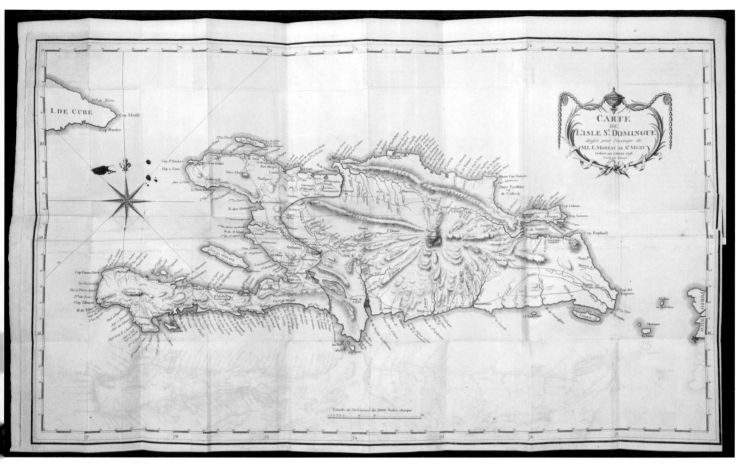

The island of Hispaniola or Saint-Domingue by J. Sonis (Philadelphia, 1796). The western end of the island was the French colony of Saint-Domingue (Haiti), while the eastern part was Spanish territory, today the Dominican Republic.

drive to free Spain's New World colonies, Haiti has struggled with political unrest and violence for much of its existence. Nineteen years of United States occupation between 1915 and 1934 strengthened Haiti's infrastructure but did little to provide stability or justice, and subsequent United States involvement in Haitian politics has produced uneven results at best. Modern authors and filmmakers have found much of interest in the career of Toussaint L'Ouverture, but the prosperity and strength he envisioned for his homeland have proved elusive. Yet, the collections of the Clements Library contain much information on colonial Hispaniola and the first century of Haiti's independence, complementing and setting the stage for resources in other University of Michigan libraries that tell modern Haiti's story. Researchers who come to the Clements to delve into the life and times of Toussaint L'Ouverture, *"le premier des noirs,"* will find his story invaluable for understanding the sweep of American history from the era of the American Revolution to the present.

Easterly's daguerreotype views of Niagara Falls, 1853.

MASTER OF THE DAGUERREOTYPE

— Clayton Lewis

How do we measure an artist's career? Commercial success, contemporary popularity or historical legacy? Some artists are successful in large part because they are attention getters– showmen along the lines of the flamboyant promoter Phineas T. Barnum. In their day, the personalities of Rubens, Whistler, Manet, and Warhol made their art famous as much as their art made their personalities famous. In the world of nineteenth-century photography, Mathew "Brady of Broadway" Brady was a model for publicizing his way to a successful career. A socially active, entertaining, and engaging personality can benefit the career of an artist, particularly a portrait artist. When portraiture made up a majority of the photographic business, as it did in the nineteenth century, even small-town photographers needed a bit of Barnum in them to succeed commercially. Building a legacy requires different criteria. The historical photographers who are best remembered today are the ones who made the news, photographed the famous and pioneered new technologies. Within the photographic collection of the William L. Clements Library are images by an American who did none of this, yet his work is of considerable importance and value.

There are only a few documents preserving the words and thoughts of American daguerrean Thomas Martin Easterly (1809–82), but they describe a personality that is introspective, dignified, smart, funny, romantic, and stubborn to a large degree—a person more private than public, essentially everything that Barnum was not. Evidence from two sources close to him, his brother-in-law and a traveling companion and fellow daguerrean, implies that Thomas Easterly was a charming but frustrating personality. Poor at business perhaps, but in the delicate daguerrean art he had few peers. He is known for insisting on the artistic superiority of the daguerreotype above all other photographic forms in the face of its irreversible decline in popularity.

Easterly had artistic vision, practiced advanced techniques, and brought a poetic sensibility to the daguerreotype process. At a time when there was plenty of clumsy painting on photographs, Easterly had a light touch, a delicate color sense, and was a master of the gilding of finished plates with gold chloride and tinting with powdered pigments. His previous career as an itinerant calligrapher and teacher of writing is apparent in the beautiful and distinctive captioning of his images. He consciously chose subjects of historical importance, and was a prolific producer. From his home state of Vermont, Easterly apparently traveled to New York to learn photography and by 1844 was taking daguerreotypes. Easterly appeared in New Orleans in the middle 1840s. He then traveled up the Mississippi and is found advertising his "exquisite colored" pictures in partnership with Frederick F. Webb in the Davenport, Iowa, *Gazette* of October 30, 1845. By 1847 Easterly was doing business in St. Louis, Missouri, under his own name.

Easterly understood that this new visual media presented a new point of view, with different capabilities and limitations from traditional artistic methods. He accentuated the medium's strengths to explore the artistic and documentary capability of the daguerreotype. These strengths included an unprecedented ability for portraiture; a responsiveness to the look of architecture and other man-made objects; and a stark, undiscriminating viewpoint that could transform the unsightly into the picturesque and the attractive into the exquisite. Above all, Easterly knew that, with the clarity and sharpness that only a fine daguerreotype could offer, the photographic image brought to the visual arts a new immediacy and a sense of time suspended.

Easterly had reason to be proud, but his pride guided him poorly in business. His advertising repeatedly stressed the beauty and quality of his photographic work while making no mention of cost at a time when most daguerreans believed that quality was irrelevant because the public didn't recognize it, and price wars were rampant throughout the trade. Although Easterly was considered a premier photographer from 1848 to 1858, he refused to produce the *carte de visite* photographs and tintypes that were phenomenally popular during the Civil War years. Modernism was in vogue then, and by 1865 his beloved leather-and-glass-cased daguerreotype plates came to be seen as antiquarian against the sleek (and cheap) new card-mounted photographs preferred by the trend-seeking public. This principled stand on artistic merit forced Easterly into selling farm implements on the side to get by. An ongoing rivalry with St. Louis photographer John Fitzgibbon was costly. Not only was Fitzgibbon the best-known St. Louis photographer and leader of the St. Louis Daguerrean Association, he was also a regular and influential contributor to several national photographic journals that were widely read by Easterly's peers. As historian Dolores Kilgo points out, these journals are often used to "reconstruct the pantheon of the daguerrean era," thus leaving the talented Easterly out. If this wasn't enough to marginalize Easterly in his own time and for posterity, a fire in his St. Louis gallery in 1865 destroyed his equipment and an unknown quantity of images, nearly ending his career. It was typical for professional daguerreans to save prime examples of their own work to display as promotional pieces. It is quite possible that the best of this master's work was consumed in the fire.

Thomas Easterly enjoyed the companionship of clever, educated people, and he found a sympathetic soul in his brother-in-law, Lieutenant Colonel Norton Strange Townshend. Townshend valued Easterly's artistic sensibilities; Easterly recognized Townshend's cultured refinement. Easterly would certainly have been impressed that Townshend had met the inventor Louis Daguerre in France in 1840. Townshend married Easterly's wife's sister Margaret Bailey in 1854, four years after Easterly's marriage to Anna Miriam Bailey. Norton Townshend took an active interest in the lives of his attractive sister-in-law and her artistic husband. Anna, known as Miriam in the family, was also smart and well read (Miriam shared Townshend's books and his library card). Orphaned with her three sisters and brother at a young age, Miriam was conditioned to be self-reliant and emotionally resilient. As her handsome husband's daguerrean business dwindled, her seamstress skills likely became the household's main source of income. Loans from Townshend kept Easterly's gallery open enough to eventually repay the debt.

This family connection brought the work of Thomas Easterly to the Clements Library. Through a generous donation by Alice Dodge Wallace, the papers of her great-grandfather, Norton Strange Townshend, are now at the Clements. The Townshend papers are a diverse and important collection. The scholarly Townshend, one of 16 medical inspectors for the Union Army, was learned and sophisticated. His multi-faceted career included studies in the hospitals of Paris, Edinburgh and Dublin. An active participant in anti-slavery societies, he served in the Ohio Senate and United States Congress.

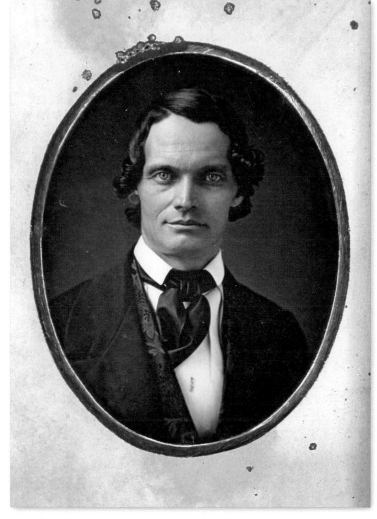

A self-portrait photograph of Thomas Easterly. Sixth-plate daguerreotype, ca. 1850.

The Townshend papers are valuable on many levels, including information on military, political, medical, educational, and social history. Like many of the Clements' manuscript collections, the Norton Strange Townshend Papers contain information in additional genre forms, including family photographs. The story told through the images in the Townshend Papers is vividly alive and full of timeless human emotion. There are many superb examples of early American portrait photography in various formats (Easterly didn't take all the family photos), including a masterly daguerreotype portrait of Dr. Townshend in uniform, taken by Easterly during the Civil War, plus four half-plate daguerreotypes in their original frame taken by Easterly at Niagara Falls in 1853. This material has been greatly enhanced by the later addition of 40 additional Townshend/Bailey/Easterly/Cahill family portraits, most by Easterly, purchased from a private collection with funds provided by the Avenir Foundation.

The same package of romantic sensitivities and stubbornness that stifled his commercial career also made Easterly a remarkable and intriguing artist. When circumstances placed him in the vicinity of the grand American spectacle of Niagara, one could only expect spectacular results. Of all American scenes, Niagara Falls has been the most frequently depicted in the visual arts. Much has been written about how the vast scale described by paintings, prints and drawings of the falls symbolizes the vast scale of the American wilderness. The awesome scene has long been promoted as evidence of God's hand in the determination of American greatness and destiny. Countless works of art assert the sublimity of Niagara by emphasizing and exaggerating the features of this natural wonder. The daguerreotype process swept across the Atlantic from France, arriving in the eastern cities of the United States in the fall of 1839 and quickly making its way to America's most popular picture-making spot. The first photographs of Niagara are likely those taken in April of 1840 by Hugh Lee Pattinson, a British geologist and chemist. The image of Niagara still represented America in allegorical form, but the daguerrean artists achieved something different from the painters.

Playing to the strength of the medium's immediacy and detail, nineteenth-century photographers of Niagara tended to emphasize the personal over the sublime. This was also where the money was. The subject for many was not the falls, but the tourist, at the falls. Indisputable visual proof, in the form of a photograph, documented that visitors really were there at the continent's most sublime spot. The quantity of photos taken at Niagara in the middle of the nineteenth century was enormous. The advent of the camera made the iconic vista of Niagara, symbol of America's eminence and assets, the backdrop for millions of personal souvenir photos of tourists. "There is no actual harm in making Niagara a background whereon to display one's marvelous insignificance in a good strong light, but it requires a sort of superhuman self-complacency to enable one to do it," Mark Twain commented in *A Day at Niagara.*

On the American side at Prospect Point, photographer Platt Babbitt secured the rights to be the exclusive photographer at that popular location. From 1853 to 1856 Babbitt made certain that his pavilion was positioned to appear in any photo taken in the vicinity. All other photographers in the area had to work around both his pavilion and Babbitt himself, who aggressively obstructed their attempts by waving large umbrellas in front of their cameras. At stake was Babbitt's steady income from pictures of unsuspecting tourists who had wandered in front of his pavilion to admire the falls and found themselves included in one of Babbitt's large, expensive, irresistible daguerreotypes.

About the time that Babbitt was striving to be the exclusive photographer of Niagara, two traveling daguerreans explored the region together. For three weeks in 1853 Englishman John Werge and his friend Thomas Martin Easterly tramped along the precipice, climbed up and down the cliffs, cleared the underbrush, felled trees, and often took great personal risks, all to obtain a better view of the falls for their cameras. Tourist portraits were not their objective.

There are no known caches of Easterly correspondence or journals to reveal his experiences first-hand, but fortunately, his companion Werge was a teller of tall tales. In his 1890 publication, *The Evolution of Photography,* Werge reminisces about their 1853 explorations of Niagara. He tells of how he and Easterly took daguerreotypes from both sides of the falls, the Whirlpool, the Cave of the Winds, the Maid of the Mist, Brock's Monument, Bloody Run, and other neighboring sites. Werge gives us a peek into the personality of Easterly, which displays both bravery and humor: "I question very much if it ever occurred to the mind of anyone, while looking at those pictures, what an amount of labour, expense, and danger had to be endured and encountered to obtain them—the many hairbreadth

Dr. Norton Strange Townshend. Quarter-plate daguerreotype by Thomas Easterly, ca. 1865.

'scapes by flood and field, of a very positive character, which had to be risked before some of the negatives could be boxed. How we actually hung over the precipice, holding on to each other's hands, to lop off a branch still in sight where it was not wanted. I hugged a sapling of silver birch, growing on the brink of the precipice, with my left arm, while friend Easterly, holding my right hand with one of the Masonic grips—I won't say which—hung over the precipice, and stretching out as far as he could reach, lopped off the offending branch. Yet in this perilous position my lively companion must crack his joke by punning upon my name … he 'guessed he was below the *werge* of the precipice.'" Werge describes repeated risks to their safety. One or the other, or maybe both men carefully crawled out to the end of a plank weighted down with rocks at one end and precariously cantilevered over the brink of the falls at the other, while pushing a camera out in front. They then reached out to remove and replace the lens cap to complete the carefully timed exposure without launching the camera or themselves into the gorge. Or so the story goes.

Easterly studied and practiced the latest modifications and advancements of the daguerrean technique, allowing him to capture beautiful sunlight and shadows on the clouds above—a rare accomplishment in the early days of photographic arts. His process often included a quick, almost

Anna Miriam Bailey Easterly, photographed with her sewing basket, ca. 1860. Sixth-plate daguerreotype by Thomas Easterly.

"instantaneous" exposure that froze the leaves on the trees and figures seemingly caught in movement. Easterly could have avoided the architecture of commerce and industry as it encroached on picturesque Niagara, but instead he featured it in several views.

The obstreperous Mr. Babbitt was gracious to these visiting daguerreans by allowing Werge and Easterly access to both the view from Prospect Point and his darkroom. As Werge recalled, "We availed ourselves of Mr. Babbitt's kindness and hospitality to develop our plates in his darkroom, and afterwards developed ourselves, sociably and agreeably, refreshing the inner man, and narrating our day's adventures." Perhaps Babbitt correctly guessed that Werge and Easterly were not a commercial threat. All in all, they had a grand time photographing Niagara.

Easterly eventually returned to St. Louis, where he was, for the time, well established. Notable in this phase of his career are the spectacular portraits he took of the Native American Sauk and Fox leaders who visited his gallery. These stand among the earliest and most important western Native American photographs ever taken. Many have survived and are now at the Missouri Historical Society in St. Louis and the Newberry Library in Chicago.

By the middle 1860s professional and amateur photographers had partly or completely abandoned the daguerreotype for cheaper, easier and more popular formats. Easterly ignored these technical "advances" and stuck to the daguerreotype process that he had so completely mastered. His efforts to promote the superior qualities of the daguerreotype failed to offset his steadily diminishing business. Among the numerous photographers at the 1866 St. Louis Fair, Easterly was the only one exhibiting daguerreotypes. The health and behavior issues that plagued Easterly late in his life may have been caused by excessive mercury exposure from daguerreotype processing. In the late 1870s the last daguerrean in St. Louis, perhaps in the nation, closed his business. Thomas Martin Easterly died in 1882 in his home state of Vermont. He implored the public to "save your old daguerreotypes, for you will never see their like again."

How is it that Thomas Martin Easterly made it into the photographic pantheon in spite of circumstances that should have kept him obscure? The large numbers of surviving plates point to his prolific output. Much credit should go to Dolores Kilgo's 1994 book *Likeness and Landscape* and the corresponding exhibit at the Missouri Historical Society. Credit goes as well to those few individuals who saved and protected these treasures during a time when many "old photographs" were tossed out. More recently, the growing interest in American photographic history has fueled a search for overlooked masters. Above all, it is the indisputable quality of Easterly's images that finally secured his reputation.

Very early American photographic images continue to be valued as interest in the photographic iconography of America rises. As the Clements builds its reputation as a resource for visual studies, these beautiful images by Easterly will undoubtedly maintain their keystone position, even within a large collection of excellent examples from the most recognizable names in early American landscape and portrait photography like William H. Jackson, Carlton Watkins, Mathew Brady, Albert Southworth, and Josiah Hawes. For aesthetic distinction and historical interest alike, the "old daguerreotypes" of Thomas Martin Easterly have timeless qualities so remarkable that scholars and collectors "will never see their like again."

A GUIDEBOOK FOR LATTER-DAY SAINTS

— *Terese M. Austin*

Westward Ho! No image carries as much American cultural meaning (or baggage) as that of Conestoga wagons, canvas flapping and frying pans rattling, heading West over the Great Plains. Families were on the move, finding new freedom, pursuing their faith, seeking the treasure—literal and figurative—at the end of the trail. But the iconic image of the wagon train, so familiar from American mythmaking, is also loaded with the larger political constructs of manifest destiny and the drive of a government and people to complete their new nation by settling it and spreading American sovereignty and values from coast to coast.

The course of westward expansion had as much to do with the period's geopolitics as it did with personal destiny seeking. Political leaders actively sought to encourage or block emigration and looked to move tokens on a chessboard of competition among the nineteenth century's Great Powers. At stake: who would control the Northwest of the vast continent. Emigrants (as they were called) were also pawns and players in the moneymaking schemes fueling the expansion of the day. Unscrupulous salesmen and empire-builders of the West sold fabricated maps, fantastical descriptions of the route and overblown expectations of the journey's end, often in order to fatten their wallets. They took advantage of the increased demand for route guidance of any kind by steering pioneers to fall in with land schemes at specific destinations. The Donner-Reed Party is the most famous of those persuaded to try a risky western route, described in less-than-honest terms and with fatal results.

We live in an era of movements aided by road maps, guidebooks and GPS navigation, and even re-locations across the continent are comfortably made in our mini- and moving vans with full knowledge of what to expect along the way. The concept of packing up one's entire family (for the vast majority of the early pioneers were family groups) and household possessions into a 4' x 12' box and setting out for a journey of thousands of miles without a clear notion of which path to take or what lay at the end of it resists comprehension. This was the reality that faced emigrants to the western frontier through the 1840s, until the thousands of gold rushers made the path impossible to miss, and the many first-person accounts defined the nature of the land at the end of the trip, as well as what to expect along the way.

Just as the early, fabricated maps used to "sell" the West were devoid of detail, so the broad strokes of the imagined panorama of wagon trains heading across the prairies obscure the particulars

THE
LATTER-DAY SAINTS'
EMIGRANTS' GUIDE:

BEING A

TABLE OF DISTANCES,

SHOWING ALL THE

SPRINGS, CREEKS, RIVERS, HILLS, MOUNTAINS,

CAMPING PLACES, AND ALL OTHER NOTABLE PLACES,

FROM COUNCIL BLUFFS,

TO THE

VALLEY OF THE GREAT SALT LAKE.

ALSO, THE

LATITUDES, LONGITUDES AND ALTITUDES

OF THE PROMINENT POINTS ON THE ROUTE.

TOGETHER WITH REMARKS ON THE NATURE OF THE LAND,
TIMBER, GRASS, &c.

THE WHOLE ROUTE HAVING BEEN CAREFULLY MEASURED BY A ROADOME-
TER, AND THE DISTANCE FROM POINT TO POINT, IN
ENGLISH MILES, ACCURATELY SHOWN.

BY W. CLAYTON.

ST. LOUIS:
MO. REPUBLICAN STEAM POWER PRESS—CHAMBERS & KNAPP.
1848.

and topography of the larger forces that shaped the journey and the textures of the day-to-day experience of this unique epoch in American history. Behind the myth and imagery of westward expansion is a deeper and more intricate picture, illuminated by the rich descriptions provided by the materials of the William L. Clements Library. Only in close reading of the actual accounts of those making the journey and contemporary contextual writings is the curtain on this epic drama pulled aside to reveal a more complex and riveting tale. One such record at the Clements Library is the rare first edition of William Clayton's *The Latter-Day Saints' Emigrants' Guide: Being a Table of Distances, Showing All the Springs, Creeks, Rivers, Hills, Mountains, Camping Places, and all Other Notable Places, from Council Bluffs, to the Valley of the Great Salt Lake* (St. Louis, 1848).

When Clayton wrote his guidebook in the late 1840s, most western American pioneers were traveling to Oregon and California, lands that were largely unexplored and unsettled. Reliable reports were few and the nineteenth-century version of spin control complicated the general scarcity of facts. During the early 1840s ownership of the Oregon Territory was very much in question. Great Britain and the United States were vying for control, and for a time it looked as if war might decide the issue. On both sides of the Atlantic, there were public figures confusing the question of emigration with exaggerations and inaccuracies. One American faction encouraged settlement of the territory as a way of committing the government to the defense of the entire region and solidifying resistance to British attempts at annexation. These proponents of settlement discounted the dangers of the trip, announcing with certainty that nothing that could be called a mountain stood in the way of travelers. A Congressman promoting the occupation and settlement of Oregon declared that the route to the mouth of the Columbia was easy, safe and expeditious. Those who did admit the existence of a western mountain range tended to compare its height to that of the Alleghenies.

Others, opposed to emigration, exaggerated the difficulties of an overland route. Horace Greeley, later famous for "Go West, young man," wrote in the 1840s that the only practice more ill-advised than attempting to migrate to the West Coast was suicide. The reasons for the anti-migration positions were varied—unwillingness to go to war with Great Britain, fear that the "natural" size of a republic would be exceeded and concerns over the possible extension of slavery. Opponents of westward expansion described the path to the coast as filled with savage Indians and the climate as that of a vast desert: arid and waterless in the summer, beset with snowy tempests in winter, sure to lead to death by attack, starvation or drowning—with some uncertainty as to where the doomed souls would drown in the desert. And at the end would be a land filled with sand and jagged rock, hardly worth the journey. The British abetted these reports with vigor, insisting that because it was impossible for Americans to travel overland and settle the Oregon territory, it should be left to Great Britain, which had an established supply route through Canada. Thus a family pondering relocation to the far West had to sort out a range of fanciful, unreliable and biased information from the outset.

A welcome antidote to these variable reports exists in several government-sponsored surveys, three important samples of which the Clements holds in original editions. The first in chronology and stature is that of Lewis and Clark, *History of the Expedition Under the Command of Captains Lewis and*

EMIGRANTS' GUIDE.

PROMINENT POINTS AND REMARKS.	DIST. miles.	FROM W QRS. miles.	FROM C of G S L miles.
Winter Quarters, Lat. 41° 18′ 53″ -			1031
The road good, but very crooked, following the ridges, and passing over a continual succession of hills and hollows.			
Pappea, ten feet wide, high banks. -	18	18	1013
Some timber on the creek, but it is difficult to water teams. After this, the road is crooked and uneven to the Elk Horn.			
Elk Horn, nine rods wide, three feet deep.	9	27	1004
Current rather swift, and not very pleasant to ferry. Plenty of timber on its banks. (See Note 1.)			
Creek, ten feet wide, steep banks. -	¾	27¾	1003¼
This creek has a good bridge over it, but little timber on the banks. There is a high post, erected near the bridge, for a guide to it.			
Platte river and Liberty Pole. - -	11¼	39	992
Plenty of timber, but you will probably have to go to the river for water—distance about a quarter of a mile. The nearest and best road to water is round the east point of the timber.			
Small Lake (narrow) south side the road.	3½	42½	988½
No timber on the Lake.			
Circular Lake, or pond, close to the road, (south.) - - - - -	¾	43¼	987¾
No timber. In the neighborhood of this, the road runs alongside a number of small lakes, or ponds, for two miles; but there is little timber near them.			
R. R. and T., road joins the river, Lat. 41° 27′ 5″ - - - - - -	9	52¼	978¾
This is a point where a branch of the river runs round an island, on which is plenty of timber. Not much water in the channel, but plenty for camping purposes.			
Indian Grave, north side the road. -	7½	59¾	971¼
This is a large pile of earth, about eighty yards north of the road.			
R. R. and T., road joins the river. -	½	60¼	970¾
Plenty of timber and water, without leaving the road.			
Shell creek, 12 feet wide, three feet deep.	2	62¼	968¾
This creek is bridged, and a few rods lower is a place to ford. Plenty of timber on it. After this you will probably find no water for twelve miles, without turning considerably from the road.			
Small lake, south side of the road. -	5¾	68	963
Plenty of water in the Spring season, but none in Summer. It was entirely dry, October 18, 1847.			

William Clayton's detailed and measured directions described the entire route to the Mormon colony in Utah.

GREAT SALT LAKE CITY, UTAH, 1867. Page 347.

Salt Lake City in 1867 showing the dramatic location selected by the Mormons for their new home.
From Albert D. Richardson, Beyond the Mississippi *(Hartford, 1867).*

Clark to the Sources of the Missouri (Philadelphia and New York, 1814), whose descriptions of the majesty of the West inspired many emigrants. The second surveying excursion, undertaken by Major Stephen Long of the U. S. Topographical Engineers in 1820 and reported by Edwin James, the party botanist, in *Account of an Expedition from Pittsburgh to the Rocky Mountains* (London, 1823), added much to general knowledge, including an important map. This was the first account to use the term "Great American Desert" to describe the land from the Rocky Mountains to roughly 200 miles east (what is now the Great Plains) and label it unfit for cultivation and uninhabitable. The route Long's party took along the Platte River would pave the way for many settlers to follow, including the Mormons. The last, possibly the best, and certainly the most popular of the books about the West in the mid-1840s was John Charles Frémont's narrative of his 1843–44 trek to Oregon, the Great Basin and California, *Report of the Exploring Expedition to the Rocky Mountains* (Washington, 1845). It became a best seller when both the Senate and House printed 20,000 copies. These accounts were valuable, but they were not meant to be guidebooks, and they did not provide the emigrant with the step-by-step instructions most of them needed to reach Oregon or California safely.

The period of crucial demand for reliable guidebooks was really only a few years long. Once travel on the trails increased, starting with the Gold Rush of 1849 and continuing steadily afterward, even the most inept greenhorn would have been able to see the path of thousands of wagons. Indeed, the trail was often littered with discarded household goods and rotting buffalo carcasses, and the choking dust inspired some travelers to don goggles. However, the earlier travelers of the 1830s and

1840s, spurred in part by population growth and positive reports of land beyond the borders of the United States, found road maps scarce at best. Into the existing information vacuum came a new set of "authorities," men who had (or claimed to have) direct experience and concrete advice specifically for emigrants. Some of the guides published at this time were not much of an improvement over the posturing politicians and newspapers of preceding years. One of the most famous of these was Lansford Hastings' *The Emigrant's Guide to Oregon and California: Containing Scenes and Incidents of a Party of Oregon Emigrants, etc.* (1845). Hastings was an adventurer with an interest in luring emigrants to California because of his business interests there. In an attempt to promote the California as opposed to the Oregon route, his guidebook encouraged the use of a "shortcut" through the Wasatch Range—which Hastings had never seen. He did manage to lead some emigrants on horseback over this route after his guide was published, without serious mishap. The Donner-Reed party, which followed his advice with loaded wagons and exhausted livestock in 1846, were not so lucky—their desperate struggle to survive a winter in the Sierra Nevada mountains, and the resulting deaths of 39 of the 87 emigrants who started on the route of the "Hastings Cutoff," is a dramatic and much-chronicled tale.

Another book held by the Clements in an original edition, *The Emigrant's Guide to the Gold Mines* by Henry I. Simpson (New York, 1848), was an outright fraud. The author tried to gain credibility by claiming to be a "New York volunteer," a member of a well-known regiment which had detachments stationed in California when gold was discovered, but this has never been verified. In fact, it is uncertain whether there actually was a Henry Simpson. In addition to making outrageous claims about the availability of gold, he included a map with scant details of the overland trail, consisting largely of Mexico, with no Rocky Mountains in sight; almost the entire region from the Mississippi to the west coast is labeled a desert. He also described the route from San Jose to San Francisco as verdant and flower strewn—in late August—while placing San Jose in a delta. Prospective emigrants took hope, no doubt, from the note on the title page claiming, "This map may be fully depended upon for its corectness." In spite of its outrageous and dangerous misinformation, *The Emigrant's Guide* sold well for a time as the first book of its kind published after the discovery of gold in California.

It is in this context that William Clayton's *Latter-Day Saints' Emigrants' Guide*—with its terse but practical and reliable advice—shines. Clayton's pamphlet consists of a table of distances and brief descriptions of landmarks and stopping places along the route from Council Bluffs, Iowa, to the Salt Lake Valley—elegantly simple and eminently useful. On its own, it would be a standout in the literature of westward expansion, but it also embodies the practicality and dedication of the unusual and significant Mormon role in the history of western settlement.

Born in England in 1814, William Clayton was an early convert to Mormonism. By the time he traveled from England to join the American Mormons in 1840, they had moved to Nauvoo, Illinois, after being hounded out of Ohio and then Missouri by hostile neighbors. They arrived in Illinois with the tacit consent of the government to establish a settlement that could be administered under their own laws, with nominal interference by outside authorities. Over time, however, their new neighbors, in a passion of suspicion and fear of the Saints' increasing political and economic power and what they considered to be the tenets of a strange and alien sect, began to use the same tactics of intimidation and physical violence against them in Nauvoo. In June 1844, a mob killed Mormon founder Joseph Smith and his brother Hyrum at the jail in Carthage, Illinois. The governor of Illinois refused to provide any protection for the Mormons, and they faced the choice of leaving or enduring further violence. They agreed to evacuate Nauvoo in 1846, under terms calling for their departure "by the time the grass came up." Not trusting the Mormons to keep their word, mobs drove them out of Nauvoo in March of 1846. Determined to head west, out of the territory of the United States, the Mormons spent four months covering almost 300 miles from the Mississippi to the Missouri River. In the spring of 1847, they sent out an advance party to find a western refuge, and later that year the main body started west under the leadership of Brigham Young.

The Mormon migration to Utah was a disciplined and well-executed initiative. Their commitment to a common future and the strength of their religious bond set them apart from the other wagon trains of the era. Because they were moving as a community, not as bands of loosely allied families and individuals, and anticipated that they would be followed by thousands of other Mormons, they had incentive to organize for the long term. At several locations along the route, they set up semi-permanent settlements to plant crops, tend herds of horses and cattle for emigrant use, and to offer rest and re-supply to the Mormons who would follow in the decades to come. By the end of the 1860s, when railroads supplanted the wagon trail as the chief mode of westward travel, some 70,000 emigrants had utilized the Mormon trail.

The character of the Mormon groups traveling together, at least when the authoritarian Brigham Young was present, was hierarchical and semi-military, with a clear chain of command. Young instituted a set of rules that made the logistics of traveling, hunting and camping predictable and efficient: reveille at 5:00 a.m.; moving out at 7:00; wagons in close order; no man to travel more than twenty rods from camp without permission, and so on throughout a well-regimented day. This minimized the squabbling and dissension that made so many of the other processions a misery of petty animosities and occasionally real conflict and violence. William Clayton, who had served as secretary for Joseph Smith until his assassination, was appointed clerk of the first Mormon emigration train. It was on this journey that Clayton kept his journal and recorded the information that would become *The Latter-Day Saints' Emigrants' Guide.*

Reportedly of a somewhat querulous and imposed-upon nature, Clayton rebelled against the inaccuracy of the usual method of dead reckoning to estimate distances along the trail. There was often a dispute at the end of the day as to how many miles had been covered, and one imagines Clayton devising a means to win an argument. Consulting with the ingenious Orson Pratt and drawing on the carpentering skills of Appleton Harmon (neither of whom is acknowledged in the guide), Clayton determined a method of precisely measuring distances using the revolutions of a wagon wheel attached to a set of wooden cogwheels, what he called a "roadometer." With his measurements, Clayton published one of the most reliable guidebooks of the decade, additionally so because he re-measured almost the whole trail on his return to winter quarters the following year. Emigrants recognized the value of Clayton's pamphlet, and there are reports of it selling for five times its retail price to travelers about to navigate the new landscape.

William Clayton wrote his guidebook not to make a profit but to make the way easier for new waves of Mormon migration. To reach the West, the Saints followed the north bank of the Platte River. The wide river was a natural highway, used by Native Americans for generations, and by the scattered fur traders and exploring parties that preceded the mass westward movement. But non-Mormon

"View of the Chasm through which the Platte flows," drawn during Stephen Long's exploring expedition. Mountains loom in the distance. From Edwin James, Account of an Expedition from Pittsburgh to the Rocky Mountains, Performed in the Years 1819 and '20 *(London, 1823).*

emigrant trains largely avoided the north bank during the years of the heaviest Saints traffic. Other travelers were leery of meeting the Mormons on the trail (perhaps because the Saints had grievances over their treatment in Ohio, Illinois and Missouri), and the Mormons were eager to isolate themselves from the armed groups they feared were pursuing them. Trail diaries and letters produce an amusing depiction of each group imagining the other, armed and waiting for a chance to attack. The Mormons worked hard to improve the trail for other Saints, and later emigrants benefited. The Mormons cleared rocks and trees, leveled the steepest pitches, and, for a fee, set up blacksmithing and ferrying services for the Gentiles. Also, in addition to recording distances and describing features of the trail in his guidebook, Clayton erected signposts along the route indicating the best camping and watering sites.

Once the Mormons were established in the Salt Lake Valley, their colony served as a welcome outpost of civilization for weary emigrants on their way to Oregon and California. Although they sought isolation, the Saints found themselves in the path of a crush of gold-rushers beginning in 1849. They quickly adapted, taking the opportunity to relieve the travelers of household goods, which they had overloaded, and selling them livestock and food supplies to replace their worn-out animals and dwindling rations. In spite of claims that Mormons in Salt Lake City overcharged for the goods they sold the desperate emigrants, they charged less than other trading posts along the route. They also made money by offering to publish an emigrant's name and projected travel itinerary in the local paper, and send it to interested parties back east, or to carve emigrants' names on Independence Rock, a landmark covered with names of passersby. In addition to benefiting the travelers, the increased commerce was serendipitous for the Mormons. The difficulty of growing crops in the arid landscape surrounding the Great Salt Lake and the continual influx of often destitute converts were straining their resources, and the influx of cash was welcome.

Another service they performed for those emigrants in need of it was the dispensation of justice. The Mormon judicial system earned a reputation for its impartiality in settling disputes arising on the trail—usually the division of property as a result of the breakup of traveling companies—and the occasional theft. Mormon deputies once traveled 200 miles to recover goods stolen from a small emigrant company. Mormon relations with Gentile emigrants were far from uniformly cordial in the Utah Territory, however. In September 1857, a contingent of Mormon militia and Paiute Indians attacked and murdered 120 Arkansas men, women and children of the Fancher-Baker emigrant wagon train at Mountain Meadows. The United States government convicted and executed one participant in the massacre, but not until 1875, and the event's impact on American perceptions of the Saints remained strong throughout the nineteenth century.

The Mormon settlement around the Great Salt Lake did have an ameliorating effect on emigrant and settler relations with the Indians. To early parties, the Native Americans were only nuisances, who occasionally harassed or stole from travelers. Later, as it became obvious that the emigrants were coming to stay and as they slaughtered buffalo indiscriminately, the Indians began to retaliate. However, the area the Mormons chose to settle was sparsely inhabited by Native Americans. The Saints also had a religious incentive to treat the Indians generously, since they believed that the Indians were Lamanites, a tribe that had been converted to Mormonism ages ago but had since fallen away from the faith. With the policy that it was cheaper to feed them than to fight them, Brigham Young's followers fostered a more harmonious environment for coexistance than that of the increasingly hostile gauntlet of the Platte corridor.

Drawn into the fabric of these pioneers' lives through quiet moments with these treasures at the Clements, and almost in spite of all the politics and discord these sources reveal, one appreciates their illumination of who we are as Americans. Our national story is one of groups like the Mormons, who made a significant contribution to the experience of westward migration and to the character of the American Southwest. William Clayton's guidebook is one example of the practicality and determination of a group of pioneers, but it is not the only one. This same stubborn persistence resulted in the cultivation of the Salt Lake Valley, populated by large black crickets and rattlesnakes when the initial wave of Mormon settlers arrived, where the arid and gravelly soil shattered plow blades in that first planting season. Although they sought isolation at the outset, as American settlement moved West the Mormons found that Utah would become a part of the United States they had been at such pains to escape when *The Latter-Day Saints' Emigrants' Guide* first informed travelers of the way to the Promised Land.

Detail from the Library's ornate bronze entry doors.

A WOMAN AMONG MEN
CORNELIA HANCOCK AND THE ARMY OF THE POTOMAC

— Bethany Anderson

James S. Schoff (1900–84) was one of the most generous donors in the 87-year history of the William L. Clements Library. A 1923 graduate of the University of Rochester, chairman of Bloomingdale's Department Store in New York City and longtime member of the Clements Library Associates board of governors, Schoff gave his impressive holdings of American Revolution and Civil War books and manuscripts to the Library in the 1960s and '70s. Today the Schoff Civil War Collections offer researchers a diverse and abundant record of the conflict that Oliver Wendell Holmes said "touched our hearts with fire." The Schoff treasures address history in its broadest sense, encompassing all aspects of mid-nineteenth-century American society. Although soldiers' letters make up the majority of the Schoff manuscripts, many of the shelves and boxes also contain the writings of ordinary civilians and non-combatants. The varied perspectives on the conflict that emerge from these papers provide a rich array of information on the war and its era.

Among the most interesting of the Schoff manuscripts are the papers of American women, including the letters of mothers, wives and daughters of those fighting in the war. These women write eloquently of the emotional, financial and physical hardships they endured. During the Civil War period, some women did not stay at home as passive spectators, as they harbored a patriotic desire to serve their country as strong as that of their male counterparts. One outlet for this enthusiasm was work in military hospitals. While the Clements has several collections concerning Civil War nurses, the letters of Cornelia Hancock (1840–1926) are exceptional. Including her years as a nurse with the Union Army, Hancock devoted her entire life to philanthropy and charity. The correspondence held by the Clements provides an interesting window on Hancock's activities, perspective and motivations. In an age when women were becoming progressively more aware of the influence they could wield as agents of social change, Hancock's letters offer a revealing meditation on a woman's role in society in Victorian America.

Cornelia Otis Hancock was born on February 8, 1840, at Hancock's Bridge, a small fishing community on Lower Alloway Creek near Salem, New Jersey. Her parents, Thomas York Hancock and Rachel were descended from English Quakers who had settled in New Jersey in the late 1600s. The family had a significant heritage that included substantial wealth and influence. Despite their Quaker

Gettysburg Penn. July 7th 1863

My dear Cousin

I am very tired to night —
have been on the field all day went
to the 3rd div. 2nd Army corps I suppose
there are about 500 wounded belonging to the second Army corp
They have one patch of woods devoted to each army corps for a hospital. I being interested in 2 nd
corps because Will had been in
it got into one of its ambulances
and went out at 8 this morning
and came in at 6 this evening
There are no words in the English
language to express the sufferings
I witnessed to day the men lie on
the ground their clothes have been
cut off them to dress their wounds
they are half naked have nothing
but hard tack to eat only as san

Soon after her arrival in Gettysburg, Cornelia Hancock wrote this letter to her cousin.

137

faith, the Hancocks were active in the American Revolution. On March 21, 1778, British General Charles Mawhood ordered Colonel John Graves Simcoe to attack the people of Salem County as punishment for their support of the Continental Army. The resulting "massacre" occurred at the site of the Hancock house, where the local militia was stationed, and Cornelia's great-grandfather, Judge William Hancock, was among those killed. The Hancock home survived the assault, and several succeeding generations maintained it as the family seat.

Their affluence notwithstanding, the Hancocks were considered somewhat eccentric within their community. In her autobiographical writings, Cornelia noted that her father was a proud non-conformist and the only resident of the Salem area "foolish enough" to vote for John C. Frémont in the 1856 presidential election. The Hancocks were also staunch abolitionists who raised their children to oppose slavery. Cornelia had four siblings, three of whom survived to adulthood. She taught school awhile before her participation in the Civil War.

When her brother, cousins and friends left to serve in the Civil War, Cornelia was eager to do her part for the Union cause. On July 5, 1863, she found her opportunity. In the aftermath of the Battle of Gettysburg, Hancock's brother-in-law, Dr. Henry T. Child, asked her to accompany him to the Gettysburg field hospitals as his assistant. Cornelia traveled from Hancock's Bridge to Philadelphia to meet Dr. Child, and then the two made their way to Baltimore. There, Hancock was placed under the care of Eliza W. Farnham, a well-known abolitionist and women's rights advocate, who was also applying to be a nurse. At Baltimore, the women were evaluated by Dorothea Dix, superintendent of the Union Army nurses, whose strict rules on appearance and demeanor made it notoriously difficult for young women to become nurses. In her later years, Hancock reminisced, "In those days it was considered indecorous for angels of mercy to appear otherwise than grey-haired and spectacled." Not surprisingly, Dix initially rejected Hancock's application to be a nurse because of her youth and "rosy cheeks," but Cornelia's resolve was unshaken. On July 6 Hancock boarded the train for Gettysburg, daring anyone to remove her from her seat. When she arrived, nobody questioned her amidst the carnage.

Hancock was assigned to the Third Division, Second Corps of the Army of the Potomac and was the first woman to reach the Gettysburg hospital after the battle. She encountered more than 500 wounded soldiers in her section. Every spare building in Gettysburg, including churches and barns, had been converted into makeshift hospitals. The men lay on the ground in disarray, half clothed, wounded and starving. From her first day, Cornelia devoted herself to feeding the wounded and writing letters for them. Although she quickly became inured to the sight of blood, amputated limbs and death, Hancock faltered as she wrote letters for soldiers to their loved ones, knowing that for many this would be the last time their families would hear from them. Cornelia's correspondence from Gettysburg began two days after her arrival, and her letters reveal the emotional impact of working with soldiers who, despite facing the prospect of death and enduring excruciating pain, rarely complained. During her first week at Gettysburg, Cornelia wrote to a cousin, "There are no words in the English language to express the sufferings I witnessed today."

Cornelia Hancock, a woman among men, poses with soldiers in their encampment.

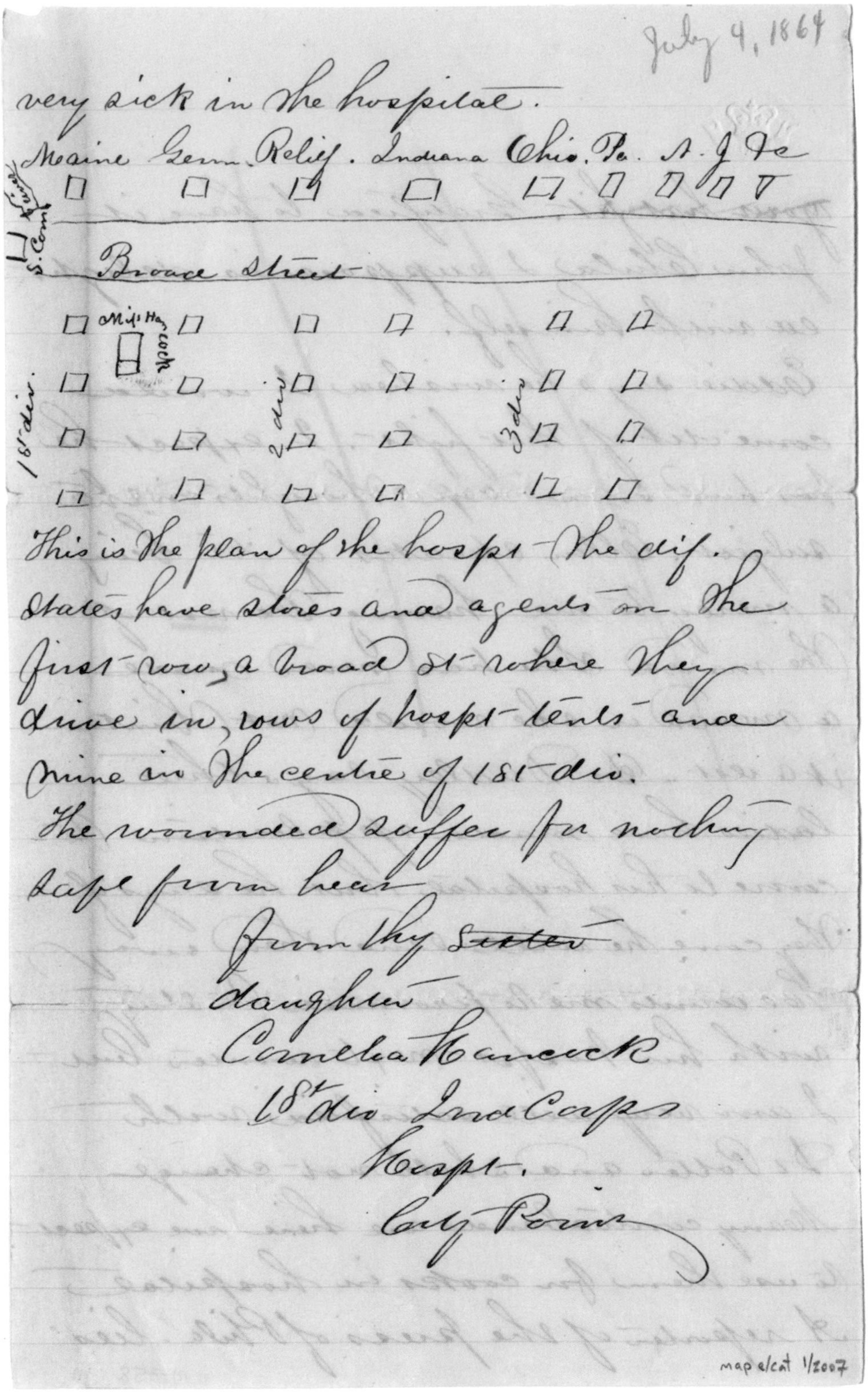

very sick in the hospital.

Maine Genn Relief. Indiana Ohio. Pa. N. J. &c

▢ ▢ ▢ ▢ ▢ ▢ ▢ ▢

S. Cont

——————————————————

Broad Street

▢ Miss Hancock ▢ ▢ ▢ ▢ ▢

1st div. ▢ ▢ ▢ ▢ ▢ ▢ ▢

▢ ▢ 2d div ▢ ▢ 3d div ▢ ▢

▢ ▢ ▢ ▢ ▢ ▢

This is the plan of the hospl. The dif.
States have stores and agents on the
first row, a broad St where they
drive in, rows of hospl tents and
mine in the centre of 1st div.
The wounded suffer for nothing
safe from heat

from thy Sister
daughter
Cornelia Hancock
18t div 2nd Corps
Hospt.
City Point

Cornelia Hancock sketched this plan of the Second Corps hospital encampment at City Point, Virginia, in a letter to her mother of July 4, 1864. She identified her own tent (upper left) and those of the agents of individual states ranged along "Broad Street."

map e/cat 1/2007

Hancock worked in the general hospital at Camp Letterman, near Gettysburg, for several weeks. Despite her inexperience, she quickly learned to dress wounds and care for patients. In late July the soldiers presented her with a silver medal of appreciation inscribed, "Miss Cornelia Hancock, presented by the wounded soldiers 3rd Division 2nd Army Corps—Testimonial of regard for ministrations of mercy to the wounded soldiers at Gettysburg, Pa.—July 1863." The respect was mutual. In her letters Cornelia repeatedly conveyed her admiration for the soldiers, especially for their bravery. It was not their bravery on the battlefield, however, which so moved her; rather, it was the silence with which they endured their injuries. She wrote to her sister and mother, "I think if you could walk this our hospital and observe the uncomplaining misery you would see. You would think sickness at home a small matter. I look in perfect astonishment at my patients. One Man said this morning if Miss Hancock only had time to fan him. The flies almost devouring his wound." Even amputees managed to find comfort in their situation. One maimed soldier exclaimed to Hancock, "What was the loss of a leg or an arm to whipping Lee out of Pennsylvania [!]"

After the situation at the Camp Letterman hospital stabilized, Cornelia returned to Philadelphia in September 1863 to await her next assignment with the Second Corps. Learning in October that nurses were needed at an African American "contraband" hospital in Washington D.C., she made her way there. The patients, many of whom were escaped slaves who had become ill from exhaustion, had come from camps in the northern part of the District of Columbia. As the Union Army advanced into the South, the hospital received more refugees each day. Although Hancock had witnessed appalling suffering at Gettysburg, she was stunned by the condition of the refugees. She wrote of one escaped slave in particular named Wilson Chinn. Having recently run away from New Orleans, Chinn bore the brand of his master's name upon his forehead. He had brought with him the instruments with which he had been tortured for 39 years, including a pronged iron collar, chains, contraptions to inflict sleep deprivation, and bells to prevent him from escaping. Female refugees were also present at the hospital, many arriving pregnant or with their children in tow. Of one woman Cornelia writes, "a more forlorn, wornout looking creature I never beheld." She petitioned relatives and friends for clothing, food and any other items they could spare for these people who were so in need.

Despite Hancock's efforts to secure resources that would assuage the dire conditions in the Contraband Hospital, she often found herself deeply disappointed and exasperated. She objected, "when you see the men who have charge here you could not help thinking where are all those good abolitionists north that do so much *talking* and so little *acting*." Indeed, she could attest to the insurmountable difficulties that the freed slaves faced. She criticized the hospital and military authorities for mistreating contrabands, noting that some were being accused of "second hand slavery." Likewise, she wondered, "Where are the people who have been professing such strong abolitionist proclivity for the last thirty years?—certainly not in Washington laboring with these people whom they have been clamoring to have freed." In spite of the disregard many had for contrabands, Hancock devoted herself to their care and education. She put her experience as a schoolteacher in New Jersey to good use, teaching at the hospital and visiting countless orphaned children.

In February 1864, at the request of Dr. Justin Dwinelle, Cornelia rejoined the Second Army Corps. Dwinelle wrote that he had 150 wounded and needed her to come immediately to his hospital at Brandy Station, Virginia. Secretary of War Edwin M. Stanton granted Hancock a permanent pass that allowed her to travel freely within the lines of the Union Army, and she made her way to Brandy Station. At the hospital, the surgeons made sure she was comfortably accommodated, building a log cabin for her residence. Cornelia immediately busied herself feeding patients and dressing their wounds. Her resentment of military authorities, however, which had shaped much of her experience at the Contraband Hospital, was again evident at Brandy Station. She writes, "I detest War and officers, if you could know of the drunkenness and bearing of our Major generals down here you would feel indeed disgusted with military affairs."

Hancock had defied many conventions in order to join the Union Army as a nurse, and she was not blind to the disapproval and potential damage to her reputation her behavior might create. Even her mother was concerned that she would fall victim to the stigma that a woman, especially a young woman, acquired in military camps. Aware of those concerns, Cornelia remained adamant in her decision to stay with the Second Corps. She constantly informed her mother that the soldiers treated her with the utmost respect, rejecting suggestions that she have a female companion sleep in her log cabin with her. Hancock wrote home, "No soldier would be allowed to come into my house without knocking even in the day time and at night they could not get in without sawing out the logs. There is no danger from any thing in the army." She could understand, however, why her neighbors in Salem gossiped about her: "I have no doubt that most people think I came into the army to get a husband. It is a capital place for that, there are very many nice men here and all men are required to give great respect to women here. There are many good looking women here who galavant around in the evening and have a good time. I do not trouble myself much with the common herd." Whether because of dedication to her work or a feminist perspective ahead of her time, Hancock remained undaunted by the specter of social disapproval.

Although Cornelia's sole intent was to alleviate the suffering of the wounded soldiers, she also developed strong bonds with fellow hospital workers. At Brandy Station she became acquainted with Dr. Frederick A. Dudley. Dudley, a graduate of Yale Medical College, had enlisted with the 14th Connecticut Infantry. At 22 he was possessed of an impervious ambition and fearless resolve, rushing onto the battlefield to treat patients and placing himself in danger to help others. Dudley remembered Hancock from Gettysburg, where she had tended to his wounds on the battlefield, bringing him tobacco for relief. At Brandy Station Dudley was the head surgeon for the Third Division. The two worked closely together, and as a result Hancock frequently mentions Dudley in her correspondence. While she wrote of his intelligence, industry and even his good looks, she was dismayed by Dudley's attitude toward African Americans. Although he was not pro-slavery, he was no abolitionist. Were it not for Cornelia's insistence, Dudley would have refused to treat African-American patients. Drawing on her faith in humanity, she hoped he would one day become an abolitionist. "Age will bring him out of many of his opinions," she reasoned.

Henry A. Simmons painted this fleeing slave during naval service on the Mississippi River in 1862. The artist titled his sketch "The Contrabands Escape, Vicksburg, July 8th." Cornelia Hancock undoubtedly heard tales of similar perilous attempts during her service at the Contraband Hospital in Washington, D.C.

When the number of wounded at Brandy Station declined, Hancock returned to Philadelphia for a brief lull that ended with news of the Battle of the Wilderness. Cornelia left immediately for Washington, D.C., but found that relief workers and supplies were unable to reach the site of the battle. The wounded had to be transported by boat to Belle Plain, Virginia. The Second Army Corps decided to locate its hospital at Fredericksburg, and when they arrived Hancock reported, "the scenes beggared all description." She estimated that nearly 14,000 wounded filled the town. Her experiences at Gettysburg had hardened her to sights other hospital workers found disturbing, but when she realized that many of her friends had been killed in the battle, she became deeply saddened and wrote, "I am glad I am here but I really thought my heart would break as one after another they told me was dead."

The Second Corps stayed in Fredericksburg for a short time before marching south, first to Port Royal, and then toward White House Landing on the Pamunkey River. After nearly two weeks of existing on little more than "hard tack," Hancock welcomed the change. During the course of their march, she lodged with "Secesh" women. Despite their cordiality toward her, she sensed their brooding resentment. The march proved to be grueling indeed, as guerrilla Rebel forces attacked the army along the way. Carrying guns and knapsacks for the weary soldiers when she could, Cornelia felt increased pity and admiration for the men. Though she feared for her safety, her loyalty to the soldiers took precedence. She wrote to her sister, "If I ever get through this march safely I shall feel thankful. If not I shall never regret having made the attempt for I am no better to suffer than the thousands who die. I think that the privates in the army who have nothing before them but hard marching, poor fare and terrible fighting are entitled to all the unemployed muscle of the North and they will get mine with a good will during this summer."

The farther the Second Corps traveled, the more Hancock's reputation preceded her. On May 31, 1864, the *New York Tribune* published an article on Cornelia's work as a nurse in the Union Army. The author of the article remained anonymous, calling himself "V," but Hancock speculated that it was Dr. Vanderpool, with whom she had worked at Fredericksburg. The article, which appeared in a number of newspapers, created a sensation in Salem, quieting many of her critics there. Cornelia's mother eagerly wrote that some even considered her a heroine. Yet though the article extended Cornelia's popularity, she also noted, "The piece in the paper has made a great stir and gained me many enemies."

In the midst of Ulysses S. Grant's Overland Campaign, the Second Corps reached White House Landing on June 2. As they awaited further orders, the Confederates staged an attack on their camp. It was the first time Hancock was endangered by proximity to shellfire. As the Rebel cavalry retreated, Hancock made her way to City Point, Virginia. Having survived the attack at White House Landing, she told her mother, "I believe I now have the confidence of more people than almost any Lady in the army." Though Cornelia had worked independently since joining the Army, at City Point the U.S. Sanitary Commission endorsed her as one of its nurses. She had mixed feelings about the Sanitary Commission but welcomed the opportunity to join the prestigious organization.

Hancock spent the rest of her wartime tenure at the City Point Hospital. After the war ended, she returned to Philadelphia to live with her sister and brother-in-law. Moved by memories of her service at the Contraband Hospital in Washington, she accepted the patronage of the Philadelphia Yearly Meeting of the Society of Friends and traveled south with fellow abolitionist and educator Laura Towne to open a school for African American children near Charleston, South Carolina. Cornelia followed that initiative by starting her own school in Pleasantville, South Carolina, where she remained for a number of years. In 1875 she returned to Philadelphia, where she helped establish the Society for Organizing Charity (also known as the Family Society of Philadelphia). The abject poverty and disaffected youth of Philadelphia's Sixth Ward became one of her main concerns, leading her to help establish the Children's Aid Society of Pennsylvania. Cornelia Hancock never married and remained active in Philadelphia charitable work for the rest of her life, devoting herself to social welfare causes until her death in 1926.

Hancock carefully saved her letters from the Civil War, bequeathing them at her death to a cousin's granddaughter, Henrietta Stratton Jaquette. Jaquette published Cornelia's correspondence in 1937 as *South after Gettysburg: Letters of Cornelia Hancock from the Army of the Potomac, 1863–1865*. In 1938 Jaquette gave the letters to the Clements as one of the Library's first Civil War collections, laying a foundation for James Schoff's donations three decades later. In 1998 the University of Nebraska Press reprinted *South After Gettysburg* under the title *Letters of a Civil War Nurse*. Unlike most of her contemporaries among American women, as the sesquicentennial of the Civil War draws near Cornelia Hancock is a recognized figure for students of the war and its impact on America.

In many ways, Cornelia Hancock followed a road that few women of her time dared to travel. Although it is estimated that nearly 5,000 women worked as nurses in the Union Army, Hancock often found she was the only woman within miles. Even at Gettysburg she wrote, "I was the first woman who reached the 2nd Corps after the three days fight at Gettysburg I was in that Corps all day not another woman within half mile." Likewise, she was the only Union woman in Fredericksburg when the army first entered the city. On the one hand, Hancock enjoyed her status as the lone woman of the Second Corps; on the other, she was gravely disappointed that more women did not volunteer. "Women are needed here very badly anyone who is willing to go," she aptly noted.

Although other women are remembered for their humanitarian and hospital work during the Civil War, the Cornelia Hancock Papers are distinctive because they allow researchers to study life in the Second Army Corps as Cornelia experienced it. Her letters, like many in the Schoff Civil War Collections, illuminate the individual tragedies and triumphs of war as well as the shifting roles women were able to fill in wartime. Few women were privy to military life behind the lines, and even fewer served as an inspiration to a whole army of men. Years after the war a soldier for whom Hancock had cared told her, "I well remember when you climbed on the back of an ambulance and commenced washing my face with water bailed from the Pamunkey River, and I said to myself although wounded right through the body, if a woman will come here and do this for us we must try to live." Though her ministrations eased the discomfort of many, it was Cornelia's courage and camaraderie that mattered most to the soldiers—and that is what makes her story so arresting.

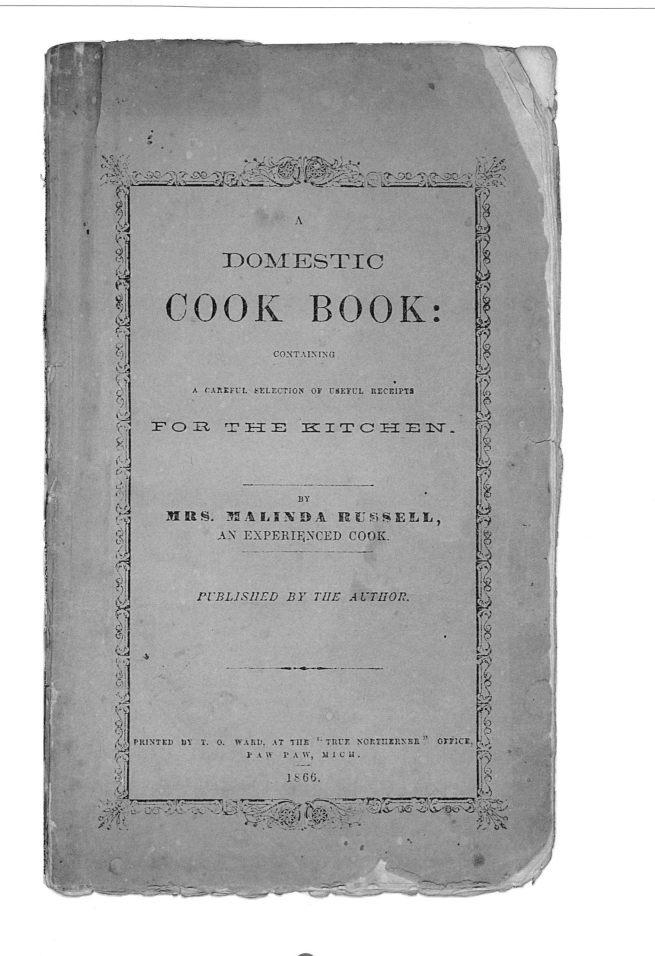

A

DOMESTIC

COOK BOOK:

CONTAINING

A CAREFUL SELECTION OF USEFUL RECEIPTS

FOR THE KITCHEN.

BY

MRS. MALINDA RUSSELL,

AN EXPERIENCED COOK.

PUBLISHED BY THE AUTHOR.

PRINTED BY T. O. WARD, AT THE "TRUE NORTHERNER" OFFICE,
PAW PAW, MICH.

1866.

MALINDA RUSSELL
AN INDOMITABLE WOMAN AND AN AMERICAN STORY

— Janice Bluestein Longone

To make the invisible visible. That is the privilege of researchers and scholars. Since culinary history is a new field of academic study, there are many contributions to be uncovered and mysteries yet to be solved. This is the story of one such mystery.

Although for many years scholars considered *What Mrs. Fisher Knows about Old Southern Cooking* (San Francisco, 1881) to be the first cookbook authored by an African American woman, culinary historians always thought that there must have been earlier such works. We were fortunate to discover one: Malinda Russell's *A Domestic Cook Book* (Paw Paw, Michigan, 1866). The very fragile copy of this pamphlet, now considered the first African American-authored cookbook, is now in the Clements Library. It is, to our knowledge, the only copy extant.

The story of its discovery and the attempt to track down its history has taken many years. It is quite remarkable that this unique copy of *A Domestic Cook Book* has survived. I do not know how many hands it passed through between its printing in 1866 and our purchase and donation of it to the Clements Library several years ago. A West Coast dealer found the pamphlet at the bottom of a box of material from the collection of Helen Evans Brown, a well-known California culinary figure in the last half of the twentieth century. Her bookplate appeared in a modern protective paper cover enclosing the volume. When my husband Dan and I received a call asking what we knew about *A Domestic Cook Book* by Malinda Russell, we answered honestly that we knew nothing about it—not even that it existed. But we very much wanted to purchase it. Fortunately, after several complications and much nail biting on my part, we were able to do so. When the pamphlet arrived, we were stunned at what it represented—an important and previously unknown piece of American culinary history.

Determined to discover more about Malinda Russell from the few tantalizing details she revealed, Dan and I spent our forty-eighth wedding anniversary in 2002 in Tennessee, Virginia and North Carolina visiting historical societies, cemeteries and government offices in the locales she mentions. Several times, we felt we had captured her or were very close, but in the end we could not be certain we had unequivocally identified her from the available documents.

A Domestic Cook Book is a fascinating first-person chronicle of a free woman of color in mid-nineteenth-century America. Malinda's was a life of "hard labor" and travail, but she overcame all of her hardships and setbacks with an indomitable spirit. It is truly an American story. All we know about Malinda Russell is what she tells us in "A Short History of the Author" and her "Rules and Regulations of the Kitchen." Her story is inspirational, and I encourage you to read her first-hand account in the facsimile discussed below, now available from the Clements Library.

Malinda Russell was born and raised in Washington and Greene Counties, in eastern Tennessee. Her mother was a member of one of the first families set free by a Mr. Noddie of Virginia: "My mother being born free after the emancipation of my grandmother, her children are by law free." We have been unable to uncover any information about Noddie. When Malinda was 19 years old, she set out with others for Liberia, but after her money was stolen by a member of the party she was "obliged" to remain in Lynchburg, Virginia. There she began working as a cook and a companion, traveling with ladies as a nurse. She also kept a washhouse and advertised in a local newspaper; she included a reproduction of one such ad in her book. In it she displays the fortitude and business acumen that appear to have been part of her character all of her life:

> Every article washed by her, she guarantees shall pass unscathed through the severest ordeal of inspection, without the remotest danger of condemnation. She can conscientiously boast of a proficiency in her business, and all clothing committed to her charge shall be neatly executed and well taken care of. She hopes to receive, as she shall exert herself to deserve, a sufficiency of patronage to insure her a permanent location.

While in Virginia, Malinda married a man named Anderson Vaughan, who lived for only four years thereafter. For the rest of her life, she used her maiden name. At the time of writing *A Domestic Cook Book* she was still "a widow, with one child, a son who is crippled; he has the use of but one hand." At some time after her husband's death, Russell returned to Tennessee and kept a boarding house on Chuckey Mountain, Cold Springs, for three years. After leaving the boarding house, she kept a pastry shop for six years, and "by hard labor and economy, saved a considerable sum of money for the support of myself and my son."

Then, for the second time in Russell's life, a robbery forced a change in her existence. On January 16, 1864, a guerrilla party stole her money and threatened her life: "Under those circumstances, we were obliged to leave home, following a flag of truce out of the Southern borders, being attacked several times by the enemy." After hearing that "Michigan was the Garden of the west," she moved to the Paw Paw area "for the present, until peace is restored, when I think of returning to Greenville, Tennessee, to try to recover at least a part of my property."

Russell tells us in 1866 that she was employed as a cook for 20 years by the first families of Tennessee, Virginia, North Carolina, and Kentucky. She learned her trade, she indicates, from Fanny Steward, a colored cook of Virginia, and she cooked after the plan of the "Virginia Housewife." This last is most likely a reference to Mary Randolph's classic and very popular work, *The Virginia House-Wife*, first published in 1824. It had at least 19 printings before the Civil War and is still in print.

RECEIPTS.

Salt Rising Bread.

To a half pint warm water, a pinch of salt; stir to a thick batter and keep warm until it rises. To one pint of this rising add three pints warm water, a little salt, and a small piece of lard. Knead the dough until smooth, make into rolls, keep warm until it rises; bake quick, but do not scorch.

Soft Ginger Bread.

Two quarts flour, 3-4ths lb lard, 3-4ths lb sugar, three teaspoonfuls cinnamon, two of ginger, one of allspice, one pint sour milk, molasses to make a stiff batter, one teaspoonful soda dissolved in milk.

Soft Ginger Bread.

One quart molasses, one cup sugar, 1-4th lb lard, three eggs; beat sugar and eggs well together; one gill sour milk, one tablespoonful soda dissolved in warm water, two tablespoonfuls ginger, flour enough to make a soft dough. Knead well, roll, and bake in a quick oven.

Cream Cake.

One and a half cup sugar, two cups sour cream, two cups flour, one or two eggs, one teaspoon soda; flavor with lemon.

Sally Dough Cake.

Three cups sugar, one cup yeast, three cups sweet milk, three eggs; beat to a thin batter, set over night. When light, add one cup butter, flour to make a stiff batter. Keep warm until it rises the second time. Paper and grease the pan before rising the last time; bake in a slow oven.

White Mountain Cake.

One cup white sugar, two eggs, one-half cup butter, one-half cup sweet milk, one-half teaspoonful soda, one teaspoonful cream tartar, two and one-half cups flour.

Forced to leave the South because of her Union principles, Russell wrote her cookbook "hoping to receive enough from the sale of it to enable me to return home." Now "advanced in age," robbed of her property and with no means of support other than her own labor she decided to write a cookbook "with the intention of benefiting the public as well as myself." Russell ended her brief autobiography with the confident assurance that "I know my book will sell well where I have cooked, and am sure that those using my receipts will be well satisfied."

Perhaps because of Russell's diverse background and varied travels, the "receipts" in her pamphlet are not distinctly southern. Nor do they appear to have been taken from Mrs. Randolph's *Virginia House-Wife*. We have not been able to uncover anything about Fanny Steward, the Virginia cook Russell mentions. Most of the recipes could come from any part of the eastern United States of the period, although there are a few southern touches, such as "Sweet Potato Baked Pudding," "Sweet Potato Slice Pie" and "Fricaseed Catfish." Most recipes are for sweets, desserts and baked goods, not surprising given Russell's years of keeping a pastry shop.

Dan and I spent a great deal of time trying to solve the mystery of this remarkable woman. We went to western Michigan, to Paw Paw and the surrounding area, only to find no answers and more roadblocks. We discovered that the town of Paw Paw had been all but destroyed by a fire within months of the printing of the Russell pamphlet by *The True Northerner,* one of the local newspapers. There were no records to be found. When we felt that we could no longer devote the time necessary to collect any new information, I chose to write about Russell for an article in my "Vintage Volumes" column in the first issue of *Gastronomica. The Journal of Food and Culture* (2001). Some of the material here was first introduced in that article.

The response, particularly from the academic community, was a bit overwhelming. Many readers wanted to know more about the author and her cookbook. The word was beginning to spread—there is a hitherto unknown nineteenth-century African American cookbook. In May 2005, J.W. "Johnny" Apple wrote a feature article in the *New York Times* on the Clements Library's first symposium on American culinary history. In the article, Apple mentioned the Russell pamphlet as one of the treasures of the Clements. But still, although many were now searching, there was little new information about Russell and her work.

When the Clements organized a second culinary history symposium in 2007, publishing a facsimile of Russell's cookbook seemed a fitting way to pay tribute to Malinda and make her work better known to a wider audience. The hope was that more people knowing about Russell and searching for her might help uncover new information. For this facsimile we added an introduction placing the pamphlet in its historical context and an index of the 265 recipes and medical and household hints to make it easier for modern culinary historians to use.

In November 2007 Molly O'Neill wrote an article in the *New York Times* entitled "A 19th-Century Ghost Awakens to Redefine 'Soul.'" The next day it appeared in the *International Herald Tribune,* and within days, newspapers, blogs, journals, historians, culinarians, and librarians the world over were talking about Malinda Russell. She was no longer invisible. O'Neill wrote that Russell's pamphlet

What Mrs. Fisher Knows About Old Southern Cooking *(San Francisco, 1881) was long thought to be the first cookbook by an African American woman.*

could challenge ingrained views about the cuisine of African Americans. She suggested that the black liberation movement of the 1960s had celebrated "soul food"—dishes with a debt to Africa (black-eyed peas, gumbo). She proposed that "neither the activists nor the scholars who later devoted themselves to black studies intended those dishes to be seen as the food on the stove of every black cook in America. But that is exactly what happened, historians say."

O'Neill interviewed several prominent scholars of African American history. Leni Sorensen, a researcher at Monticello outside Charlottesville, Virginia, said, "Southern poverty cooking was mistakenly established as the single and universal African American cuisine."

And then the volume by Malinda Russell surfaced. Toni Tipton-Martin, a journalist and food historian in Austin, Texas, who has spent more than a decade researching the cooking of African American women, agreed with this interpretation: "It is an Emancipation Proclamation for black cooks. In isolation, Malinda's book might appear to be an aberration." But in the context of the black-authored cookbooks that followed, many of which reflected a sophisticated international kitchen, Russell's work "dispels the notion of a universal African American food experience, which is why the term 'soul food' doesn't work for so many of us."

Culinary historians agree that the evidence of a single cookbook is not enough to rewrite culinary history. Yet the Russell pamphlet suggests that a more nuanced view might be in order. Here was an African American cook who was already two generations removed from the plantation kitchen by the time Lincoln died. When interviewed for the O'Neill article, Sandy Oliver, publisher of *Food History News* in Islesboro, Maine, indicated "no cookbook alone can provide an accurate view of African American food ways in the 17th and 18th centuries." Scholars are still debating these questions.

After the O'Neill article appeared, the Clements Library staff responded to many visitors, phone calls, emails, and letters about Malinda Russell and her cookbook. Recipes from Russell's pamphlet have been served in restaurants, in school and community programs and in private homes from California to Michigan to Virginia to New Jersey. The Learning Network of the *New York Times* proposed a lesson plan for using Russell and her cookbook to help students learn about the discovery of an American culinary history treasure and the history of family artifacts. There have been lectures about Russell and her cookbook throughout America. Russell has been entered into various halls of fame, according to the blogosphere, both on African American and culinary sites.

Orders for copies of the facsimile came in from all over the United States as well as diverse foreign countries. The great majority of those who contacted us about Malinda Russell thanked us for bringing her to life. Here is an excerpt from one such letter:

> *Allow me to introduce myself. I am a special education teacher in the Trenton Public School District in Trenton, NJ. For the past two days my American Literature class has been reading your article.... The class loved it. We are using your article to support and incorporate the importance of food into our cultural diversity appreciation.... As we read the article, we went on a hunting expedition ... with you and Professor Longone. It became our quest to find her. I have never seen my class so excited and hopeful. Every trip you took to towns caused my students and me to pray that the journey would yield a positive result.*

The Clements Library's unique Malinda Russell cookbook is one of the four nineteenth-century culinary works by African Americans that have so far come to light. Although *A Domestic Cook Book* is now considered the first cookbook written by an African American, there are two earlier manuals on household management and hotel and dining room work by professional African American men: Robert Roberts' *The House Servant's Directory* (1827) and Tunis Campbell's *Hotel Keepers, Head Waiters and Housekeepers' Guide* (1848). The fourth book by a nineteenth-century African American is Abby Fisher's *What Mrs. Fisher Knows About Old Southern Cooking* (1881).

The House Servant's Directory by Robert Roberts was the first book of any kind by an African American issued by a commercial American publisher. Of major gastronomic importance, the book was published in 1827 in Boston by Monroe & Francis with two additional printings in 1828 and 1843. Roberts was a butler in the household of Christopher Gore, U. S. Senator and governor of Massachusetts. Roberts' book is noteworthy for several reasons. It offers one of the most detailed discussions of that period on the proper management of an upper-class New England household. It gives advice to servants on how to behave, how to perform their work and how to use the variety of new household utensils and equipment then becoming increasingly available. Although Roberts comments on the responsibilities of the employer, he is generally more interested in teaching other servants how to act. His work is one of the first to help encourage young black men to become the finest professional house servants. He offers specific, detailed suggestions to them to ensure their advancement and tenure. In addition to his influence on black employment patterns, Roberts was active in various organizations promoting black interests. One indication of the influence of *The House Servant's Directory* is its inclusion in the library at the Hermitage, President Andrew Jackson's home. One of a handful of culinary books in the Hermitage library, it shares honors with Mrs. Randolph's *The Virginia House-Wife*, the first southern cookbook.

Tunis Campbell's *Hotel Keepers, Head Waiters and Housekeepers' Guide,* published in Boston in 1848, is known to bibliographers but has been little examined due to its rarity. Born in New Jersey early in the nineteenth century, Campbell attended an Episcopal school in New York and trained for missionary work in Liberia. But he became increasingly opposed to the planned removal of blacks from America to Africa, "having long since determined to plant our trees on American soil." Between 1832 and 1845, Campbell was a social worker, reformer, abolitionist, and an active participant in antislavery causes. During this time he worked in New York as a hotel steward, the last three years as the principal waiter at the Howard Hotel. Then for an undetermined period he worked at the Adams House in Boston. While there he wrote his *Guide,* one of the earliest manuals written by any American on the supervision and management of first-class restaurants and hotel dining rooms.

Campbell's book is evocative of a military manual. He gives detailed, exacting instructions, with illustrations, for the dining table service brigade. As careful as he is to instruct and train his waiters for their responsibility, he is equally voluble in telling the employers that *they* also have a responsibility to treat their help with respect and dignity.

Hotel Keepers, Head Waiters and Housekeepers' Guide deserves to be better known, but only a few copies of the original exist, and, to my knowledge, there is no facsimile in print at present. Campbell is

THE
HOUSE SERVANT'S DIRECTORY,

OR

A MONITOR FOR PRIVATE FAMILIES:

COMPRISING

HINTS ON THE ARRANGEMENT AND PERFORMANCE OF

SERVANTS' WORK,

WITH GENERAL RULES FOR

SETTING OUT TABLES AND SIDEBOARDS

IN FIRST ORDER;

THE ART OF WAITING

IN ALL ITS BRANCHES; AND LIKEWISE HOW TO CONDUCT

LARGE AND SMALL PARTIES

WITH ORDER;

WITH GENERAL DIRECTIONS FOR PLACING ON TABLE

ALL KINDS OF JOINTS, FISH, FOWL, &c.

WITH

FULL INSTRUCTIONS FOR CLEANING

PLATE, BRASS, STEEL, GLASS, MAHOGANY;

AND LIKEWISE

ALL KINDS OF PATENT AND COMMON LAMPS:

OBSERVATIONS

ON SERVANTS' BEHAVIOUR TO THEIR EMPLOYERS;

AND UPWARDS OF

100 VARIOUS AND USEFUL RECEIPTS,

CHIEFLY COMPILED

FOR THE USE OF HOUSE SERVANTS;

AND IDENTICALLY MADE

TO SUIT THE MANNERS AND CUSTOMS OF FAMILIES

IN THE UNITED STATES.

By ROBERT ROBERTS.

WITH

FRIENDLY ADVICE TO COOKS

AND HEADS OF FAMILIES,

AND COMPLETE DIRECTIONS HOW TO BURN

LEHIGH COAL.

BOSTON,
MUNROE AND FRANCIS, 128 WASHINGTON-STREET.
NEW YORK,
CHARLES S. FRANCIS, 189 BROADWAY.
1827.

Robert Roberts, The House Servant's Directory *(Boston, 1827), the first book by an African American to be issued by a commercial publisher in the United States.*

better known to American historians for his non-culinary contributions, including many years as a powerful force in Reconstruction politics in Georgia.

Abby Fisher's *What Mrs. Fisher Knows About Old Southern Cooking* was printed in San Francisco by the Women's Co-operative Printing Office in 1881. Until the discovery of Malinda Russell's work, this book was considered to be the earliest black-authored American cookbook. Mrs. Fisher was an ex-slave who could neither read nor write. Born in South Carolina, she achieved fame in San Francisco, where she had a business of pickles and preserves manufacturing. Her cookery received medals and diplomas at several California fairs, including two medals in San Francisco (1880) for "best pickles and sauces and best assortment of jellies and preserves." Mrs. Fisher's collection of recipes, with origins in the plantation kitchens of the pre-Civil War South, was published with the assistance of named benefactors in San Francisco and Oakland. Because of its scarcity it was little known until recently, but several facsimiles have made the book more widely available. Currently, a number of culinary historians are trying to unravel the contradictory facts known about Mrs. Fisher.

Scholars who studied early books by African American authors such as Robert Roberts and Tunis Campbell tended to see their blend of Yankee, European and Southern recipes as a reflection of who was being served more than who was doing the serving. The plantation kitchen recipes in books like that by Mrs. Fisher—"Beat Biscuits," "Ochra Gumbo," "Jumberlie—A Creole Dish (Jambalaya)"—were championed by some historians as a better mirror of the African American kitchen. Molly O'Neill's article in the *New York Times* closed with the following comments:

> *Locating the woman they call Malinda seems, therefore, increasingly unlikely. But to the Longones, abandoning the research is unthinkable.... "Our needle in the haystack gets smaller and smaller," Mrs. Longone said softly, "but we'll find her. She wants to be found, and we got some great new leads."*

Malinda Russell's story is an African American story. It is an American story. She has overcome. Stop Press! A new reference to a Malinda Russell has recently emerged on the Internet. In the Montgomery County, Virginia, Register of Free Negroes, 1823–1847, the following notice appears:

> *No. 30, 6 August 1844, Malinda Russell a free woman produced in court her register made in the county court of Washington in the state of Tennessee ... being at the time a dark mulatto with dark curly, kinkey hair about 24 years of age ... registered in this court as being about the age of 25 years ... five feet three inches high.*

Is this our Malinda Russell?

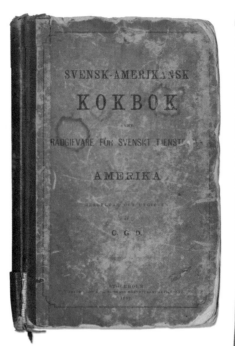

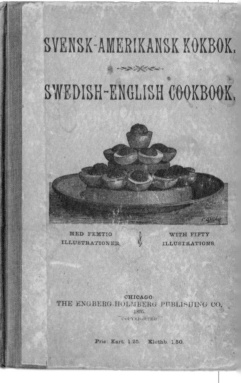

SWEDISH AMERICAN COOKBOOKS

— JJ Jacobson

The Janice Bluestein Longone Culinary Archive is a remarkable collection. One of the strengths of the archive is our holdings of cookbooks (and related materials) that reflect the many regional and ethnic communities of the United States. Food and other matters of domestic life are expressions of culture, and there is much to learn about the details of daily life by examining them. For an immigrant community, food ways show both ties to the old country and acculturation in the new one. Among our holdings of Swedish and Swedish American cookbooks are three that shed light on the food ways that formed part of the Swedish American experience. Two are from the late nineteenth century and were meant to aid the Swedish immigrant in America; the third, published in 1936, is a translation of a prestigious Swedish cooking school's cookbook, aimed at an American audience, which would naturally include second and third generation Swedish Americans.

Sweden sent a large group of immigrants to America, and the Swedish American population of the nineteenth century was cohesive enough to form an extensive and busy system of contacts for prospective and new immigrants. A network that included both personal ties and formally organized enterprises—emigration societies in Sweden, steamship companies, aid societies, employment agencies in the United States—wove across the Atlantic to connect the old country and the new. In 1930 Sweden had a population of roughly six million, but since 1850 it had lost more than one million inhabitants through emigration, with the bulk of them going to the United States. The causes were a mixture of push and pull, with both dissatisfaction with life in Sweden and the prospect of a better life in the United States playing a part.

Emigration from Sweden varied during the latter half of the nineteenth century, as economic conditions there and in the United States became more or less favorable, and as boom times and crises in agriculture or industry prompted higher or lower numbers. During the 1840s the yearly average was fewer than 2,000 a year, but during the next decade the average was more than 12,000. Emigration rose to a peak of 46,000 in 1887; after that, although improved economic conditions in Europe and the 1893 depression in America reduced the flood somewhat, in the 1890s and 1900s emigration still averaged 25,000 people annually.

Both social and economic push factors came into play. Speculation in Swedish agricultural lands in the early 1860s produced bankruptcies and heavily mortgaged farms. There were crop failures from 1867 through 1869 and a further agricultural depression in the 1890s. These fell particularly hard on Sweden's landless laborers, tenant farmers and the "cottagers" who received a bit of land in return for a specified number of days of labor per year. Another goad was the limited political franchise, which excluded those who did not own their own land. The right to vote did not extend to all Swedish men until 1909, and female suffrage not until 1919. Taxes were not, however, restricted to landowners, adding a further burden in lean years. Military training and service were compulsory for Swedish men when they reached their twentieth year, and the length of the required service grew as the nineteenth century progressed, adding incentive to emigrate for male laborers and famers' sons.

Religious intolerance also played a part. Until 1860 the Conventicle Act of 1726 forbade all religious assemblies outside the state church. While the act had originally targeted the Pietist movement of eighteenth-century Sweden, in the first half of the nineteenth century it came to stand for the authority of the state church, particularly against the revivalist movement that objected to the rationalism prevalent in the state church's doctrine. The state church was a pervasive part of Swedish life; any citizen who did not formally resign was considered a member, and membership meant tithes. Social penalties for those who did resign included loss of employment or ineligibility for jobs. The Erik Janssonists were the best-known group to emigrate to the United States for religious freedom, but less extreme religious minorities also sought tolerance in America, making religion a significant factor in Swedish emigration.

In *The Background of Swedish Emigration, 1840–1930,* Florence Edith Janson neatly summarizes the economic factors of migrating to America:

> *Wages were higher in the United States because of the scarcity of labor in a new country. The overpopulation of the rural districts before the industrialization of Sweden tended to make the wages low, and even after industry developed there was a large labor supply. Though the cost of living was higher in the United States the laborer could obtain a higher real wage in the newer world. It was easier for him to accumulate some capital and establish himself in agriculture or in industry. His standard of living was higher. In the new world he hardly ever felt the burden of taxation until he became a landowner; in Sweden the numerous burdens on land were often paid by the tenant and the early introduction of income tax made the laborer feel the pressure of direct taxation.*

Another pull factor was what Janson calls "publicity, the creator of demand." Letters from friends and relatives in the United States were a persuasive form of information about American opportunity, shaping opinion and firing the imagination, especially when they contained prepaid tickets or promises of employment. Sometimes former emigrants came back in person to brag of prosperity in the New World and return with friends and relatives in tow, the trip financed by commissions from land developers or transportation concerns. The Swedish press also published letters from immigrants in America.

An array of commercial and social enterprises enticed and smoothed the way for the immigrant. Emigrant societies in Sweden published and distributed literature with information about opportunities in the United States, and organized parties of emigrants. Steamship companies and American

Pyramid af kräftor.   Pyramid of crabs.

HUMMER OCH KRÄFTOR. | CRABS AND LOBSTERS.

Anmärkning. Humrar äro goda året rundt, men bäst emellan mars och oktober. Hanhummerns kött är fastare, men honhummern är mest omtyckt på grund af rommen, som begagnas för såser och garneringar. I motsats till den allmänna meningen kan det sägas att hummerns alla delar äro goda och hälsosamma med undantag af

Remarks: Lobsters are good the year round, but are preferable between March and October.   The meat of the male is the most solid, but the female is generally preferred on account of the eggs, which are used for sauce and garnishing. Contrary to general belief all the parts of a lobster are good and nutritious, with the exception of

(73)

From the Fullständigaste Svensk-Amerikansk kokbok *(Chicago, 1897).*

372. Smoked Hog's Head
(6 servings)

Select a lightly cured and lightly smoked hog's head. Wash and scrub the head well, removing any bristles which may remain. Soak in cold water overnight, wrap in a cloth, being careful not to displace the ears, and boil slowly in a covered kettle for about 2-2½ hours or until meat is tender but not overdone. Allow the head to partially cool in its own liquor, then remove from liquor and chill thoroughly. Garnish with creamed butter forced through a fine pastry tube. Fill each ear with a bunch of curly parsley.

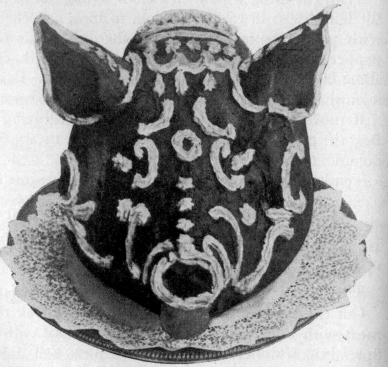

172

From Jenny Akerström, The Princesses Cook Book *(New York, 1936).*

land developers advertised in Swedish rural newspapers, distributed literature and sometimes maintained agents in Sweden to encourage prospective emigrants. After the Civil War a number of states and territories—Wisconsin, Iowa, Minnesota, Maine, the Dakotas, Kansas, Vermont, and Nebraska—actively competed for Scandinavian immigration to counter the influx of the "wrong" kind of immigrants coming from eastern and southern Europe. By 1900 East Coast ports of entry and cities across America also featured ethnic employment agencies for newcomers.

Swedish immigrants came from a wide class spectrum, but the majority originated in Sweden's landless agriculturalists. Some came with connections in established Swedish American frontier communities or with funds to rent or purchase land. But some immigrants had only been able to scrape together the money needed for their passage and so arrived in need of immediate employment. Employment agencies found jobs in domestic work for many of these individuals. Of two late nineteenth-century, dual-language Swedish American cookbooks in the Longone collection, the 1882 *Svensk-amerikansk kokbok: samt rådgivare för svenskt tjenstefolk i Amerika (Swedish American Cookbook: As Well as Advisor for Swedish Servants in America)* clearly represents a class of works published for this population. We also have another in a similar format, the 1897 *Fullständigaste Svensk-Amerikansk kokbok (Popular Swedish American Cookbook).*

All immigrants encounter and make some accommodation to the food ways prevalent in their new surroundings. This is important for any immigrant, but much more so for newcomers who find employment that in some way involves food—both in public professions (grocers, butchers, bakers, cooks) and in private domestic service. For those whose living depends on preparing food for the native or naturalized consumer's palate, it is crucial to understand the cuisine of their new country. They need to become familiar with dishes and ingredients, recognize names and gain facility with modes of preparation. That is what the first of these two volumes could facilitate. Both books are printed in side-by-side columns of Swedish and English, with the Swedish in the left-hand column. Both assume some familiarity with cooking techniques, as is typical for cookbooks of this period. Both have an index in Swedish and English, and both contain some explanatory material, if only in the form of asides, to orient the reader to specifics of American cooking.

For it is on American cooking that both works concentrate. Each contains directions for preparing some number of traditional Swedish dishes, but the majority of the recipes are consistent with what you would find in other late nineteenth-century American cookbooks. Recipes make much use of cornmeal—cornbread, johnnycake, mush, rye, and Indian bread—and there are numerous recipes with explicitly American names, such as Boston brown bread, Saratoga potatoes (the precursor to that American culinary marvel, the potato chip) and Hartford election cake.

The earlier of the two works, the 1882 *Svensk-amerikansk kokbok: samt rådgivare för svenskt tjenstefolk i Amerika, bearbetad och utgifven af C. G–d.*, had a long life. We know of further editions in 1888, 1890, 1893, 1901, and 1923. Our 1882 edition carries advertisements in both English and Swedish for an employment agency in New York (where the vast majority of Swedish immigrants landed) owned by Carl Grimsköld (presumably the C. G–d of the byline). The ads address different audiences, however. The one in English is clearly meant for prospective employers:

> *First Class Employment Agency for Swedish, English, German, and French Male and Female Servants for all Capacities I can give my patrons advantages in selecting help, that they cannot obtain elsewhere.*

This is the book's only advertisement in English, but its presence suggests that some English speakers were expected to be among the readers. The Swedish ad aims at immigrants, specifically those in need of work as domestics. In translation, it says:

> *Women who are looking for places in New York may find same by applying to Carl Grimsköld's office, where there are always situations for cooks, housemaids, nannies, cleaners, waiters, washerwomen, and ladies' maids, with salaries from $10 to $50 a month. Men as well as women workers should, as soon as they arrive in New York, come to my house, where they will receive the best lodging and food, while they choose jobs. Other travelers can avail themselves of room and board at the cheapest prices during their stay in New York. CARL GRIMSKÖLD Employment office 154 East 29th Street, New York City.*

At the end of the book, besides the Swedish and English index there is a chapter of

Hushållsordres (domestic orders), with side-by-side Swedish and English for sentences an employer might say to a domestic worker. They cover a variety of household positions, mirroring those advertised. For the general housework servant we find, "Give me the pan and I will show you how to cook oatmeal" and "You shall keep your own room in as good order as the other rooms." For the nurse there is, "The baby shall have a bath every evening at 7 o'clock" and "The waiter doesn't understand the children, you know." The cook, washer and ironer may be told, "You need not iron the wash today" or "Tomorrow we give dinner for 20 persons." The housemaid may hear, "Always bring fresh water before breakfast" or "You can go to church in the afternoon but must be home at a quarter to ten." For the more specialized housemaid and seamstress there is, "When you are at liberty, play with the children" and "I suppose you can cut and fit a dress?" The waiter is informed, "The first thing you do, is to look after the furnace" and "You have to take off the mustache" (he is, however, allowed to keep his side-whiskers and goatee). And the coachman may be told, "We take a drive through Central Park" or "Mr. John and Miss Bessy's saddlehorses should be saddled at a quarter to seven in the morning when it is clear weather."

It is tempting to think that these give us a glimpse into typical interactions and expectations. It's not certain, however, how this section would have been useful. Would the employer have pointed out sentences so the employee could read the translation? Would either have tried to pronounce the sentence in the other's language? Was it meant as an aid for the immigrant to learn the English relevant to domestic employment? There is also a section on furniture and utensils with Swedish and English names opposite one another in columns. The index gives the English terms after the Swedish ones, and is set up for use by the Swedish speaker, with headings alphabetical by the Swedish terms, which suggests that the main user the author had in mind would be the immigrant employee. The English, while clear, has awkward constructions and other infelicities that suggest that the Swedish was written first and translated by someone unfamiliar with American usage.

The recipes in the book are typical of those found in other late nineteenth-century American cookbooks: broiled shad, Brunswick stew, green corn fritters, maple sugar biscuit, pone, Delmonico-pudding, and steamed and baked Indian puddings. Many recipes sport American names such as Hartford election cake, Connecticut cake, Goshen-cake, Federal cake, Rochester jelly cake, Washington pie, and Wisconsin cake. Some reference American locales, such as "Clam Soup (Hartford)" or "Stufvad fisk (Astoria)" (literally stewed fish, but the English is "a very nice chowder"). Occasionally, information is added to the Swedish title to orient the Swedish-language reader. For instance, we find, "Sally Lunn (Frukostkaka)" (breakfast cake) and "West Point-kornbrod (Kadetter)" (cadets). In some cases the recipes are attributed by name, such as "Swedish plumpudding (Mary Håkanson)." There are a number of recipes identified as being Swedish in origin, grouped together in some sections but in others scattered among the American recipes.

The 1897 work, *Fullständigaste Svensk-Amerikansk kokbok* (we also know of an 1895 edition), is half again as long and somewhat more comprehensive. It was published in Chicago, at that time a jumping-off point for many Swedish immigrants headed for frontier communities and home to a sizable Swedish American community. The book is not as obviously tied to a specific enterprise; the preface merely says, "In response to an often-repeated request the public is herewith presented with a Swedish American Cook-Book, printed in parallel columns." A testimonial from "Fru Doktorinnan Sophia Lindahl," one of the few parts of the book not translated into English, recommends it to Swedish American housewives setting up housekeeping, for its detailed recipes for the dishes of the new country and its coverage of unfamiliar ingredients such as maize, "for whose use the Swedish cookbooks, quite naturally, do not give any instruction." Here then was a cookbook meant for daily use in the home by Swedish Americans but also accessible to English speakers. It includes Swedish and English indexes, obviously composed separately, as the listing is alphabetical by name in the language used. The book ends with twelve pages of publisher's ads, in Swedish.

Fullstandigaste Svensk-Amerikansk kokbok also served as a household manual. The preface signals this with its general reflections on cooking (including remarks on nutrition and digestibility), outlines on the two alternative manners of serving and an explanation of the *Smörgåsbord* custom:

> *The French way of serving is to put all dishes on the table before the meal, the Russian way to bring them from the kitchen warm and carved in the order they are to be served. The best way appears to be to make use of both methods, cold dishes being on the table at commencement of the meal, warm ones brought in as needed. Otherwise the Russian way of serving appears to be best for dinners, the French way for suppers. An original Swedish institution mentioned in the last chapter is "Smörgåsbord," served before meals either on a small side table or passed around, generally disposed of in a standing position. The "smorgasbord" is supposed to sharpen the appetite of those participating therein.*

In addition, a paragraph of general remarks on the availability, preparation and nutritive value of foodstuffs, and the service of the dishes, precedes each section. For instance, we learn that "Eggs that give a gurgling sound when shaken are bad." The section on bread begins with several recipes for making yeast, and there are two sections on preserving food: one on jellies and fruit preserves and one on preservation more generally ("Pickles and salted goods") that contains directions for drying fruit and keeping vegetables in sand or earth over the winter as well as recipes for drying or salting them. Dill and parsley are considered sufficiently important to the culinary regimen to require recipes for preserving them in salt or butter for the cold months. The same section contains directions for salting down beef and pork, and preparing and smoking hams in both the Westphalian and the American manner.

At the end of the book is a section of "General Observations" with household directions "to make hens lay in winter," "to preserve steel pens," "to test nutmeg," and "to enamel shirt bosoms." There is also a series of menus, which begins with a table of the time it takes different foods to digest. There are sample menus for *smörgåsbord,* small dinners, grand dinners, and suppers, plus simple menus by season.

The recipes in the *Fullstandigaste Svensk-Amerikansk kokbok* are chiefly American, comparable to what one would find in contemporary cookbooks designed for modest households, albeit with some variation and elaboration. For instance, there are three recipes for roast turkey: the French way, stuffed with veal, kidney, lard, and ox marrow flavored with brandy, then lined with slices of salt pork and the whole laid in a cool place for three or four days "in order to get the taste of the stuffing in the meat" before roasting; the English way, with a bread stuffing, roasted and basted with a mixture of butter, water and pepper, glazed at the last with egg white, served with giblet gravy made in the roasting pan and garnished with fried oysters; and the American way, steamed and then stuffed with oysters and a dressing of bread crumbs and butter, roasted ("about half an hour before it is done, baste with butter alone and dredge with a little flour, which will give the turkey a frothy appearance") and served with a giblet gravy enriched with cream. There are a few distinctly Swedish recipes, such as fruit soups, rye mush and graflax (or gravlax, a preserved salmon).

Like all immigrants, Swedes coming to America brought their food ways with them. They needed to adjust to the available foodstuffs of their new home for their own cooking, just as they learned to make other accommodations to their new surroundings. These two volumes, published with recent immigrants in mind, address specific and immediate needs faced by the target population. By contrast, a later book of Swedish cookery, translated into English, is a publishing venture of a different kind.

The Princesses Cook Book from 1936 is an edited and translated version of a very status-conscious volume of recipes from the cooking school of author Jenny Akerström. The school's graduates included three Scandinavian princesses, to whom the book is dedicated, with pictures of them on the cover and following the title page. Inside the back cover we read that "These Swedish recipes of good taste are recommended by their Majesties Margaret, Martha, and Astrid to her majesty the American housewife." The book's stated purpose was to introduce the cooking of Sweden to Americans:

> *Some of Sweden's famous dishes have found their way to this country but there are many others which might enrich our American cookery.... In choosing the material for this condensed English edition, preference has been given to those recipes which are most typically Swedish.*

But because Akerstrom saw the American cookbook reader as her audience, we wonder about the recipes selected for inclusion and what she chose to present as typical of Sweden. From what we gather from the recipes, the cooking of Sweden in 1936 (at least at the Princess-at-cooking-school level) was rich, refined and cosmopolitan. The book is reminiscent of the English translations of Escoffier's *Guide Culinaire* published about the same time, being similar in construction with numbered recipes and references from recipe to recipe ("Prepare ground praline as directed for almond brittle ice cream in recipe No. 480....Make a sponge cake after directions in recipe No. 617"). However, traditional recipes with obvious agrarian roots are also prominent, so that breaded sheep's head, rye mush, clabbered milk, and black soup (blood is a key ingredient) stand alongside veal fillet à la Oskar, Soup à la Moliere, and an "Oriental lobster soup" in which the lobster is enveloped in veal stock, egg yolks and cream and the result is garnished with curried rice.

Persiljekyckling. Parsley Chicken.

Kyckling med champig-noner.	Chicken with champig-nons.
Fullväxta kycklingar sönder-skäras och fräsas öfver frisk eld i smör med hackade cham-pignoner, litet peppar och salt. Brynes lätt på alla sidor. Se-dan tillsättes mjöl och buljong så att det blir en tjock sås. Efter några minuters fräsning upplaggas kycklingarne på ett varmt fat. Såsen redes med	Take some fullgrown chick-ens, cut them and fry them slightly over a brisk fire in butter and champignons, pepper and salt. See that they are a little brown on all sides. Add flour and bouillon, making a pretty thick sauce. When they have fried a few minutes, put up the chickens on a warm platter.

From Fullständigaste Svensk-Amerikansk kokbok *(Chicago, 1897).*

The Princesses Cook Book is a luxurious production, boasting on the back flap about its superior construction, paper and ink. It is easy to conjecture that it was constructed to tempt the eye, to be given as a gift, perhaps with the idea that it was suitable to hand down to succeeding generations. Reading a recipe is an act of imagination, and there is an element of fantasy in any luxury cookbook. This volume's idealized picture of Swedish food ways combines those of the elite townhouse or country estate and the bustling farmstead—an agreeable image for a reader in Depression-era America.

A group's food ways are an aspect of its cultural identity. For an immigrant community, food habits show both ties to the old country and acculturation in the new one. Cookbooks can help us trace these food ways as they evolve over time, and as repositories of social history they provide us with a window onto some of the day-to-day details that make up identity. These Swedish American cookbooks are merely one example of the Clements' culinary ethnic resources. It was typical for immigrant communities to create cookbooks for their members, and our collection contains a number of these "in America" works, in the native languages of the immigrants. We have five such volumes for German-speaking immigrants in America (the earliest from 1850), one for Danish and Norwegian speakers, three in Finnish, two in Yiddish, and we are in the process of acquiring others in Greek, Chinese, Armenian, Czech, and other languages. We also have a more than a dozen such works for the Jewish community in America, such as the *Jewish Cookery Book: on Principles of Economy, Adapted for Jewish Housekeepers* from 1871, and *Modern Kosher Meals: Recipes and Menus Arranged for Each Month of the Year Based on Current Food Supplies* from 1934. The Longone Archive also includes culinary works representing other distinct American ethnic communities, such as *The Creole Cookery Book, Edited by the Christian Woman's Exchange of New Orleans* (1885, one of half a dozen Cajun and Creole cookbooks) and *The Old Dutch Cook Book* (1881, one of many Pennsylvania Dutch cookbooks). For these two communities, ethnic cooking shades into regional cuisine, but other regions have distinct food ways without representing the cooking of a particular ethnic group; we have ample representation of culinarily distinct regions such as the South and New England that allow researchers to trace the evolution and cultural profile of local food ways.

Then there are the "adoptive" cookbooks, which like the "Princesses" volume instruct Americans how to cook dishes from cuisines brought to America by immigrant groups. Works such as the 1901 *The Cook's Decameron: A Study in Taste: Containing Over Two Hundred Recipes for Italian Dishes* and the 1911 *Chinese Cookery in the Home Kitchen: Being Recipes for the Preparation of the Most Popular Chinese Dishes at Home* allow us to examine the ongoing American curiosity about and developing taste for the many cuisines assimilated here throughout the nineteenth and twentieth centuries. The Library's extensive holdings of community and charity cookbooks, many of them from church groups or other ethnic community organizations, also show us something about American ethnic identity as it evolved, allowing us to track what dishes from the ethnic traditions were retained in everyday cooking, how they were modified to suit changing tastes and habits and how they accommodated American ingredients.

Each of these genres of cookbooks picks out humble but important threads in the tapestry of everyday life in America. The earlier ones show us the daily concerns of immigrants as they grappled with life in their new home, with its new foodstuffs and food ways, its unfamiliar demands and expectations, and other immediate necessities. The later ones show us how a composite American cuisine came into being at the juncture of taste, identity, convenience, market forces, distribution networks, and other elements of public and private life. What was relished? What was marketed? What constituted sustenance, nourishment, hospitality, or luxury? The culinary and domestic resources of the Clements Library illuminate American history from fresh perspectives and offer new insights into the social life, customs and contemporary concerns of our nation.

*Leather-bound clothing
trunk once owned by
General Sir Henry Clinton
(1738?–95). His
papers are in the
Clements Library.*

HORRIBLE, SUBLIME AND TRIVIAL EVENTS

THE WORLD WAR I DIARIES OF STEPHEN DOUGLAS BROWN

— Cheney Schopieray

"On reading some of this junk over, I find that the composition is crude and the grammar punk. You must excuse this on account of the conditions under which this is all written. There is always someone singing, yelling or rough-housing. Excuse also the writing, we did away with the desk. The subject matter is rather hashed up, sort of spontaneous-like, but I have to put things down as I think of them, or else they might be teetotally lost."

— Stephen D. Brown diaries, September 29, 1917

Stephen Douglas Brown was born August 20, 1892, in Philadelphia, though he lived the better part of his life in Lansdowne, immediately to the west of the city. His father, William, was a Scottish immigrant and coal merchant. On July 13, 1917, just over three months after the United States' declaration of war on Germany, Stephen Brown enlisted in the Pennsylvania National Guard, First Engineers, Company E. He was part of a large influx of volunteers during the summer of 1917; between April and August, National Guard strength doubled to approximately 377,000 troops.

In 2006, the William L. Clements Library acquired four diaries of Stephen Brown, which he kept from the time of his enlistment until his return from France in July 1919. Stephen's diaries are notable for their consistent, extraordinary detail, their candid and thoughtful reflection, their comprehensive daily entries, and the circumstances of their creation. Written and illustrated on approximately two thousand 3 3/4-inch x 6 7/8-inch pages, with interleaved mounted photographs, pasted-in newspaper clippings, letters, ephemera, and maps, the Brown diaries are made up of materials sent home to his parents. Scattered throughout the often lengthy, daily entries are indications that the pages were intended both to share his experiences with his parents and to be brought together into their present bound form for the sake of memory. Stephen Brown's writing

Steven Brown's voluminous diaries.

is non-discriminatory in its detail; he describes with equal fervor bridge building under heavy fire during the Aisne-Marne offensive and the contents of his pack. His writing documents the absolute horrors of death and loss associated with military conflict; sublime feelings of patriotism, camaraderie and achievement; and minute, trivial, repetitive occurrences that are vitally important to understanding the everyday life of the soldier.

Stephen Brown and his fellow members of the Guard remained at the 33rd Street Armory in Philadelphia until departing from the Reading terminal on August 12, 1917. Their first stop was Mount Gretna, northwest of Philadelphia, where they remained, performing basic drill but also swimming at Lake Gretna. On the 20th of August, 1917, they left the Gretna station for the long train journey to Georgia. Brown's diaries note various attempts at entertainment along the way. In one case, he recorded on August 21, "a bunch of fellows from the car in front, headed by a banjoist came in to serenade us, but being attacked with pillows from both uppers and lowers, retreated in disorder." The troops arrived at their destination, Camp Hancock, outside of Augusta, Georgia, on the 22nd of August. There, the First Pennsylvania National Guard was re-designated and re-organized, and Brown found himself in the 28th Division, 103rd Engineers, Company E.

As inoculations and medical tests were completed, training commenced. Whether performing almost daily drills according to "Butts' Manual" (Edward L. Butts' *Manual of Physical Drill*); dreading weekly inspections; loading, sighting and shooting rifles; practicing bayonet exercises; digging trenches; practicing skirmish movements; playing a variety of sports, from piggy-back races to boxing; performing on his violin; making short trips to Augusta; or adjusting to the social and cultural environment of military life, Stephen Brown sent highly detailed reports to his family. In the camp environment, military rigor was matched almost equally by amusements and pranks. "There being too much racket in the tent," he wrote on October 7, "I went to the mess hall to read. On my return at tattoo, I found all of the straw in my mattress at one end of the tick, and all the basins, buckets and miscellaneous junk in the tent on top of my bed. Really, the army is the best place in the world to learn control of temper. I retaliated by vigorously clashing the buckets and basins together, waking up the pestiferous seven, who by this time were fast asleep."

September 18 saw Brown's permanent appointment as a reconnaissance engineer. To provide his family with clarification, he explained ten days later, "Reconnaissance is a crude sort of surveying." During this period, his engineering training included learning to use "crude" (though surprisingly effective) slope boards with plumb bobs and strings; sketching, drafting and map making; bridge building; laying barbed wire; and other tasks.

Brown was proud and patriotic, and his diaries are filled with reflections on the value of his training: "If there ever comes a time when universal military service comes up for vote, I want the family to say 'yes'. If every flat-chested corner-loafer and ballroom expert could be put thru stuff such as we are getting, for a year, when about 19 or 20, we would have a different lot of citizens," he wrote on October 20. "The camps for such doings should be away from cities, sale of tobacco and junk eats prohibited, recreations supplied in the camp itself, and see if we wouldn't be better off physically as well as nationally militaristically. The industrial loss would be more than made up by improvement in individuals. A year is not much of a bit out of a fellows life. This sort of life suppresses bullyism and brings out the backward."

Few furloughs were granted at Christmas time, but on December 21 Brown recorded what must have been a popular (and very likely apocryphal) story of one instance: "One fellow in F Co. received a telegram reading 'Come home at once, your mother is dead.' He was given a furlough at once, but when his case was investigated, they found that his mother had been dead eight years. He was arrested, brot back and court martialed, but they could not get him, as the telegram was correct. He was freed." And so, after several months of training, Brown spent Christmas Day burning tin cans at the officers' tents. He did not regret missing the Christmas service as "the fellows said that it was a highfalutin Episcopalian communion." A fourteen-day furlough followed the Christmas season, and then came uninterrupted exercise and training from January until May. In February, Companies D, E and F spent a week hiking and camping, drilling, blasting, ditch digging, and road building on an artillery range in Georgia. The following is a related excerpt from Brown's February 11, 1918, entry. The depth of detail and his contrasting of required procedure with *actual* practice are typical of the larger portion of entries throughout the volumes:

> An enormous list of everything that we were supposed to take was posted. We had to collect all articles, have them inspected then packed them up. We were supposed to wear winter underwear, woolen pants, trench shoes, woolen shirt and service hat. Duffle bags, to be carried on the wagons were filled with overcoat, blouse, extra socks, 1 blanket, and any personal articles we wished. In the pack we carried mess kit, toilet articles, 2 blankets, poncho, tent pole & pins, shelter half, canteen full of water, bayonet, and belt, suit of underwear & socks. That is, we were supposed to - I slipped the heavy poncho & underwear in the duffle bag slyly. Then last was the gun. It was a hefty load.... The scheme of progress is to march 50 minutes, and rest 10. A fellow doesn't realize what work is until he marches with a full pack & gun. I guess I am soft from office work, for I sure am tired.

On May 9, with stateside training over, Brown took the train north to Camp Mills on Long Island, where he had a visit from his family before embarking at Brooklyn on the 18th. After a relatively uneventful North Atlantic voyage, he arrived in Liverpool, England, on May 30. From this point onward, military censorship appears to have become more rigid, and so, until his return, Brown kept a "meagre" record of principal dates, events, and places to be later incorporated into the diary being kept by his parents. The men traveled by railway past London to the Dover station and crossed the English Channel to Calais aboard a Belgian vessel, escorted by sub chasers. After packing their gear, by foot and by train, the men of the 103rd made their way to a billet between Bellebrune and Belle-et-Houllefort, where they quartered with the British Fifth Army and received additional training with the help of their allies:

A colonel, three other officers and six non-coms of the Northumberland Fusiliers were assigned as training staff. At intervals there would be talks, either by the colonel or by a pink-cheeked boy officer, who strolled around the circle while talking snapping off daisy-tops with a cane. The colonel was an old Scotchman, and his stories, all having a valuable lesson for us, were comical on account of his accent and queer ways of expression.

"Now, min, whin ye go into the trinches, ye want to mak frens wi' the mon who doesn't drink. For while ye're waiting to go over the top, they come roun wi a drap o' rhum, just whin ye're cauldest and wettest. Then stick next to ye're teetotaler fren. I tell you it's guid.

"And whin ye're on duty in the trinch, niver stick ye'r whole heid up to look aroun. On my estate in Sooth Efrica, I go huntin monkeys sometimes. The little beasts are wise – whin they want to tak a luik at ye, they don't come out in the open and stare at ye wi' both eyes. No, they stick one eye out around a rock, take a quick peep at ye, and draw back. So be lik the monkeys, stick yer tin hat over the parapit, and if a sniper is waitin, he'll shoot at it. Then pop up one eye, tak a quick look, and drop down agen.

"Be careful of any officer ye don't know. Sometimes they sind over an officer dressed as one of yours and speakin guid English. He'll try to order ye oot of the trinches, and lead ye to the Boche lines to be captured. Once I got in a trinch wi a lot of Canadians, who didn't lik my accent, an kept me until their own colonel came along."

Gas and bayonet work was about the same systems as we had had in Georgia. The gas drill was varied by having races and contests between two sides, to see which could be first to have all men masked, one man at a time doing this, then giving the signal to his next man. Bayonet drill became very tiresome (June 7, 1918).

A grueling march from Bellebrune to Desvres on June 22 made the Pullman car ride to Paris particularly welcome. From Paris, an eight-mile hike to Viels-Maisons, some eight miles south of Château-Thierry took them to the front lines. The first casualties suffered by the 28th Division were members of E Company, 103rd Engineers. Eight men were wounded while the 103rd moved into billets at Bonneil, some two miles from the front.

On Bastille Day, July 14, the 28th Division was stretched from Chézy to Vaux, the U.S. troops serving to fill in gaps or thin stretches of the line of French soldiers concentrated around Château-Thierry. From the night of the 14th to the 21st, Pennsylvania troops along the eastern line (including Brown's company) were exposed to heavy artillery fire. The German line pressed south, successfully laying pontoon bridges over the Marne, and members of the 103rd Engineers fought alongside infantrymen to resist. German advances met with counter-offensive maneuvers. Stephen Brown, however, was fortunate to have been appointed a "runner" or message carrier. Rather than engaging in the frontal assault, Brown moved communications between platoon leaders scattered along the Marne near Rouvroy, just over a mile down the Marne from Château-Thierry. Not entirely out of harm's way, Brown wrote of night bombing raids and a close call on the 16th in which he narrowly missed being

Say it with Kodaks.

Stephen Douglas Brown, photographed while using his Kodak camera. Many of Brown's informal snapshots are laid into the earlier volumes of his diaries.

hit by a barrage of shells. The following passages, written during the Aisne-Marne offensive, contain, blended together, grand and horrifying scenes of war and observations on the mundane and everyday:

The shell . . . exploded, throwing dirt & limestone all around, and puffing off an acrid irritating smoke. Then at nicely timed intervals, perhaps 3 or 4 seconds, I heard three more sing across land, and explode, with me hugging the ground at every shock. All landed close together. The first was bad enough, but the suspense of hearing the others coming and waiting for the explosions was worse. Ordinarily, when shooting at a somewhat indefinite target, they spread their shells a little on each side of the first. Lucky for me that they didn't this time. I was choked by the fumes, stunned and dazed by the concussions and some-what deafened, and sprinkled all over with dirt. Five or six more came across at a little greater range, and exploded back a ways. As soon as I realized that the range had in-creased, I scrambled up, ran over thru the little vineyard to an unoccupied traverse of the trench, and made an inspection of self. Total inventory was one grand fright, slight case of shell-shock, neckful of dirt and a hole thru the front rim of the helmet about as big as a dime (July 16, 1918).

On July 21, Brown made his way through Château-Thierry:

I struck directly north thru the woods, got lost for awhile. In there I saw a dead soldier for the first time. He was a fine looking Frenchman of about thirty five years, with part of his jaw shot away and a big hole in his abdomen. I finally came out at a place where I could see the river road, and saw that there was a solid column of French artillery, trucks, wagon trains and ambulances moving forward. We had noticed that firing had decreased, but had no idea until then that the Germans were in retreat. . . . On the edge of the city all of the streets were flooded, little strips along the houses, and the center of the road being dry. Everyone had to slosh thru the water whenever a conveyance passed by. It was a bright moonlit night, and we could see clearly the buildings along the way. On account of the shelling, the men were being hustled thru as fast as possible, and with regret I had to keep my eyes on my front buddy's feet, for safety's sake, instead of enjoying a slant at the cathedral as we passed by. We turned to the left at a broad, tree-lined cross street, directed by an MP on duty there. Someone, I don't know with what organization, stood there, too, and as we passed gave each man a little stick of chocolate candy. That didn't go bad under such circumstances. We got out of town by a winding steep road. On the far edge was a monster shell hole directly in the middle of the road, with several dead boys in the gutter nearby. One of their packs had been ignited by the flash of the explosion, and the wool blankets were smouldering, giving off unpleasant burning-wool odors.

Brown's company made their camp about a mile outside Château-Thierry. On the 25th:

I walked back to Chateau Thierry, to try to get some eats and smokes for the com-

pany.... The YM[CA] had established itself in a fine residence near the cathedral. They
had a canteen with lots of smokes chocolate, and paper obtainable. The reading room was
a splendidly decorated place, with large mirrors and much gilded carved work. In back,
seen thru large French windows, was a neat formal garden. I had to wait there for a new
truckload of supplies to arrive, and took a walk meanwhile up to the cathedral. This was
in a too crowded section of the city, and altho a fine structure in itself, did not show up well
because other buildings were too close. It was a massive Gothic building, with the fine
carvings on the outside chipped in many places by shell-fire. The interior was in confusion,
broken chairs and rubbish were piled around. Some of the religious paintings had been cut
from the frames, and some that remained had been slashed. Breaks in the windows had
probably been caused by shell-splinters. Many civilians had returned to their home towns,
and a few, evidently prominent church members, were sadly observing the destruction and
disorder in the church. I secured a lot of chewing gum cigarettes and cake chocolate to take
back to the gang, and rounded up a few men of the company who had skipped away on
sightseeing trips, to help carry it back. To finance these purchases, I had borrowed money
from different men. These fellows let me keep their cash for weeks at a time, to be used for
company purchases. I carried it in a money belt. The stuff was taken back and distributed
pro rata to the platoons.

From late July to August 4, the 28th Division was ordered to pursue the retreating German army. They moved from near Château-Thierry to Verdilly, along muddy roads in the woods to the hills of the Marne at Mont-Saint-Père. In two lines, American and French infantry, engineers, signal corps, and others marched through dense woods, calf-deep mud, and ripe wheat fields, sometimes during the day and other times during the night. From Stephen Brown's locations he could frequently see and hear artillery duels and aircraft dogfights. His regiment laid barbed wire and camouflage screens of green burlap. They made their way through Le Charmel, Cierges, Chamery, Coulonges-Cohan, Dravegny, and to Chéry-Chartreuve. Along the way, Stephen worked at repairing roads. On arrival, they camped on the side of a deep valley south of town. The Germans had retreated back to the opposite side of the Vesle River, where high ground gave them an artillery advantage over anyone attempting to cross.

The 103rd Engineers were part of an effort to construct bridges across the river to facilitate troop movement into the occupied Fismette, across the river from Fismes. Brown's often-harrowing bridge-building efforts continued from August 10 until the 12th. For the next week or so, he laid barbed wire and repaired roads near Dravegny and moved camp to an area west of Arcis-le-Ponsart. Wire work and periodic shellfire continued while Brown spent some of his time running to procure canteen supplies from distant Red Cross stations and YMCA warehouses. On the 12th of September, following seventy-two days within the range of German shells, the 28th Division was relieved. However, after a drive to Charmont, the men received an order to shift course ninety degrees east to meet with General John Pershing's newly formed 1st American Army. The truck train stopped in Revigny, south of the Argonne forest and the 103rd Engineers enjoyed 10 days of "army rest" (drilling and short jaunts to

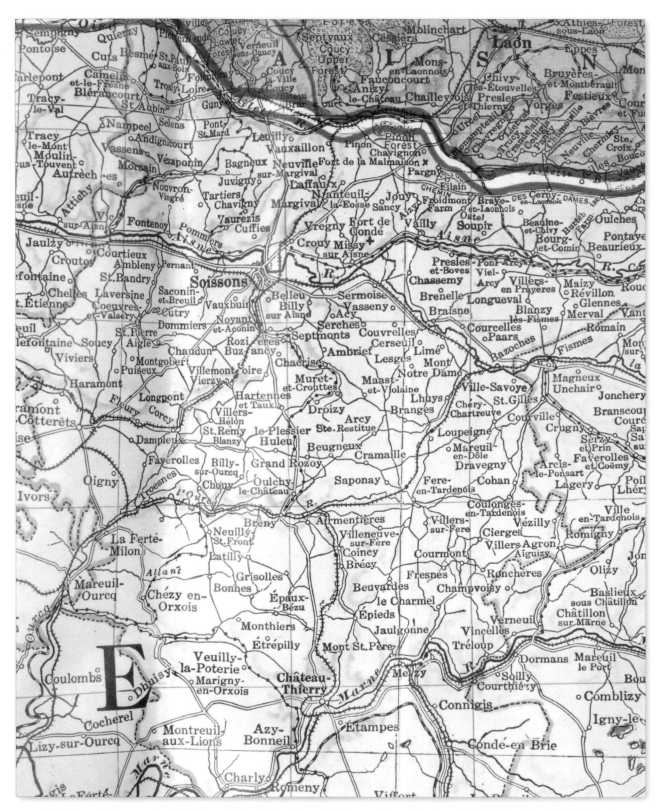

The Château-Thierry area from The Literary Digest Liberty Map of the Western Front of the Great World War Showing the Battle Line of Liberty as it Stood May 1st 1918 *(New York, 1918). The front line is depicted as it was in the spring of 1918.*

nearby villages). The 28th Division moved to about two miles from the front lines on September 24. The former National Guard of Pennsylvania was only one of nine U.S. divisions, and the whole of the American contribution to this campaign covered about twenty-one miles of a roughly fifty-four-mile front. The following is an excerpt from Brown's long description of the first day of the Meuse-Argonne offensive, September 25–26, 1918:

> No one had any idea that this was the great day for the American Army, but we began to realize that something unusual was at hand when the chaplain made us a little speech, then prayed for those who were about to die. This was a woozy beginning of the day's work . . . the American artillery barrage began. We had heard the French barrage on the Marne, and battery shooting on other fronts, but had never heard such a volume of sound as lasted throughout this barrage. There was a constant roar, so that the only discharges we could hear were the louder ones of nearby guns. All along the front, to right and left, were the flashes visible. . . . Finally a relief came in the form of a job. We left packs & rifles in the trench, and hiked back a little ways, finding three or four trucks there that did not dare go forward on the main road, on account of the noise made by their motors. They were loaded with bridge material and loose timbers. I do not see why they were afraid of being heard, because the noise of firing had increased by this time, the machine guns having started in with a barrage of their own, in addition to the artillery. We pushed the trucks, steered by their drivers, up to the edge of the mine crater, and unloaded the material. The trucks started up their motors, and beat it away as fast as they could in the semi-darkness. Of course they had no lights. We worked hard getting the bridge material down to the stream, where our new roadway crossed. The Germans threw over three or four shells, hitting the road where the trucks had just been. Fortunately none of our gang happened to be getting lumber at the time, and so no one was near enough to be hit. We wondered how the Germans knew when to fire, because it seemed impossible for the sound of the truck motors to be heard above the artillery. This was the only time during the preliminary barrage when they returned the fire, and considering the volume of our barrage, one wonders how they had the chance to shoot. One gang of carpenters started to work on the bridge, digging two deep holes in the bed of the shallow stream for the supports to rest in. The rest of us cleared the camouflaging sod away from the roadway, and made the cuts necessary to get from our roadway to the bridge. The machine guns and artillery continued to shoot, more loudly than ever just before dawn. It became very misty, but yet we were able to see a few of the big squadron of tanks clattering across the field, on their way to join the infantry. We did not see the infantry going over, but judged that it was shortly after the tanks joined them. By this time there were a number of vehicles, ammunition trucks, ambulances and field kitchens lined up back of our cut in a very dangerous closeness.

Finally bridge and roadway were ready, and we had the satisfaction of seeing several ambulances run down it, cross the bridge, and go up the other side. So we gathered up tools and packs, and started forward. On the ridge just beyond the stream, we had a good elevated view of what had been No Man's land. The road itself, originally a macadam roadbed, was overgrown with long coarse grass, that had found a strong foothold between stones in the four years during which it had not been used. The stones were entirely out of sight. The two lines of trees, such as border so many French Roads, were nothing more than splintered trunks near the trench lines. All of the foliage and branches had been shot away. The French trench line was not battered up at all, because up to this day, this Argonne front had been a very quiet place. The fields were covered with the same kind of coarse grass as was the road. We found that our divisional sector was out in the open. The main forest lay about a quarter mile to our left, and this main road from Neuvilly to Varennes ran down the center of it.

Along the sides of the road was a snarl of cut telegraph wires, on the ground because the poles had been all cut down by shell fragments. Broad paths of barb-wire, so rusty that they made brown decorations on the landscape, zigzagged around in short straight lengths, with frequent sharp angles, all over the fields between the two trench lines. Away off to our right, was a high hill rising abruptly from the general flatness. This must have been an important point, because even from our distance, we could make out that the whole surface, from top to bottom, had been so plowed up by bursting shells that not a bit of the green grass remained.... We got out of the gutter, found the road uninterrupted where the French front line had crossed it, and passed on over No Man's land. There was a continual crackle of rifle and machine gun fire from a little ways in front, but we could not see a man of either side, they kept concealed so well.

The trench across the road of course obstructed it for vehicles, and our job was to fill it in. First we had to pull up a lot of barb wire stakes, and drag the wire off to the side of the road. Then there were some heavy chevaux de frises, built up of angle irons and barb-wire ... and placed end to end, completely obstructing the road. These had to be pulled aside also. Our platoon remained here to fill in the trench, while the rest of the company went ahead a short distance to repair the arches in a stone bridge over another stream near Bourevilles. We first shoveled the stuff that had been used as a parapet into the trench, which was unusually wide and deep. Then we had to go over to the destroyed houses and carry over building stones to throw in the hole. Some of the company had remained behind to do further work on the road and bridge at the mine crater. The stone carrying was a slow and tedious job, so we took our shovels again, and started to throw clay into the hole. Soon the colonel arrived, and Lt. Oakman got a fierce bawling-out for using clay. The old boy said that it would pack so much that in a few days the hole would appear again. So we had to return to stone carrying and it was not until late afternoon that we finished.

Pvt. 1st. Cl. Brown.

My place card at Company E Christmas dinner.

This caricature of Brown, drawn by a fellow soldier, served as his place card at Christmas dinner in 1917. Brown took his violin to training camp in Georgia.

There is one good point in army discipline in the field. At camp, in Georgia, the personal doings of a man, such as condition of equipment and location of pup-tent (when on artillery range) was subject to orders from officers. But in France they let us do as we pleased after the work was over. Some of the boys this night just flopped in the field nearby, some went all the way back to the French trenches, and about a dozen of us found an old French dugout, where we turned in for the night. It was dug into a little reverse hill-side, thru a limestone formation, and had been well braced with timbers, like a mine gallery. It was ankle deep with water, but the former occupants had made duck-boards to walk on, so that we didn't get wet on entering. A line of double-decker bunks was on each side of the aisle, each bunk filled with a meager supply of damp straw. I prepared for bed by removing glasses, too tired even to take off shoes. We soon found that the place was inhabited by rats, and one big fellow, scampering down along the bunk, put his wet feet on my face. Too lazy to move out into the field, I pulled the blanket up over my face, and slept, letting the rats run wherever they would (September 25, 1918).

Stephen Brown's description of the Aire River Valley and the area around Varennes continues extensively. Following the first day of the battle, the 103rd Engineers spent their time repairing existing railways and roads and constructing new ones, working at the heels of the infantry units, facilitating the transport of supplies from the rear. "At Château Thierry and Fesmes we didn't know what ruined villages were," he wrote. "There the houses were full of shell-holes, but here, the houses are only piles of debris. No man's land is a very desolate-looking place." The soldiers spent days drilling and exploring villages around Lamarche-en-Woëvre. October 21–29 were the 103rd Engineers' last days at the front. Brown was called upon to sketch locations of troops at the front lines in the muddy forest beyond the nearby town of Beney-en-Woëvre, northeast of Lamarche, where the troops repaired a stretch of railway that had been severely damaged by the retreating German soldiers. After the signing of the armistice with Germany on November 11, 1918, the 103rd Engineers remained near Lamarche and Stephen Brown's entries become shorter and shorter as the days pass by. In early January, he trekked south to Toul and to villages to its southwest until February when he returned to Paris by train, spent several days sightseeing, then traveled to Toulouse where he remained until departing for home in July 1919. Here, Stephen Brown's diaries come to a close. He returned to Lansdowne, Pennsylvania, where he later pursued a career as a chemical engineer.

Twentieth-century military materials, such as Stephen Brown's diaries, do not conform to the Clements Library's founding collection scope of early Americana or to the current terminal date of 1900 for most of our collecting. Until the donation of James S. Schoff's extensive collection of Civil War letters and diaries in the 1970s, the Clements' holdings represented the antebellum period and earlier. Over the past twenty years, however, substantial quantities of later wartime manuscripts and graphics have been acquired, extending the chronological scope of those areas of the Library's collection beyond the Civil War to include the Spanish-American War, World War I, World War II, Korea, and even Vietnam.

The value of twentieth-century military collections to the Clements Library lies in their relationship to similar materials embodying similar human experiences in earlier times. The training and education of military personnel, the activities of soldiers and other persons in the field, and the lives of their families back home are also key components of our eighteenth- and nineteenth-century holdings. The experiences recorded in Stephen Brown's diaries and the writings of other participants in post-1900 conflicts can be compared and contrasted to those recorded by soldiers from the French and Indian War to the Civil War. Together, they document what, in August of 1918, Stephen Brown described as "soldier philosophy"—"a grand mixture of horrible, sublime and trivial events."

Bust of Thomas William Coke, earl of Leicester (1752–1842). This 1824 sculpture by John Francis came to the Library with the Christopher Hughes Papers.

TRADITION
FADES BUT THE
WRITTEN RECORD
REMAINS
EVER FRESH

*One of a pair of adages
composed by Professor
Ulrich B. Phillips for the
south façade of the Library.*

CONTRIBUTORS

Bethany Anderson was formerly Information Resources Assistant, Clements Library.

Terese M. Austin is Information Resources Assistant, Clements Library.

Barbara DeWolfe is Curator of Manuscripts, Clements Library.

Brian Leigh Dunnigan is Associate Director and Curator of Maps, Clements Library.

J. Kevin Graffagnino is Director of the Clements Library.

David Hancock is Professor of History, The University of Michigan.

Emiko Hastings is Curator of Books, Clements Library.

Katie Heddle is a freelance writer and formerly a volunteer in the Manuscripts Division, Clements Library.

JJ Jacobson is Curator for American Culinary History, Clements Library.

Martha S. Jones is Associate Professor of African American Studies and Associate Professor of History, University of Michigan.

Clayton Lewis is Curator of Graphic Materials, Clements Library.

Janice Bluestein Longone is Curator of American Culinary History, Clements Library.

Mary Hrones Parsons is a volunteer in the Manuscripts Division, Clements Library.

Mary Sponberg Pedley is Assistant Curator of Maps, Clements Library.

Cheney Schopieray is Assistant Curator of Manuscripts, Clements Library.

Diana Sykes is Information Resources Assistant, Clements Library.

Christine Walker is Graduate Student Instructor of History, University of Michigan, and formerly Curatorial Assistant in the Manuscripts Division, Clements Library.

This small oil painting of the tug Champion *is one of many pieces of original documentary art in the collection of the Clements Library. Little is known of the vessel or of this ca. 1880 work by an anonymous artist. It was purchased for the Library in 1946.*

ACKNOWLEDGMENTS

Any volume such as this is the work of many hands. In addition to the authors of our essays, listed on the Contributors page, the editors are grateful to the following for their assistance on this project:

First and foremost, the McGregor Fund of Detroit, Michigan. Tracy W. McGregor was a staunch supporter of the Clements Library until his death in 1936, and his foundation has continued that tradition in the decades since. Substantial support for the publication of this book is only the most recent example of generosity to the Library, and we are most appreciative of all the McGregor Fund has done for the Clements.

Clayton Lewis for the photography on illustrations for the book and Diana Sykes for additional assistance with photography.

Terese Austin for proofreading and other copy work on the typescripts.

Kathy Horn for designing the book and shepherding it through the printing process.

Fine Books & Collections for publishing an earlier draft of the introduction in its August 2009 issue.

Our predecessors on the staff of the Clements. This Library's collections reflect the dedication and hard work of our founder, three previous Directors (Randolph G. Adams, Howard H. Peckham, John C. Dann), curators (Lloyd A. Brown, Colton Storm, William S. Ewing, Richard W. Ryan, David Bosse, Don Wilcox, Georgia Haugh, Joyce Bonk, Arlene Shy, J. Clements Wheat, Douglas W. Marshall, Christian Brun, Elizabeth B. Steere, and others), and too many donors to list here. Today's Clements Library staff realize that we stand on their shoulders in caring for this extraordinary institution, and we are grateful to all of them for shaping it into one of the world's great libraries of primary sources on early American history.

William L. Clements Library
909 S. University Ave.
Ann Arbor, MI 48109-1190

(734) 764-2347
Fax: (734) 647-0716

www.clements.umich.edu

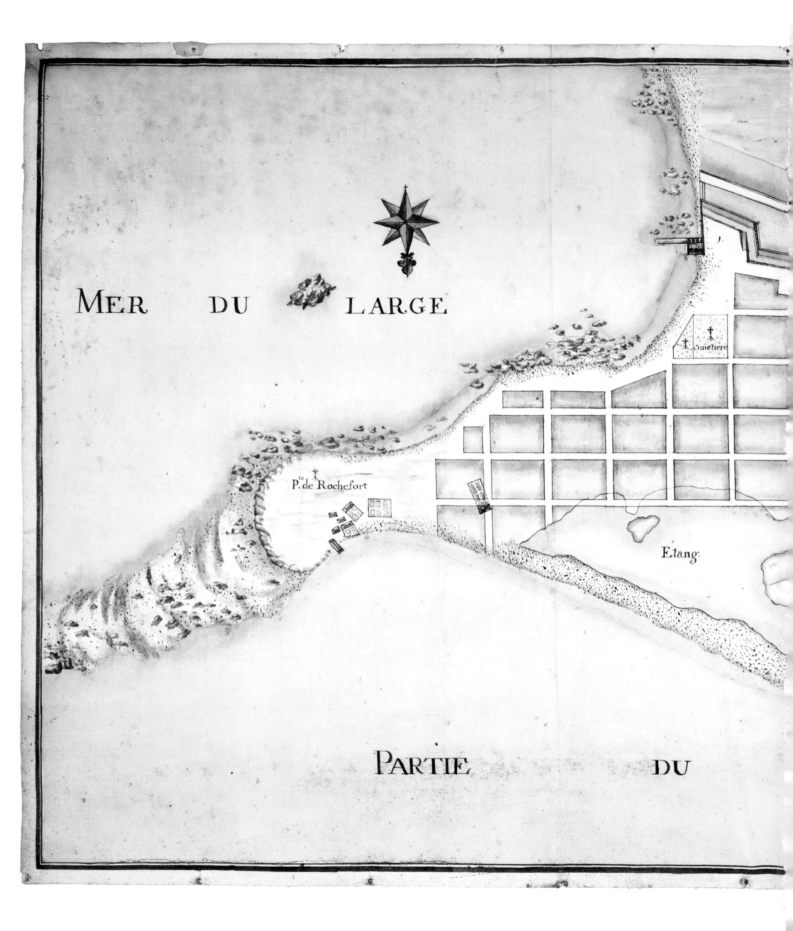

MER DU LARGE

Pte de Rochefort

Cimetiere

Etang

PARTIE DU